# A JUSTIFICATION OF RATIONALITY

# A JUSTIFICATION
# OF
# RATIONALITY

John Kekes

State University of New York Press
Albany · 1976

JOHN KEKES

is professor and chairman of the philosophy department
at the State University of New York at Albany

First published in 1976 by
State University of New York Press
99 Washington Avenue, Albany, New York 12210

Suggested form for citation of this book
in bibliographical references:
John Kekes, *A Justification of Rationality*
(Albany: State University of New York Press, 1976).

**Library of Congress Cataloging in Publication Data**

Kekes, John.
A justification of rationality.

Includes bibliographical references and index.
1. Rationalism.   2. Skepticism.   3. Metaphysics.
I. Title.
BD181.K36   1976      149'.7      76-16069
ISBN 0-87395-356-8

This book is
dedicated
to
Jean Y. Kekes

# Contents

CONTENTS

# Preface

The aim of this book is to defend rationality against its enemies and to assure its uneasy friends that a rationalist need not be rigid, arbitrary, dogmatic, cold, and unimaginative. Rationality is an ideal which represents the best in our civilization. The ideal, however, must be reaffirmed from time to time and this is done here by expressing it anew in a contemporary idiom and by defending it against new doubts.

This is a philosophical study, but it tries not to be technical, narrow, parochial—in a word, academic. It is written for an audience of literate, thoughtful, and perhaps intellectually troubled people who have had no special training in philosophy beyond one or two basic university courses. But this is also a *philosophical* study which aims to make a contribution to epistemology.

To many philosophers these two aims appear to be inconsistent. But these philosophers are mistaken. During the last one or two generations philosophy has become of interest only to philosophers. For over two thousand years preceding this deplorable development, however, philosophers spoke to all the cultured men in their society. This work aims to return to that excellent tradition.

Many people helped me in writing this book. My greatest debt is to my wife who read the entire manuscript and suggested innumerable substantive and stylistic improvements. But much more importantly, she was the first audience and the first critic of most of my ideas. For being an intellectual partner, my conscience, and my friend, I dedicate this book to her with love and gratitude.

Donald F. Henze read all the chapters, some of them several times, and I have benefited greatly from his vast historical knowledge, critical acumen, and fine style. My views on the nature of philosophy and rationality have been deeply influenced by our correspondence over the years.

First lengthy conversations and then correspondence with Herbert Feigl set me to face the problems which I attempt to solve here. But even in his absence, he acts as a kind of intellectual censor leading me to ask myself about an idea or an argument: what would Feigl say about that? I am deeply indebted to him for his teaching and for his help and encouragement when these were badly needed.

The following philosophers helped me in conversation and correspondence: Max Black, Roy Edgley, Josiah Gould, Richard Hull, James Kellenberger, Joel Kupperman, Jack Meiland, Robert Meyers, Harold Morick, Steven Nathanson, Campbell Purton, William Reese, James Thomas, Henry Veatch, and Gershon Weiler. I now thank them for the time and effort they spent in helping me.

The manuscript was typed by Helen Somich with her usual incredible accuracy, and I thank her for this and much else.

I gratefully acknowledge grants from the following institutions: The Canada Council, State University of New York at Albany, and the University of Saskatchewan.

I have published portions of this book in philosophical journals. The published material has been revised, sometimes substantially, to fit in with the rest of the book and to strengthen the argument. Thus the portions incorporated in the book bear various degrees of resemblance to their original version. I acknowledge permission to use material from the following journals: *Metaphilosophy*, 2 (1971) and 4 (1973) in Chapters One, Eight, and Nine; *The Philosophical Quarterly*, 25 (1975) in Chapter One; *Philosophy and Phenomenological Research*, 31 (1971) in Chapter Two; *The Philosophical Forum*, 1 (1969) and *Philosophica*, 15 (1975) in Chapter Three; *The Personalist*, 52 (1970) in Chapters Four and Eleven; *American Philosophical Quarterly*, 9 (1972) in Chapter Five; *Philosophy of the Social Sciences*, 3 (1973) and *Philosophical Studies*, 26 (1974) in Chapter Six; *International Philosophical Quarterly*, 12 (1972) in Chapter Eleven; and *Idealistic Studies*, 2 (1972) in Chapters Twelve and Thirteen.

# Introduction

*"Things fall apart; the center cannot hold;*
*Mere anarchy is loosed upon the world,*
*The blood-dimmed tide is loosed, and*
*everywhere*
*The ceremony of innocence is drowned;*
*The best lack all conviction, while the worst*
*Are full of passionate intensity."*
—W. G. Yeats, *"The Second Coming"*

The need for justifying rationality arises out of the context of a long-standing conflict between faith and reason. Some defenders of faith contend that in the last analysis no belief or action can be rationally justified. They argue that the standards upon which the supposed justifications rest do, themselves, need justification. But this justification cannot be provided because the processes of justifying one standard by another must lead either to infinite regress, or to nonrational commitment to some standard. Opposed to this is the view to be defended here: that the rational justification of beliefs and actions is possible.

If it were true that nothing could be justified by reason, then all honestly held convictions would have an equal claim upon general acceptance, and argument would, indeed, be replaced by "passionate intensity." This would be a dangerous and undesirable situation, for the inevitable conflicts could then be settled only by force. The civilizing restraint of debate and criticism would disappear. If rationality is abandoned, then either "anarchy is loosed upon the world," or dogmatism supported by brute force would prevail.

Rationality, however, is besieged by criticisms. It is charged with damaging man by denying a rightful place to feeling, imagination, and creativity. It is said to lead to "bad faith" and to "inauthentic" life by suppressing parts of human nature. It supposedly rigidifies thinking, forcing everything into a Procrustean bed of "bloodless categories." It handicaps the exercise of that "negative capability" which renders us receptive to the mysteries, ambiguities, and uncertainties of existence. Some claim that the "whore reason" leads us astray by licensing false pride and the illusion that salvation is in human hands. Others accuse rationalism of fostering ideological tyranny which is the death of liberty. One of its very restrained critics expresses some of these charges by writing:

> To be rational, to be reasonable, is a good thing, but when we say of a thinker that he is committed to rationalism, we mean to convey a pejorative judgment. It expresses our sense that he conceives of the universe and man in a simplistic way, and often it suggests that his thought proceeds on the assumption that there is a close analogy to be drawn between man and machine . . . the poet's mind was the normative mind of man. It grew . . . not through the strengthening of its powers of analysis and abstraction, but through the development of feeling, imagination, and will.[1]

Thus the moderate use of reason is viewed as a virtue, but excessive attention to it is liable to produce inhumanity in subject and object alike.

All of these attacks are symptoms of the most fundamental kind of scepticism. Their target is not one or another instance of reasoning, but the very possibility or, at the very least, the extreme undesirability, of rationality. It would be natural, therefore, to expect to find that philosophers have devoted considerable time and energy to combatting this most serious of all challenges. But somehow this is not the case, and the bulk of philosophical attention to scepticism falls into two categories.

The first attempts to belittle scepticism through *ad hominem* arguments. When Russell, for instance, dismisses the issue by delivering himself of the *obiter dictum* that "scepticism, while logically impeccable, is psychologically impossible, and there is an element of frivolous insincerity in any philosophy which pretends to accept it," [2] he expresses the sentiments of many philosophers. The other category comprises refutations of versions of scepticism that are much weaker than the scepticism directed against the possibility of rationality. The author of a recent work on scepticism is quite right in remarking that "the arguments of Moore, Wittgenstein, Ayer, Chisholm, and Strawson against such scepticism have created a philosophical climate in which philosophical scepticism is not taken seriously." [3]

Cultural currents, however, are not influenced by the lack of philosophical attention. In fact, philosophical smugness about scepticism contributes to the flourishing of such flowers of unreason as existentialism and mysticism, drug cults and transcendental meditation, ideologies and dogmas of higher consciousness, astrology and palmistry, fundamentalism and Jesus freaks, Kierkegaardian revivalism and Pascalian logic of the heart. Philosophical arguments against scepticism have not even approached an adequate response to the challenge these regressions to the Dark Ages present.

Oddly enough, then, a justification of rationality must not only argue against the champions of irrationality, it must also persuade those who would be its natural allies that there is an urgent problem requiring solution. On occasion, the second task seems the more formidable. Accordingly, it is the dual aim of Part One to state the problem and to show that scepticism constitutes a threat which cannot be ignored. It begins with an examination of the frequently refuted Humean scepticism and then demonstrates how scepticism can be greatly strengthened by dropping the faulty assumptions that made the refutation of Humean scepticism such a relatively easy task.

Part Two is concerned with showing why standard philosophical arguments fail to refute the strengthened version of scepticism. Appeals to pragmatic conditions, common sense, ordinary language, science, all fail, as does the attempt to show that the sceptical challenge is illegitimate. Each of these approaches, however, contains elements to be used later in the refutation of scepticism.

Part Three opens with a discussion of the requirements of a theory of rationality. It goes on to provide a statement and defense of a theory of rationality which comprises standards not open to the charge of arbitrariness, and which rests on grounds more secure than faith.

In Part Four the theory of rationality is deployed against two forms of scepticism. The first is the view that belief in the existence of anything outside of one's mind is rationally unsupportable. The second is that while it may be rational to believe *that* something exists outside of one's mind, there is no rational way of deciding between various accounts of *what* it is. The conclusion is that solipsism is irrational and that it is possible to make rational decisions concerning the merits of different and conflicting ways of looking at the world. Another way of expressing the point of Part Four is that metaphysics within the bounds of reason is possible. In fact, the possibility of metaphysics will be seen to be intimately tied to the possibility of rationality.

# PART I
# THE PROBLEM

# 1 The sceptical challenge to rationality

*"If reason be considered in an abstract view, it furnishes invincible arguments against itself."*—David Hume, *Dialogues Concerning Natural Religion*

## Introduction

There are many positions that might properly be called sceptical, but only the most fundamental kind will be examined here. All other forms of scepticism grant considerably more to their opponents than does the thoroughgoing, radical scepticism which aims to call into question the very possibility of reason. The term "scepticism," then, is reserved for the attack upon reason. And since it will be convenient from time to time to refer to the target of the sceptical attack, "rationalism" will be used for this purpose. "Rationalism" is also used to designate some of the philosophical views of Descartes, Spinoza, Leibniz, and of others, and to contrast their views with those of the empiricists. In the present context, however, rationalism is used in contrast with irrationalism. This usage renders empiricists, as well as their traditional rivals, rationalists.

Rationalism is commonly held to be the attitude of the man who holds rational beliefs and who acts, when the need arises, in accordance with his beliefs. To be rational is desirable because rational beliefs generally have a far better chance of being true than do beliefs that are held independently of or in the face of reasons. A man acting rationally is much more likely to achieve his goal than one who acts on other grounds.

The rationality of a belief is intimately connected with justification: to justify a belief is to offer good reasons for it. What counts as a reason is decided with reference to such standards of rationality as, for instance, logic or science provides. Conformity to these standards certifies the rationality of a belief, failure to abide by them leads to loss of rational support.

7

This common view is attacked by sceptics, since they dispute the very possibility of rationality. Rationalists, in turn, attempt to defend their position, but their rebuttals rarely damage scepticism seriously, for rationalists usually argue against the weaker forms of scepticism.

The best criticism should aim at the most formidable challenge scepticism can present. If rationalism can be defended against the strongest arguments, the weaker ones will fall by the wayside. The procedure in this book will be to present initially a weak form of scepticism. The sceptical argument will, however, gradually grow stronger as it survives objections. Slowly, its full force will emerge, and it is this final position that must be refuted.

## Humean scepticism

The sceptic attacks the reliability of reason by arguing that all standards of rationality are irrational, arbitrary, lacking in justification. Hume [1] illustrates this form of scepticism, when he holds that "all is uncertain, and that our judgment is not in *any* thing possesst of *any* measure of truth and falsehood." [2]

> This sceptical doubt, both with respect to reason and the senses, is a malady, which can never be radically cur'd, but must return upon us every moment, however we may chace it away, and sometimes may seem entirely free from it. 'Tis impossible upon any system to defend either our understanding or senses; and we but expose them farther when we endeavour to justify them in that manner. As sceptical doubt arises naturally from a profound and intense reflection on these subjects, it always encreases, the farther we carry our reflections. [3]

Hume accompanies these melancholic thoughts with unruffled common sense. Thus, unavoidable as the sceptical conclusions are, "neither I, nor any other person was ever sincerely and constantly of that opinion." [4]

> Whoever has taken the pains to refute the cavils of this *total* scepticism, has really disputed without an antagonist, and endeavour'd by arguments to establish a faculty, which nature has antecedently implanted in the mind, and rendered unavoidable. [5]

When the results of philosophical reflection and the natural urgings of common sense conflict, which should be heeded?

> Shall we then establish it for a general maxim, that no refin'd or elaborate reasoning is ever to be receiv'd? Consider well the consequences of such a principle. By this means you cut off entirely all science and philosophy: You proceed upon one singular quality of the imagination, and by a parity of reason must embrace all of them: And you expressly contradict yourself; since this maxim must be built on preceding reasoning, which will be allowed to be sufficiently refin'd and metaphysical. What party, then, shall we choose among these difficulties? If we embrace this principle, and condemn all refin'd reasoning, we run into manifest absurdities. If we reject it in favour of those reasonings, we subvert entirely the human understanding. We have, therefore, no choice left but betwixt a false reason and none at all.[6]

Implicit in this conclusion is a view about reasoning.

The task of reasoning, according to Hume, is to lead to conclusions that result in knowledge. The guarantee that a particular kind of reasoning is reliable is that if its rules are followed knowledge is attained, and the conclusions reached are thereby justified. The best, most reliable kind of reasoning is deductive, because provided only that its rules are followed, the conclusions require no further justification, and so truth is apprehended and knowledge is attained.

Once this view of reasoning is accepted, scepticism is unavoidable. Therefore, the view and the assumptions upon which it rests must be made explicit.

## The first assumption: induction and deduction

The first assumption underlying this view of reasoning is expressed by Hume in the well-known passage:

> If we take in our hand any volume; divinity or school metaphysics, for instance: let us ask: *Does it contain any abstract reasoning concerning quality or number?* No. *Does it contain any experimental reasoning concerning matter of fact?* No. Commit it then to the flames: for it can contain nothing but sophistry and illusion.[7]

9

The assumption is that valid arguments must be either deductive or inductive. If a putative argument fails to be one or the other, it can contain "nothing but sophistry and illusion."

The consequence of the rigidity that allows only two forms of legitimate reasoning is just that "total scepticism" the cavils of which Hume so eloquently regrets. For the sceptic needs only to ask for a rational justification for accepting any method of reasoning. Suppose that the sceptic starts by questioning inductive arguments. His challenge cannot, of course, be met by offering inductive arguments as the required justification, for it is inductive arguments that the sceptic challenges. Since, on Hume's account, there are only two kinds of arguments, the sceptical challenge can be met only by a deductive justification of induction. Such attempts are naturally foredoomed, because if there really are two different types of arguments, then they must be logically independent of each other; nondeducibility is a consequence of logical independence. Furthermore, even if a deductive justification of induction were possible, deduction itself would have to be justified. But to offer either a deductive or inductive justification in favor of a deductive justification of induction would be hopelessly question-begging. And so, *if* all reasoning is either deductive or inductive, reason "furnishes invincible arguments against itself."

Humean scepticism has been criticized on the ground that induction and deduction are not the only forms of reasoning. But scepticism is not committed to sharing Hume's assumption; dispensing with it will strengthen scepticism, even if it weakens the Humean version of it.

The obvious way to rebut the assumption that there are only two forms of reasoning is to present alternatives to them. Are there, then, any rational disagreements that cannot be settled either by an appeal to facts or by an appeal to formal or informal linguistic convention?

Consider, first of all, disagreements about value judgments. To say, for example, that an argument is valid is not merely to describe and classify it, but also to evaluate it as being worthy of acceptance, as being reliable, as providing a dependable conclusion; it involves an appeal to a standard by which the argument is favorably judged. The demonstration of whether or not the argument *can* be judged by a certain standard is a mixture of deductive and inductive considerations of what the argument actually is, as well as questions about classification. But the question of whether or not arguments of that kind *should* be judged by that standard is neither deductively nor inductively answerable. For example, Hume's argument that all non-sophistical arguments must be deductive or inductive is neither deductive nor inductive, but an argument about the standards by which all arguments should be judged.[8]

A second kind of reasoning that is neither deductive nor inductive concerns disagreements about regulative principles which guide the construction of theories and the method of testing them. A regulative principle of physicalism, for instance, is to explain all events in terms of physics. Physicalism, at least in this respect, cannot be refuted merely by deductive or inductive arguments, for the regulative principle is based on neither kind of reasoning. To point at an event that cannot be analyzed physicalistically is not an objection to the regulative principle. For the physicalist can and would hold out for the possibility of an explanation, and he attributes the lack of it to ignorance or to other human limitations. Nor is "every event is physicalistically analyzable" a necessary truth, for its denial is not self-contradictory. Similar arguments hold for mechanism, determinism, psychoanalysis, and for many other theories. The aim of regulative principles is to guide the arrangement of observed data into intelligible patterns, so that what was previously puzzling will appear understandable. Such principles are arguable on the grounds that some patterns are more illuminating than others, but these arguments are neither deductive nor inductive.[9]

A third kind of reasoning that cannot be accommodated in the Humean scheme involves arguments about criteria of demarcation. Consider, for instance, debates about the empirical meaning criterion whose task it is to demarcate cognitively meaningful and meaningless utterances. The disputes about the respective merits of strong and weak verifiability, confirmability, falsifiability, translatability into an empiricist language cannot be deductive, because it is not supposed to be a matter of definition whether or not there could be a connection between an utterance and some relevant set of facts. Nor can the dispute be inductive, since what is at stake is whether inductive considerations are at all applicable to the utterance. Quite generally, whenever a problem of demarcation exists between one kind of consideration and a logically different kind, be it the distinction between rational and irrational, fact and value, animate and inanimate, mental and physical, the subsequent argument cannot be merely deductive or inductive. For the argument is about the very question of what inductive evidence and what deductive considerations are relevant for the rational appraisal of a kind of utterance.

But the sceptical attack on reason can easily abandon the Humean commitment to induction and deduction as the sole forms of reasoning. For the sceptic's point is that rationality requires that only those beliefs be accepted that are supported by some reliable method of reasoning, and he need not restrict reliability to induction and deduction. A method of reasoning is judged to be reliable if a justification for reasoning that way is derivable from standards of rationality. Of course these standards themselves are in need of justification, and their justification, if it were offered, would also have to be justified. In the end, therefore, no method of reasoning can be rationally supported. And so it should make no difference to scepticism how many different forms of reasoning are offered.

The fact is, however, that historically it did make a difference what forms of reasoning were held to be even candidates for reliability. The explanation lies in the existence of a second assumption underlying Humean scepticism.

## The second assumption: the ideal of certainty

The Humean sceptic regards knowledge as the aim of reasoning. To know, it is supposed, is to be free from error, to have the right to be certain. Various forms of reasoning are evaluated with reference to their propensity to avoid error and approximate certainty. Deduction has the best chance of conforming to the ideal, because provided only that its rules are followed, certainty is unfailingly attained. Induction, too, is in the running, because it could provide certainty if the Sisyphean task of amassing all the relevant facts were completed. The trouble with other forms of reasoning is that not only do they fail to achieve the ideal, but also that it is impossible to specify what would count as certainty within areas to which they apply. Reasoning about standards, regulative principles, criteria of demarcation require decisions which may or may not be felicitous. But not even the most finely honed sense of judgment could provide certainty in these shifty, changeable matters. Since the purpose of reasoning is to attain certainty, and since deduction and induction alone can do so, only deduction and induction are acceptable forms of reasoning. Deduction and induction, however, are themselves rationally uncertifiable, so no form of reasoning is acceptable.

The second assumption underlying Humean scepticism is that different forms of reasoning constitute a hierarchy. Beliefs, it is thought, all resemble each other in that they aim at certainty. They can be arranged in an order depending upon how closely their ideal is approximated. Beliefs based on deduction, then, occupy the peak of the hierarchy, and various inductively supported beliefs follow in a rapidly descending order. The price of entry into the hierarchy is the adoption of the ideal, and since nondeductive and noninductive forms of reasoning cannot pay the price, beliefs based upon them are excluded.

But why should this model be accepted? It is based on the assumption that all forms of reasoning have an essential feature in common which accounts for the reliability of that form, and the model is an exemplification of this feature. When the Humean sceptic finds that no form of reasoning, not even deduction, approximates the ideal of the model, he concludes that no form of reasoning is reliable. There is, however, another conclusion possible: when particular cases conflict with the model, it may be the model that is at fault.

The justification of the model cannot be that it is a generalization from beliefs that are commonly regarded as justified. For, then, the model could not be used for the purpose that it was constructed, namely, to call into question the common view that very many beliefs are justified. A model based on a generalization cannot be used to prove that very many of the cases upon which the generalization is based are not cases that fall under the aegis of the generalization. If the proof were successful, the generalization would fail, and the model based upon it would be groundless. The Humean sceptic's claim, however, is even more extreme than this: he argues that *all* the cases upon which his model rests fail as cases of justified beliefs. The model cannot therefore be a generalization from instances of justified beliefs. If there are such instances, the Humean sceptic is wrong; if there are not, he could not have derived his model from them.

The alternative, then, may be to think of the model as embodying an ideal, a standard, a paradigm with reference to which beliefs are evaluated. Clearly, there is no necessity inherent in beliefs dictating their analysis in hierarchical terms. Why should they be justified only with reference to the ideal of certainty? Why should all beliefs have something in common? The answer leads to the third assumption of Humean scepticism.


## The third assumption: the traditional view of classification

Another assumption of the Humean view is that the reason why particulars are labelled by a common epithet is that they resemble each other in some important way. If they did not, there would be no reason for calling them by the same name. The resemblance of particulars that are members of the same class is supposed to be a necessary condition of their class-membership.

This assumption derives from the traditional analysis of classification. It is immaterial for the present purposes whether the resemblance is interpreted realistically, as holding between characteristics inherent in the resembling particulars, or whether the resemblance is understood nominalistically, as resting on the judgment of the person who performs the classification. The important point is that Humean sceptics, as well as many of their opponents, accept this analysis of classification, and this is what gives a certain plausibility to the idea that all beliefs must resemble each other.

The traditional view of classification, and by implication the third assumption of Humean scepticism, has been challenged. The antinominal answers of realism and nominalism are not the only possible solutions of the problem of how particulars are classified. These answers lead to an apparently insoluble conflict and to the subsequent inability to explain what they set out to explain, namely, how we can classify particulars. So there is at least a *prima facie* case for needing a new answer.

The idea underlying the new analysis of classification is that particulars classified together may resemble each other as members of a family do and need not resemble each other in respect to one commonly held characteristic. While the traditional analysis leads to a confused search for the one characteristic shared by all the particulars in the same class, the new analysis renders such a search unnecessary. In this inquiry, as in so many others, philosophers were motivated by a "craving for generality." Humean scepticism is a symptom of an unsatisfied craving for generality.

> This craving for generality is the resultant of a number of tendencies connected with particular philosophical confusions. There is— (a) The tendency to look for something in common to all the entities which we commonly subsume under a general term. —We are inclined to think that there must be something in common to all games, say, and that this common property is the justification for applying the general term "game" to the various games; whereas games form a *family* the members of which have family likenesses. Some of them have the same nose, others the same eyebrows, and others again the same way of walking; and these likenesses overlap. The idea of a general concept being a common property of its particular instances connects up with other primitive, too simple, ideas of the structure of language. It is comparable to the idea that *properties* are *ingredients* of the things which have properties; e.g. that beauty is an ingredient of all beautiful things as alcohol is of beer and wine.[10]

If one follows Wittgenstein's advice to look and not think in order to see what different particulars have in common

> we see a complicated network of similarities overlapping and criss-crossing: sometimes overall similarities, sometimes similarities of detail.[11]

If it is not, in general, a necessary condition of classification that all members must resemble each other in some one respect, then members of the class of justified beliefs need not share one common feature either. If different beliefs are justifiable differently, then a particular belief would not be unjustifiable just because it fails to fit the model of deduction and induction. If justification is separated from the ideal of certainty, then the hierarchical conception of justified beliefs collapses and it can no longer be thought necessary to offer justifications by appealing to one and only one standard.

## *Summary*

Humean scepticism has been severely attacked for accepting the three assumptions. It is possible, however, to reformulate Humean scepticism, or, if it is preferred, to formulate another version of scepticism which is free from these vulnerable assumptions and thus far stronger. The ground upon which this version of scepticism ("scepticism" from now on) attacks rationalism is its incapacity to provide a rational justification for standards of rationality. The sceptic does not handicap himself unnecessarily by allowing only two methods of reasoning to be used for justification; nor does he suppose that different forms of reasoning must all aim at certainty; and he drops the demand for a common feature of all forms of reasoning.

What remains, then, is a challenge to the notion that it is possible to justify rationally any belief. For such a justification requires appeal to standards of rationality and these need to be, and according to the sceptic cannot be, rationally supported. The sceptic attacks the possibility of knowledge, certainty, or justified belief only indirectly. His primary target is the process—reasoning—which allegedly yields the reliable conclusion. If reasoning is successfully challenged, then the rationality of any of its products becomes *ipso facto* dubious.

## Rationality and justification [12]

Our Cartesian heritage prompts us to regard rationality as involving the acceptance of all and only those beliefs that are justifiable. The justification of beliefs is provided by reasoning, and a belief is rational if it is held as the conclusion of a reliable method of reasoning. Reasoning, then, is reliable if it conforms to one or another standard. Both sceptics and many rationalists accept this analysis of rationality; they merely draw opposite conclusions from it. The difficulty the rationalist meets occurs when he finds he must demonstrate that standards of rationality are themselves rational.

## Postulational rationalism

The first line of defense attempts to meet the sceptic by postulating some standard of rationality and admitting only those beliefs as rational that are held in accordance with the standard. The deductive ideal is one such standard, but there are many other candidates: the Cartesian clear and distinct ideas, the sense data of phenomenalism, the "given" of traditional empiricism, the protocol sentences of early logical positivism, and so forth.

No matter what standard is chosen, appealing to it involves the same problem. For if rational justification consists in appealing to a standard of rationality, then how can the standard itself be rationally justified? And if the standard is judged rational by its own testimony, then postulational rationalism is question-begging. If the standard, however, is justified by an appeal to another standard, then the same question arises about the credentials of that other standard, and so postulational rationalism leads to a never-ending regress of justificational attempts. Postulational rationalism is thus an easy prey for the sceptic who can point at the ultimate lack of justification for any of the standards to which appeal is made.

There are two strategies for countering the sceptical challenge. One is to argue for its illegitimacy, while the other is to meet it by providing a ground upon which standards of rationality can be founded. The first approach is taken by analytic rationalism and it fails. The second approach will eventually bring about the demise of scepticism. But a great deal must be said before this promise is kept.

## Analytic rationalism

The idea of the analytic rationalist is to accept that justification consists in appealing to some standard of rationality, while denying that the question of that standard's rationality can arise. The reason he gives is that "rationality" has meaning only with reference to some standard. Hence questioning the rationality of standards of rationality is like questioning the length of the standard meter rod.

The virtue of analytic rationalism is that it avoids the necessity of opting between begging the question or pursuing the justification that does not need justification. Analytic rationalists accept that if one can ask for the rational justification of standards of rationality, then rationalism surrenders to scepticism. They strive, therefore, to rule the question out of order. Ayer, arguing as an analytic rationalist, points out that any justification of induction will

> assume that the future can . . . be relied on to resemble the past. No doubt this assumption is correct, but there can be no way of proving it without its being presupposed. So, if circular proofs are not to count, there can be no proof. . . . This does not mean that the scientific method is irrational. It could be irrational only if there were a standard of rationality which it failed to meet; whereas in fact it goes to set the standard: arguments are judged to be rational or irrational by reference to it.[13]

The argument can be further strengthened by noticing that not only do analytic rationalists accept the standards of rationality, but their critics do so as well. The sceptical arguments presuppose the standards that they were supposed to undermine. If the standards fail, the sceptical arguments fail. If the standards are defensible, the sceptical arguments are unsuccessful.

Analytic rationalism, however, does not withstand the sceptical assault. Part of the problem is that the nature of the account of standards of rationality is unclear. If it is supposed to be a *description* of how arguments as a matter of fact are judged, then analytic rationalism is simply false. Rhetoric, propaganda, flattery and threat, guilt and greed play a considerably greater role in the judgment of arguments than does the judicious weighing of evidence.

If, however, it is supposed that analytic rationalism offers a *prescrip-*

*tion* of how arguments ought to be judged, then it is perfectly proper to demand some support for the recommended standards. The demand is made much the more acute, because alternative standards— utopian, religious, aesthetic, superstitious, political—are presented in frightening abundance.

Nor does it help to avoid scepticism to *define* "rationality" as "satisfying such-and-such standard" because the whole problem is whether or not arguments should be judged favorably by their satisfaction of standards that analytic rationalists are inclined to accept. Why believe because it is reasonable, why not believe with the beatific Tertullian because it is absurd?

Yet another part of the problem lies in the fact that the sceptical challenger need not be disconcerted by the charge that he makes use of the standards he attacks. For the sceptic's point is that *all* standards are arbitrary in that they lack the possibility of rational justification. The logic of the sceptical challenge is *reductio ad absurdum:* it is to assume for the sake of argument the rationalist's standards and show, in their own terms, that they are arbitrary.

Thus given only postulational and analytic rationalism, rationalism is untenable. The very general reason for this is that justification consists in appealing to standards of rationality and the standards must be and have not been rationally justified. The sceptical challenge is based on the charge that the justifications offered by rationalists are, in the last analysis, no less arbitrary than the fideistic appeal to faith, revelation, insight, instinct, taste, or what have you.

## Psychological and epistemological scepticism

Scepticism is frequently attacked on grounds of inconsistency. Its critics do not have logical inconsistency in mind, for they do not suppose that scepticism is committed to two or more contradictory propositions. Rather they charge that the sceptics behave inconsistently, that they do not really hold the philosophical views they avow. Thus a sceptic is committed to denying the rationality of believing in the existence of the external world, yet his behavior belies his commitment: he talks to people, he opens doors, sits on chairs, none of which he would be doing were he consistent. This is perhaps what prompted Russell's remark about the "frivolous insincerity" of scepticism and Hume's pronouncement that nobody holds scepticism "sincerely and constantly."

This criticism, however, rests on a misunderstanding. Scepticism is not a psychological attitude. There is, of course, such a thing as the sceptical frame of mind or the sceptical temperament. What this comes to is a certain overscrupulousness about demanding evidence, a tendency to be suspicious, not to be trusting, wanting more persuasion that what would satisfy most people. This, however, does not constitute a philosophical argument. It is merely a tendency to doubt and until supported by arguments it remains a psychological scepticism having very little philosophical interest.

Epistemological scepticism, on the other hand, is the philosophical threat and that is what is being discussed here. It is a thoughtful, argued attack on the possibility of rational justification and it rests on the contention that standards of rationality are arbitrary.

The epistemological sceptic can behave just like everybody else, and he can, with perfect consistency, hold all those nonphilosophical beliefs that people generally hold. He can, for instance, believe in the existence of objects, animals, people, he can hold that some actions are right and others are wrong, he can hold beliefs about the past, and so on. The main point on which he differs from other people is the question of the rational justification of these and other beliefs. Many people accept that it is possible to rationally justify these beliefs, but the epistemological sceptic denies it. His denial need not affect his holding them, nor need his conviction about the inadequacy of reason have any reflection upon his ordinary behavior. The epistemological sceptic is a person whose philosophical reflections have led him to reject reason as a guide for life.

If questioned about the grounds for accepting his beliefs, the epistemological sceptic has several options. He can simply deny that there are any grounds and explain that he just holds these beliefs because they strike him as true, but that he neither desires nor is able to prove them so. Another option is to appeal to authority. His beliefs are held because his father, teacher, textbook, newspaper, political party, or king said that they are true. Or the epistemological sceptic may become a fideist and justify his beliefs by an appeal to faith. The epistemological sceptic need not be without grounds for his beliefs— he must only eschew rational grounds.

It might be asked then what difference does it make whether or not a person is an epistemological sceptic? The main difference is that if epistemological scepticism were correct, then any belief would have precisely the same verisimilitude as any other. It would be impossible to criticize, improve upon, or to make more reliable what anybody believes. So science and pseudoscience, history and myth, medicine and quackery, considered judgment and rabid prejudice, would be equally acceptable. Furthermore, rational argument as a method of settling disputes would disappear and those old stand-bys, force and propaganda, would take its place. The difference it would make is that if scepticism were correct and if it were accepted, life would be ugly, brutish, and short.

## Scepticism: a summary

The most fundamental kind of scepticism is directed against the rationality of standards of rationality. It demands a rational justification of these standards and its challenge is the claim that such justifications turn out to be question-begging, lead to infinite regress, or are, themselves, merely disguised fideistic appeals.

Scepticism can afford perfect liberality in respect to the various forms of reasoning whose reliability rationalists advocate; in this respect it is much stronger than Humean scepticism which rigidly insists upon the exclusiveness of induction and deduction. Nor should scepticism be thought to stem from the quixotic quest for certainty. It, although not its Humean predecessor, would be satisfied with some examples of reliable reasoning even if such examples provided conclusions that fell short of certainty; it is the method of obtaining conclusions, not the conclusions themselves that the sceptic directly attacks. Furthermore, scepticism is not committed to either a realistic or a nominalistic analysis of classification. There is no reason why the successor to Humean scepticism cannot take the Wittgensteinian analysis in its stride.

Scepticism should be thought of as an epistemological doctrine, not as a psychological attitude. The personality and the behavior of the sceptic are as little relevant to the philosophical merit of the position as are similar *ad hominem* considerations directed against any other theory. Scepticism has been associated with a doubting frame of mind for all too long. What it should be associated with is a persistent attack on the grounds of reason. It is this attack which must be met.

# PART 2

# INCONCLUSIVE ARGUMENTS AGAINST SCEPTICISM

# 2 The pragmatic argument: Carnap

*" [I]n the 'practical use' of reason we find grounds for accepting those important propositions which are its postulates, but which speculative reason is demonstrably powerless to establish. . . . practical reason yields, so to speak, a bonus or dividend not procurable by any other means."*—G. J. Warnock, *"The Primacy of Practical Reason"*

## The pragmatic answer to scepticism

The pragmatic answer to scepticism is that the sceptical challenge is misconceived. The challenge appears dangerous because it is misinterpreted by both sceptics and champions of rationality. If scepticism is thought of as demanding a theoretical justification of rationality, then it can never be met, because one theoretical answer necessitates the support of another, and all theoretical answers cannot have theoretical support. But there is no need to strive for the theoretical justification of rationality because there is another kind: the practical.

The reliability of reason is proven by the favorable outcome of activities which rely upon reason. Thus the proof of rationalism is its usefulness. Reason can be vindicated in practice, but it cannot be validated by theory.[1] Scepticism derives its deceptive power from the misguided search for theoretical validation. What needs to be done to counter the sceptical challenge is to stop looking for the impossible and to call attention to our signal practical achievements.

The most persuasive contemporary statement of this position is Rudolf Carnap's in his article "Empiricism, Semantics, and Ontology."[2] The argument there is not directed explicitly against scepticism, but against the adoption of an allegedly mistaken view of external questions. However, since scepticism rests upon that view, it is necessary to examine Carnap's objections.

## Carnap's argument

The crux of Carnap's case is the distinction between theoretical and practical questions. His argument is directed toward the conclusion that the sceptical challenge should be understood as posing a practical and not a theoretical question. Carnap elucidates the distinction with reference to the notion of a linguistic framework. Carnap explains what he means by "linguistic framework" in three ways. First, he describes it in terms of its purpose:

> If someone wishes to speak in his language about a new kind of entities, he has to introduce a system of new ways of speaking, subject to new rules; we shall call this the construction of a linguistic *framework* for the new entities in question.[3]

Second, he describes the essential steps in the construction of a linguistic framework together with an account of their constituents:

> The essential steps are. . . . First, the introduction of a general term, a predicate of a higher level, for the new kind of entities, permitting us to say of any particular entity that it belongs to this kind. . . . Second, the introduction of variables of the new type. The new entities are values of these variables; the constants . . . are substitutable for the variables.[4]

Presumably the introduction of meaning and referential rules in accordance with which the general terms and variables are used is also an essential step. Third, Carnap gives examples of linguistic frameworks; these are: "the world of things," "the system of numbers," "the system of propositions," "the system of thing properties," "the system of integers and rational numbers," "the system of real numbers," and "the spatiotemporal coordinate system for physics."

The material object framework, for instance, has "material object" as its general term; "table," "rock," "car," etc., as its variables. The rules determine how sentences can be constructed out of these terms and of logical constants, and also how these sentences can be used to refer to various aspects of the world. The material object framework enables its users to think and speak about the world in a certain way.

With the help of the concept of linguistic framework Carnap introduces the distinction between external and internal questions:

> We must distinguish between two kinds of questions of existence: first, questions of existence of certain entities of the new kind *within the framework;* we call them *internal questions;* and second, questions concerning the existence or reality *of the system of entities as a whole, called external questions.* [5]

Questions like "Is there a white piece of paper on my desk?", "Did King Arthur actually live?", "Are unicorns and centaurs real or merely imaginary?" are internal to the material object framework. They can be answered by making use of the rules and procedures of the framework. If one asks, however, "Are there any material objects?" or "Are material objects real?" then one asks questions external to the material object framework.

Carnap's position is that internal questions are a kind of theoretical—by which it is meant factual or logical—question, while external questions are a kind of practical question. When the sceptic demands a justification for rationality, he is asking an external question. It can be answered by justifying the practical decision involved in its acceptance:

> The acceptance cannot be judged as being either true or false because it is not an assertion. It can only be judged as being more or less expedient, fruitful, conducive to the aim for which language is intended. [6]

If it is recognized that the justification demanded by the sceptic rests on a misunderstanding, then the lack of theoretical justification of rationality will be regarded as a symptom of the illegitimacy of the sceptical demand, and not as a sign of its profundity.

## Internal criticisms of Carnap's argument

"Linguistic framework" may mean "language as a whole." In this sense, if there were no linguistic framework, it would be impossible to speak or to write. "Linguistic framework," however, may mean only "a part of language." Language may be taken to consist, *inter alia,* of the totality of linguistic frameworks. In the second sense, a linguistic framework is only a particular way of speaking or writing.

27

If Carnap is understood to accept the first interpretation, then it must be granted that external questions cannot have cognitive significance. But Carnap's argument would then amount to the utterly trivial point that no question can be asked outside of language. Indeed, questions have to be framed within language.

Naturally, Carnap meant to do more than to make this trivial claim. The correct interpretation is that linguistic frameworks are parts of language, and this is supported by Carnap's examples: "the world of things," "the system of numbers," "the system of propositions," etc., are all parts of language. There is no one framework whose generality is the same as that of language.

Consider "Are there any material objects?" Given the linguistic framework for material objects, this is an external question. It should, therefore, be understood to be a practical question about the usefulness of that linguistic framework. Answers to it that appear to have truth-value are actually without cognitive significance. The framework does not commit the user to a belief in the existence of material objects; the affirmation or the denial of their existence is neither sanctioned nor permitted by the framework.

"Are there any material objects?" may indeed be interpreted along these lines, but there are other perhaps more plausible interpretations as well. The question could be regarded as asking "Is it true that material objects exist?" Carnap would argue that this is a question about the usefulness of the linguistic framework for material objects. One may agree that the question is partly about the usefulness of the framework and deny that it is purely a practical question. The cognitive element both in it and in possible answers is the same as the explanation of the framework's usefulness, namely, that material objects exist. One reason why a linguistic framework may be useful is that it is not used to describe chimerical entities.

Carnap's rejoinder would be that there is no way to settle external questions, unless they are interpreted as practical questions. For the discussion about an entity can proceed only within the framework designed for conducting that discussion. The point of using a framework is precisely that no other framework is suitable for discussing the relevant kind of entity. So Carnap poses a problem: external questions are either pseudoquestions or practical questions. In the former

28

case, they need not and cannot be answered. In the latter case, the answer is a decision about what to do, not a cognitive assertion about the existence of a kind of entity.

This predicament can be avoided if it is recognized that linguistic frameworks are not sharply distinguishable from each other. Hence a question external to one framework could be reinterpreted as an internal question in another framework.

Consider how the key general term is introduced into a linguistic framework. At least a partial definition is a necessary step in the construction of a framework, otherwise no one would know what the framework is about. The initial definition must be either ostensive or be given in terms of another framework. Whichever it is, Carnap's point fails. For if the initial definition is ostensive, then the thing defined exists; otherwise the definition could not be ostensive. Consequently the framework that uses an ostensively defined general term is committed to an existential presupposition. Thus questions about the existence of ostensively defined entities cannot lack cognitive significance. If, however, the general term is initially defined in terms of another framework, Carnap's point still does not hold. Suppose that the problem is the introduction of "material object." The first step is specifying another framework in terms of which "material object" could be defined. Let us assume with Carnap that the framework for sense data may qualify.[7] The next step is to formulate a partial definition in sense data language that is at least roughly synonymous with "material object." This may be done by saying that "material object" is roughly synonymous with "the cause of certain specifiable collections of sense data." The initial definition thus obtained may be substantially altered by a fully developed framework for material objects. Defining the term in this way does not commit one to a presupposition about the existence of material objects, but it has the consequence that the existence of at least one framework is a necessary condition of the construction of any other framework. If this were not the case, the general term could not be given meaning (unless it were defined ostensively, but that, as we have seen, does not help Carnap's case).

If there must exist a framework before a new one can be constructed, then what Carnap says cannot be done can be done. Maybe

"Are there material objects?", interpreted as "Is it true that material objects exist?", is external to a framework. Perhaps if only one framework were in existence, then answers to it would not have cognitive significance—but, of course, there is at least one other framework. Therefore, for each external question there is a question that is both roughly synonymous with it and that is internal to the framework in which the general term was initially defined. The question in this case is: "Is it true that certain collections of sense data (those in terms of which "material object" was defined) have a cause?"

The second question is not about the sense-data framework, so it cannot be objected to on the grounds that it is either a call for a practical decision about the continued use of the framework or a question to which no answer is possible. Nor can the second question be criticized for not being even roughly synonymous with the first, since one was initially defined in terms of the other.

If a general term is initially defined in terms of another framework, then questions about the existence of its referents do have cognitively significant answers. Now it may be that Carnap would object to calling the roughly synonymous formulations external questions, but nothing substantive depends on this. If the objection is just the expression of preference for one formulation of the question over a roughly synonymous phrasing, then it is quite innocuous. But Carnap did not mean to argue for this trivial point; he meant to make it meaningless to engage in the sort of existential inquiry to which external questions traditionally lead.

The second internal criticism is that any explication of "linguistic framework" is bound to be incompatible with Carnap's analysis of external questions. It is not sufficient to describe a linguistic framework as a way of talking about a kind of entity. Suppose we regard our way of talking about elephants as a linguistic framework. "Do elephants exist?" is, then, an external question. But it can be treated also as an internal question in the material object framework. What Carnap needs is a criterion for being a linguistic framework that makes it impossible to interpret external questions as internal questions in another framework. What would satisfy this requirement?

A criterion-candidate may be to regard a way of talking about a kind of entity a linguistic framework if any discussion about the entity presupposes that way of talking. For instance, talk about elephants presupposes the linguistic framework for material objects, while talk about material objects is, in some sense, fundamental so that it presupposes nothing for settling internal questions about material objects. On this criterion external questions could not sensibly arise, because linguistic frameworks would be fundamental.

The difficulty is that there are alternative and equally fundamental linguistic frameworks. Carnap recognizes this. In connection with the relation between the material-object framework and the framework for physics he notes that an entity may be described either in terms of "qualitative predicates," like "hot," or in terms of "physical magnitudes," like "mass" or "temperature," etc., depending on which framework one chooses to use.[8] But if this is true, then the possibility of asking cognitively significant external questions is not excluded. For a question external to a framework could always be reinterpreted as an internal question in an alternative, equally fundamental framework. "Is it true that material objects exist?" could be reinterpreted as: "Is it true that space-time points occur in certain conglomerations (in those that are known as "material objects")?" This latter interpretation, however, is internal to the framework for physics, so that if this criterion were adopted, Carnap's argument about external questions would not follow.

Yet another candidate needs only to be mentioned to be shown inadequate. It would not do to say that what makes a particular way of talking a linguistic framework is that one and only one kind of entity is being discussed. For this would allow a fantastic number of frameworks: one for elephants, one for tigers, one for lions, etc. And what appeared as external to one framework would be an internal question in a more general framework, for instance, in the one for mammals.

It might be thought possible to improve upon the above criterion-candidate by combining the requirement of there being one and only one kind of entity discussed with the requirement that the kind of entity be fundamental. One would mean thereby that that way of talking is so general that other ways can always be subsumed under its heading. The number of fundamental ways of talking then would be the number of linguistic frameworks.

This would meet the objection raised previously by disqualifying ways of talking about tigers, elephants, etc., from being linguistic frameworks. Only such fundamental entities as material objects, numbers, space-time points, propositions, and the like would qualify for linguistic frameworks.

It must be remembered, however, that an entity being fundamental cannot be understood as an ontological thesis, for then Carnap's argument that the acceptance of a kind of entity commits one to no belief about the existence of the entity would fail. So it must be understood as the linguistic thesis that a way of talking about a kind of entity is more fundamental than another way of talking about another kind of entity. One might see how, in a sense, talk about material objects is more fundamental than talk about elephants.

There are two reasons, however, why this criterion-candidate cannot be used to support Carnap's thesis. First, Carnap's examples contradict it: several linguistic frameworks are dependent upon other linguistic frameworks. The system of thing properties presupposes the system of things; the system of integers and rational numbers and the system of real numbers both presuppose the system of natural numbers. Second, even if we disregard Carnap's own examples, this criterion-candidate would not do, for there are alternative, equally fundamental, ways of talking about a kind of entity. For instance, material objects can be discussed either in the material-object framework or in the framework for physics; the same is true of properties of material objects. The problem is not just that we do not have the necessary procedure for settling which of these alternative frameworks is fundamental, but it is also that a question external to one of these frameworks can always be treated as an internal question within the other framework.

Thus none of the criterion-candidates discussed provides a satisfactory interpretation of "linguistic framework." Failing this, Carnap's argument that external questions lack cognitive significance also fails. The reason why the required criterion-candidate has not been provided is that a criterion enabling us both to give a clear interpretation of "linguistic framework" and to exclude the possibility of there being cognitively significant external questions cannot be provided. There is a dilemma buried in the effort.

The dilemma is that the criterion for a way of talking, being a linguistic framework, must be either linguistic or ontological. If the criterion is ontological, it necessarily involves presuppositions about the existence of the entity discussed. And so it is possible to question the existential presupposition, and hence ask a cognitively significant external question. If, however, the criterion is linguistic, then another difficulty arises. There are alternative ways of talking about a kind of entity, and a question external to one way is internal to another way.

## Existential presuppositions and metaphysical theories

A way of avoiding the dilemma might be to deny that the first lemma presents a coherent alternative. It might be argued that no sense has been given to the possibility that external questions involve existential presuppositions. But this argument fails, since there are existential presuppositions involved in all linguistic frameworks that have a descriptive use and it cannot lack cognitive significance to question these presuppositions.

If a linguistic framework has a descriptive use, it follows that there is at least one existential presupposition involved in its use: its users must explicitly or implicitly accept the truth of the statement asserting the existence of the entity that is being described. Otherwise the users would be in the absurd position of employing a framework for describing an entity whose existence they do not accept.

The descriptive use of a linguistic framework requires the acceptance of an existential presupposition. However if an existential presupposition is accepted, it follows neither that a metaphysical theory about the nature of the entity is also accepted, nor that the presupposition is true. The acceptance of a metaphysical theory implies commitment to an existential presupposition, but an existential presupposition may be accepted without even considering any metaphysical theory. An existential presupposition commits one to the existence of a kind of entity. A metaphysical theory invites acceptance of some analysis about the nature of the entity.

External questions may be about existential presuppositions or

33

about metaphysical theories. Carnap interprets them exclusively in the second way, while they should, at least sometimes, be interpreted in the first way.

Perhaps external questions about metaphysical theories are practical questions, but it does not follow that external questions about existential presuppositions must also be treated in the same way. Consider again: "Is it true that material objects exist?"; it is about the analysis of the causes of perception. The analysis, given in terms of a metaphysical theory, requires the acceptance of the existential presupposition that perception has an external cause. The external questions whose existence Carnap failed to recognize are about presuppositions to which metaphysical theories are inevitably committed. When the sceptic presents his challenge he questions the existential presuppositions assumed by metaphysical theories.

Carnap might object that answers to external questions construed in this way cannot be tested and therefore cannot be cognitively significant. For testing existential presuppositions is possible only if some view is adopted about what it is whose existence is presupposed and such a view is a metaphysical theory. So an existential presupposition can be tested only by testing the metaphysical theory in terms of which the presupposition is expressed. The objection is double-barrelled: first, since existential presuppositions cannot be tested, answers to external questions about them cannot have cognitive significance; second, existential presuppositions are indistinguishable from the metaphysical theory in terms of which they are expressed and so no separate question can arise about existential presuppositions.

In reply to the first point, it is sufficient to note that it evokes an extremely narrow version of the verifiability principle. The objection holds only if the cognitive meaningfulness of a statement depends upon the actual, immediate possibility of testing. There is, however, very little in favor of this criterion of meaningfulness. If it is recognized that existential presuppositions can be tested when they are expressed in terms of metaphysical theories, then the argument for external questions about them having cognitively significant answers will stand even in the face of less indefensible versions of the verifiability principle. But, of course, there are good reasons for rejecting the positivist account of cognitive significance. So while it is true that existential presuppositions cannot be tested until there is a metaphysical theory offering an analysis of the entity which is the object of the existential presupposition, it is not true that the acceptance or the rejection of the existential presupposition before there is a way of testing is devoid of cognitive significance. And this leads to the second part of the objection.

The objection is that existential presuppositions cannot be distinguished from the metaphysical theory in terms of which they are expressed and tested. This can be met by showing that the distinction follows from some of the things Carnap himself says. Carnap writes:

> If someone wishes to speak in his language about a new kind of entities, he has to introduce a system of new ways of speaking, subject to new rules; we shall call this procedure the construction of a linquistic famework for the new entities in question.[9]

The following points can be derived from Carnap's position: (1) At the time when a new linguistic framework is introduced there already is a language in existence. This is supported by Carnap's remarks about "the introduction of a system of *new* ways of speaking," [my italics]. For there to be new ways, there must have been old ways. (2) There must be a time when the existence of the new entity is accepted, yet there is no way of speaking about it in the existing language. That the new entity cannot be spoken about in the existing language follows from Carnap's remarks about *"having* to introduce a new way of speaking . . . for the new entities," [my italics]. That the existence of the new entities is accepted follows from Carnap's statement that "someone *wishes* to speak in his language about a new kind of entities" [my italics]. If an existential presupposition were not accepted, why would anybody wish to speak about the new entity? The old kinds can be spoken about in the old language. (3) The acceptance of the new entity cannot be understood *merely* as a decision to use a particular framework. For at the time of the decision there can be no suitable linguistic framework; if there were, there would not be a problem about discussing the new entity. The existing framework has to be enlarged precisely in order for discussing the new entity. Nor can the decision be to use the new framework, because at the crucial time the new linguistic framework is not yet in existence. Acceptance of a new entity, therefore, cannot amount to a decision to use either the old or the new framework, since the first is inadequate and the second does not yet exist.

On the basis of (1), (2), and (3), implied by Carnap's argument, we can reject the core of Carnap's thesis that

> we may still speak of "the acceptance of new entities" . . . but one must keep in mind that this phrase does not mean for us anything more than the acceptance of the new framework. . . . Above all, it must not be interpreted as referring to an assumption, belief, or assertion of "the reality of the entities." [10]

The acceptance of the new entity must be prior even to the decision to construct, let alone accept, a new linguistic framework.

## External criticisms of the pragmatic argument

A defender of the pragmatic refutation of scepticism might acknowledge that Carnap's formulation of the pragmatic position has internal defects. He might, however, attribute the defects to formulation's peculiarities, such as the incoherence of the notion of linguistic framework and the survival of the verifiability principle. He would hold that the pragmatic position is not damaged by these incidental shortcomings, for it can be expressed in unobjectionable language.

The pragmatic point is that of any theory (not linguistic framework) there can arise internal and external questions. The theory can either handle internal questions, or it is shown to be defective. External questions are about the theory and so they cannot be answered in terms of that theory. Many external questions can perhaps be reformulated as internal questions in another theory, but there is an external question—the one the sceptic is asking—that cannot be reformulated. For the sceptic wants to know what justification there is for constructing theories and adhering to them in our actions. Since the question is about the justification of theories, no theoretical answer can be satisfactory. But that is no cause for concern, because there is a

36

practical answer: the justification is that theories are useful because they aid us in achieving our purposes. This, it may be argued, is the hard core of pragmatism, and while Carnap's formulation perhaps obscures it, all the same it also contains the point.

The reformulated pragmatic answer is very plausible. The difficulty is that it does not, by itself, meet the sceptical challenge to rationality, for given the pragmatic answer only, no goals can be rationally justified nor can theories provide explanation.

The pragmatic answer to the sceptical doubt about theories is that their justification depends on the contribution theories make toward the achievement of our goals. A sceptic may grant this and go on to question the rationality of the goals. The usefulness of a theory does not guarantee its rationality, for a useful theory may serve an irrational goal. How is one to decide whether or not a goal is rational? How can goals be rationally chosen, especially given the multiplicity of frequently conflicting goals?

Consider, for instance, how the sceptic might attack the pragmatic justification of scientific theories. He starts by asking: what is the goal that scientific theories help to achieve? The answer might be that it is understanding and subsequent ability to cope with problems posed by the environment. So the injunction to the sceptic is: if you want to cope with your environment, do science. Scepticism has frequently been made to look foolish by supposing that the sceptic, at this stage in the argument, would attack the consequent of the conditional. But the profound question the sceptic poses is about the antecedent. Why should it be one's goal to cope with the environment? Perhaps that is a trivial activity distracting attention from the really important purpose of life, which is, say, worship of God, the appreciation of beauty, or the achievement of a mystical union with nature. The sceptic's point is not that these goal are more worthy than the one scientific theories help to achieve, but that these are alternative goals and the scientific ideal needs to be justified vis-a-vis its rivals. The justification cannot be pragmatic because that rests upon having already accepted certain goals. So adherence to a goal must be justified nonpragmatically, if it is justified at all. Hence, the pragmatic answer to scepticism is incomplete.

Suppose, for the sake of argument, that the goal of coping with the environment is accepted. We all follow the scientific method and our activities are graced by success. The difficulty with pragmatism is that it makes it impossible to explain why we are successful. Scientific theories work, but why do they? It cannot be because they reveal how things are. For

> [a]n alleged statement of the reality of a system of entities is a pseudostatement without cognitive content. . . . To be sure, we have to face at this point an important question; but it is a practical, not a theoretical question. . . . The acceptance cannot be judged as being either true or false, because it is not an assertion. It can only be judged as being more or less expedient, fruitful, conducive to[our] aim.[11]

We are urged here to sever the connection between the acceptance or rejection of a theory and its truth or falsity. Expedience, not verisimilitude, is to count as the relevant criterion of rationality. Theories are no longer expected to give an explanation, instead they are to be recipes for action. The result is that while we may be successful in action, we do not know why we are successful. Is it that science works because it correctly depicts the nature of reality or because God is good or because we are lucky? Are we successful because failure goes unrecognized? Given only pragmatism, these are unanswerable questions.

## Conclusion

The argument between scepticism and pragmatism has now reached the following stage. Carnap's attempt to render harmless the sceptical challenge by interpreting it as posing an external question that has only a practical answer fails. The failure is due to the incoherence of the notion of linguistic-framework to which questions are supposedly external and to the tacit evocation of a particularly rigid version of the verifiability principle. The principle is used to attack the distinction between existential presuppositions and the metaphysical theories about the nature of the things whose existence is presupposed. But the pragmatic position can be reformulated in terms of external and internal questions about theories, and it can also be acknowledged that not all external questions need to lack cognitive significance. The important pragmatic point is that the sceptic's question about the rational justification of theories is an external question to which only a practical answer can and need be given. And that answer is in terms of the usefulness of the activity of constructing theories and acting upon them.

Pragmatism insists on a feature of rationality which is undeniably important. Rationality, to be worth anything, should be a more successful policy than those recommended by its rivals. The rational pursuit of a goal should be demonstrably more efficient than other ways of acting. So let us grant to pragmatism that a necessary condition of rationality is that rational activity should tend to be successful. But success is not sufficient for rationality, for one may be successful in an irrational pursuit. To meet the sceptical challenge it has to be shown also that the pursuit of rational goals is demonstrably preferable, on rational grounds, to the pursuit of nonrational goals. Pragmatism, by its own strategy, is disqualified from this attempt. For if rational justification consists in the successful achievement of goals, then goals themselves could never be rationally justified. Pragmatism offers a necessary condition of rationality, but it is incomplete because the sufficient conditions are lacking.

But not only has pragmatism provided the beginning of a way of meeting the sceptical challenge, it has done so by using the distinction between external and internal questions—a distinction which will prove very useful. Carnap's employment of it is too rigid; there is no need for equating external questions with practical questions and internal questions with theoretical considerations. The usefulness of the distinction comes from its providing a precise way of separating questions *within* a theory from questions *about* a theory. This distinction and the principle that rational activity should tend to be successful are the gains from our examination of pragmatism.

# 3 The appeal to common sense: Moore

*"This, after all, you know, really is a finger: there is no doubt about it: I know it and you all know it. And I think we may safely challenge any philosopher to bring forward any argument in favour either of the proposition that we do not know it, or of the proposition that it is not true, which does not at some point, rest upon some premiss which is, beyond comparison, less certain than is the proposition which it is designed to attack."—G. E. Moore "Some Judgments of Perception"*

## Common sense

A possible way to counter the sceptical challenge is to argue that it goes against common sense and since common sense is rationally justified, scepticism is mistaken. The oustanding contemporary advocate of this approach is G. E. Moore. Moore's defense of common sense has attracted much criticism, and this, in turn, has forced the strengthening of the original position. The view considered here is a strengthened version of Moore's argument.

"Common sense" may be used normatively and descriptively. In its normative use "common sense" means "good, sound judgment," the opposite of being hairbrained, flighty. In its descriptive use "common sense" means "common belief," "what is generally accepted as true." "Common sense" is used here exclusively in the descriptive sense. This avoids accusing anyone who questions common sense of lacking in sound judgment, a charge which Moore did not always eschew.

The plan of discussion is to present the common sense view of the world ("common sense" from now on) and then argue for its primacy. The difficulty that a Moorean defense of common sense faces, however, is that since the justification of common sense does not follow from its primacy, sceptics can accept its primacy and deny its rational justifiability.

Moore, in "A Defence of Common Sense," [1] presents a list of hard-core common sense beliefs. Common sense includes these beliefs and it may include many more in addition. The statements expressing these beliefs fall into three groups. In the first belong statements about one's body, such as that it exists and has existed for some time, that it is a human body, that it has occupied various positions in contact with or close to the surface of the earth, that there exist other bodies as well as other things each of which has shape and size in three dimensions, and that some of these other human bodies ceased to exist before one's body was born. The second group comprises statements about one's experiences, such as that one has often perceived his own body and other things in the environment, that one has often observed such facts as that his body is closer to the mantelpiece than it is to the bookcase, that one is aware of facts which he is not now observing, that one has expectations about the future and many beliefs of various kinds, some of which are true and others false, that he has had dreams, imagined things, and also that there exist very many other human bodies which have had experiences of a similar kind. The third group consists of the single statement that just as one knows that the statements belonging to the first two groups are true of himself, so also many human beings know statements of a similar kind to be true of themselves.[2] Moore claims that these statements are "truisms, every one of which (in my own opinion) I *know* with certainty to be true."[3]

Moore offers two clarificatory remarks. The first is that "all propositions . . . [listed], and also many propositions corresponding to each of these, are *wholly* true."[4] He thereby rejects the interpretation that the statements are only partially true, or that they may be partially false.

The second clarificatory remark concerns the distinction between the meaning and the analysis of these statements. Moore writes:

> I have assumed that there is some meaning which is *the* ordinary or popular meaning of such expressions as "The earth has existed for many years past". And this, I am afraid, is an assumption which some philosophers are capable of disputing. . . . It seems to me that such a view is as profoundly mistaken as any view can be. Such an expression as "The earth has existed for many years past" is the very type of unambiguous expression, the meaning of which we all understand. Anyone who takes

> a contrary view must, I suppose, be confusing the question whether we understand its meaning (which we all certainly do) with the entirely different question whether we *know what it means,* in the sense that we are able to *give a correct analysis* of its meaning. The question of what is the correct analysis . . . is, it seems to me, a profoundly difficult question. . . . But to hold that we do not know what . . . is the analysis of what we understand by such an expression, is an entirely different thing from holding that we do not understand the expression.[5]

Understanding the meaning of the expression is to know how to use it; being able to give the correct analysis is to know the true philosophical account of the expression. So one may know perfectly well when to say "the table is brown," without knowing whether idealism, naive realism, or phenomenalism gives the proper analysis of the statement. Moore's point is that philosophers who doubt common sense beliefs confuse knowing their meaning with being able to give the correct analysis. They must know what each of these expressions means, for "it is obvious that we cannot even raise the question how what we understand by it is to be analyzed, unless we understand it."[6]

The fundamentally important question that Moore has to face is: what justification is there for claiming that common sense beliefs are known with certainty if it is admitted that their correct analysis is not known? Or, to put it slightly differently: how does it follow from one's knowing the meaning of a common sense expression that one has the right to claim that the expression is certainly true? The final answer is that one has no such right, and consequently the appeal to common sense does not refute scepticism. But this conclusion is reached in two stages: the first is to argue for the primacy of common sense, and the second is to argue for its justification. Moore, or a Moorean-type argument, does indeed establish the primacy of common sense, and this has important consequences. But it does not follow from the success of the first stage that common sense is justified, nor do Moore's supporting arguments succeed in establishing it.

## The primacy of common sense

The kingpin of the Moorean defence is the removal of common sense from the ranks of competing theoretical options. Theories, at some point or another, must rest on pretheoretical data, and common sense is thought of as providing that data. The implication is that theories must do justice to the data with which they start, and so it is to common sense that such theories must do justice. It cannot be the legitimate result of a theory that it contradicts the data which it is supposed to explain—for such contradiction is an infallible sign of something having gone awry. What is true of theories in general is true also of philosophical theories. If a philosophical theory starts with common sense, it cannot end by going against its own starting point. This is the significance of Moore's remark that

> This, after all, you know, really is a finger: there is no doubt about it: I know it, and you all know it. And I think we may safely challenge any philosopher to bring forward any argument in favour either of the proposition that we do not know it, or of the proposition that it is not true, which does not at some point, rest upon some premiss which is, beyond comparison, less certain than is the proposition which it is designed to attack.[7]

The consequence is not that common sense beliefs are necessarily true, nor even that they are contingently so; they may well turn out to be false. However, if a belief is part of common sense, then it is a belief that one has all the reason for holding and no reason at all for doubting. For common sense is the most secure part of our system of beliefs.

Strictly speaking, common sense cannot be proven if we mean by "proof" a conclusion that logically follows from proven premises. And if the only proper use of "to know" is in cases where error is logically impossible, then nobody knows that any common sense belief is true. But, of course, if by "proof" is meant "giving good reasons to believe and removing grounds for doubt," then there is a proof of common sense. Furthermore, if "to know" is used to mean "to have a right to believe and it being unreasonable to doubt," then we do know that common sense is true. And this leaves very little scope for scepticism. For though sceptics can claim that it is logically possible that common sense is false, logical possibility is not a proper ground for doubt. If all that scepticism amounts to is a reminder that it is not self-contradictory to deny common sense, then it has been rendered harmless.

We must ask, however, what reason there is for thinking of common sense as primary and of theoretical concerns as secondary, and further, whether it is true that no sceptical attack can succeed against common sense.

## Common sense and physiology

One reason for accepting the primacy of common sense is that it is physiologically basic. This means that, apart from a very small minority with genetic or acquired abnormalities, people come to hold common sense beliefs, because this is the information that their senses provide. It is simply a fact about human beings that they perceive the world in five sense modalities. So in the most innocuous possible sense, it is "natural" for human beings to believe that what they see, hear, taste, touch, and smell exists.

An immediate objection is that there is no "pure" perception because whatever is perceived is subject to interpretation. The interpretation reflects a conscious or unconscious theoretical bias, and this may and does change what is perceived. Perception is influenced by past experience, expectations, by the accepted categories of classification. Since these change from person to person and especially from culture to culture, there is nothing that is "naturally" perceived.

In reply, let us argue a particular case. Suppose that the perception in question is what a musically knowledgeable person in this culture would describe as listening to a Bach recording being played. It goes without saying that interpretation has an enormous role in this description of the event. Nor, of course, is the statement that "I am listening to a Bach recording" part of common sense. Consider what would happen if the same piece of music was heard by a snake-charmer with his basket still shut, a tone-deaf burglar poised outside the window, and a New Guinea head-hunter. Their respective interpretations would, of course, be vastly different. But beyond their interpretations we find that they all hear sounds. The sounds are interpreted variously, but the raw material is perceived by all.

Perhaps there is interpretation involved even in the experience of hearing sounds. Could it not be that the head-hunter does not hear it as a continuous melody, but merely as a series of discrete auditory stimuli? This, too, is possible, but it does not alter the fact that they all hear sounds. The fact that given a stimulus of a certain sort people will have auditory, visual, olfactory, etc., experiences, establishes that common sense is physiologically basic. For common sense is that part of human experience that a human being cannot help having. The compulsion comes from being human.

Common sense being physiologically basic does not mean that if a belief is part of common sense, then it is true, nor that it is free of interpretation. For it may well be that the human physiological apparatus consistently misinforms, and, so, while our experiences are physiologically determined, they are misleading. And it is also possible that an animal or an extraterrestrial being would perceive the same stimulus and interpret it differently from the way we do. The point of arguing for common sense being physiologically basic is not to attempt to render it immune to criticism or falsehood, but to establish it as the base from which any human being must start. The primacy of common sense amounts to no more, and to no less, than the recognition that the point of departure for theories about the world is not arbitrary, but determined by the human physiological apparatus.

Not only are the modalities in which human beings perceive the world determined by our physiology, but the repertoire of possible responses is also bound by the capabilities of the human body. Consumption and elimination, pain and pleasure, sleep and wakefulness, rest and motion, maturing and aging are some of the enevitable dimensions of being human. Of course there are immense individual, cultural, and historical differences between people, but these differences are due to the manner in which different people at different times and in different social groups have coped with the limits imposed by their bodies. Common sense marks the outer limits of human possibility; variations and differences occur within these limits.

The primacy of common sense does not mean, however, that these limits cannot be overcome; pain can be alleviated and pleasure produced by manipulating the brain; sleep may be induced and wakefulness artificially sustained; consumption can be replaced by intravenous injections and elimination drastically reduced; the time when aging is controlled need not be very far distant. And, of course, scientific instruments can be used to supplement existing senses and thereby enormously enlarge the humanly perceivable part of the world. Telescopes and microscopes enable us to perceive what is too far off or too small; X-ray machines and ultraviolet sensors inform us of what we could never perceive by relying upon the senses only. None of this, however, changes the fact that even the most sophisticated scientific instruments must be calibrated with reference to the human senses and the success or failure of all techniques designed to manipulate physiological functions must be judged by the criterion of human experience. X-ray functions well if we can actually *see* what is otherwise beyond our reach, and pain is alleviated only if the person suffering from it no longer *feels* it. Common sense is primary, because it is the view with which a normal human being must start. Refinements and alterations and the acquisition of depth and breadth occur against the background of common sense, but it is common sense which is being refined, altered, deepened, or broadened.

## Common sense and problems

The other reason for accepting the primacy of common sense is that it forms the background against which many problems occur. Normal human habits and expectations are basically influenced by the picture of the world that common sense provides. But our habits and expectations, justifiably derived as they are from common sense, are sometimes disrupted and disappointed. Dangers, threats, surprises and problems occur, and they indicate that there is more to the world than common sense has allowed for.

These problems may be primitive, such as the occurrence of pain without injury, the failure of limbs, for no apparent cause, to carry their accustomed burden, the occasional unreliability of the senses, natural disasters like earthquakes or tidal waves. Or the problems may be social, such as coping with undeserved humiliation, with authority, insanity, or injustice. Yet another source of problems has to do with great surges of feeling in oneself, such as grief at the death of someone loved, or the experience of naked, gratuitous evil.

Common sense is adequate when everything is going as expected. But when the routine is upset and expectations are basically disappointed, when crises occur, then the picture of the world that common sense presents must be supplemented and made more sophisticated. Scientific theories, religions, metaphysical systems all attempt to provide answers where common sense has proved inadequate. Part of the task of such theoretical efforts is to construct a picture of the world that is capable of accommodating anomalies which have proved too difficult for common sense. In so doing, theories may help solve practical problems by presenting a picture of the world that renders events understandable.

Different theories aim at different goals, but there is a feature they all share: the point of any theory is the solving of some problem. And of course the presence of problems not only gives point to a theory, but it also provides a way of evaluating it. The success or failure of a theory depends, in part, upon the extent to which it is capable of solving the problem that gave rise to it.

There are many problems whose roots are other than the conflict between common sense expectations and subsequent anomalous experience. Problems may occur because two or more theories, designed to supplement common sense, give contrary accounts of a segment of the world; or they may be due to disagreement about the nature of the theory that is needed; problems may be methodological or logical, arising in the course of the construction of theories; another type has to do with discerning the practical, political, or moral implications of various theories. All these problems, however, are parasitic upon theories, and theories arise because common sense is disappointed. The primacy of common sense derives from its being, directly or indirectly, the background to very many problems.

There is a picture that goes with the primacy of common sense. The picture is true, but the questionable uses that have been made of it cast a shadow over it. The picture is that in certain ways all men, everywhere, respond to their environment similarly. The type of information they can receive and the type of responses they are capable of making are similar because all men, by virtue of being members of the species, are similarly built: they are equipped with the same physiology.

Common sense is the label for the world view that a human being cannot help having. The reasons for accepting common sense are that the world certainly seems to be as common sense depicts it and when one responds to the environment on the assumption that it really is that way, then by and large the responses are successful.

The truth is, however, that the responses are not always successful. Furthermore, there are situations in which common sense prompts no response at all, or even worse, in which it prompts a harmful one. Because common sense is occasionally inadequate, it has to be improved, and various theories aim at improving it. Such theories, be they scientific, religious, political, or philosophical, may solve the problems that common sense cannot. But no matter how sophisticated the human theoretical approach becomes, the primacy of common sense remains indisputable. For the ultimate test as well as the initial starting point of all theories must be the original problem situation that is composed of common sense and some anomaly or another. And the "must" derives its force from the physiological boundaries that human beings inevitably have.

## The rational justification of common sense

The justification of common sense does not follow from its primacy, for it may be that common sense is physiologically basic and that it gives rise to problems that prompt various theories, and that, at the same time, common sense beliefs are false. A sceptic may admit that the world comes to us filtered through our physiology and deny that there is any rational justification for accepting those beliefs that are physiologically based. The sceptical position is that common sense can be rationally justified only if some reason is given for the reliability of our method of acquiring information. The argument for the primacy of common sense does not provide such a justification. The discovery of a necessary starting point is compatible with the starting point being rationally indefensible.

A possible argument at this point is to combine the primacy of common sense with pragmatism. The sceptical challenge could perhaps be met then by offering as a rational justification of common sense our practical success in coping with the world when acting on the assumptions of common sense. But this argument fails to counter the sceptic.

The very general reason for its failure is that there are independent sceptical objections against each of these positions. The combination of two attempts that failed to counter scepticism will be at least as vulnerable as they were severally. Pragmatism, it will be remembered, was objected to, *inter alia,* on the grounds that pragmatic justification cannot be a rational justification. For success in action is determined by the achievement of goals, and the rationality of the goals cannot be pragmatically decided. Thus either there is no rational justification of any goal, or goals can be justified rationally, but such a justification cannot be pragmatic.

The difficulty pragmatism faces is in no way lessened if the goal turns out to be coping with the environment on the basis of common sense, for the sceptic can accept that all human beings pursue this goal and still question its rational justifiability. It is after all possible that all human beings pursue an irrational goal. And of course the importance of the sceptic's question emerges when common sense faces a religious, moral, mystical, or political challenge which may dictate going against common sense in pursuit of an allegedly more worthwhile goal. Common sense and pragmatism have no rational answer ready to cope with asceticism, theocracy, Nazism, Kamikazi pilots, and transcendental meditators.

Another difficulty that sceptics can mention is that reliance upon common sense is not all that successful. Most practical human achievements are due precisely to having gone beyond common sense. If we relied on common sense only, our species would be in no better position than any other. The spur to success is the anomaly with which common sense cannot cope. The challenge is either met, or the species is endangered. So pragmatism and common sense are not very happy bedfellows.

A Moorean defender of common sense is obliged, therefore, to offer other than pragmatic arguments for the rational justification of common sense. And Moore does offer two related arguments for passing from the primacy to the rational justification of common sense: first, a negative one, that any argument against common sense involves the person so arguing in inconsistency; and second, a positive argument, that common sense is justified because one has all the reasons for accepting it and no reason at all for rejecting it.

## The negative argument: scepticism is inconsistent

Moore develops one of his arguments for the inconsistency of scepticism while examining some epistemological views of Hume.[8] Commenting on Hume's scepticism, Moore writes:

> These sceptical views he did not expect or wish us to accept, except in philosophic moments. He declares that we cannot, in ordinary life, avoid believing things which are inconsistent with them; and, in so doing, he, of course, implies incidentally that they are false: since he implies that he himself has a great deal of knowledge as to what we can and cannot believe in ordinary life.[9]

The structure of Moore's argument is as follows: first, Hume believes in his philosophical moments that we cannot know any facts about the external world; second, Hume states that in ordinary life he and others cannot help holding beliefs that are inconsistent with the philosophical belief that we cannot know any facts about the external world; third, knowing the truth of Hume's statement, namely, that in ordinary life he and others cannot help holding beliefs that are inconsistent with Hume's philosophical belief, depends upon the possibility of knowing at least one fact about the external world, namely, that in ordinary life he and others cannot help holding beliefs that are inconsistent with Hume's philosophical belief; fourth, since Hume himself implies that he knows what are the ordinary beliefs of himself and others, it follows that Hume's philosophical belief is mistaken, because knowing the ordinary beliefs of himself and others is knowing at least one fact about the external world.

Moore's argument can be generalized so that it supports all common sense beliefs against scepticism. The first part of the generalized argument concerns the method of refuting philosophical beliefs that are inconsistent with common sense beliefs. The refutation consists in showing that the person holding the philosophical beliefs also holds the common sense beliefs that philosophical beliefs contradict.

The second part derives from the recognition that the refutation of philosophical beliefs cannot be only that they are inconsistent with common sense beliefs. For the sceptic could counter it by abandoning his common sense beliefs, The refutation must be based both on the inconsistency and the primacy of common sense. It is this combination that makes it impossible for the sceptic to disavow his common sense beliefs.

Moore's refutation of Hume's position then is that Hume, in his common sense phase, believes that he and others know many facts about the external world. In his philosophical phase, however, Hume denies that he or anyone knows any facts about the external world. Yet in his philosophical phase Hume makes statements that imply that he knows facts about the external world, and so Hume implies that his own statements expressing the philosophical beliefs in question are false.

## Criticism of the negative argument: psychological and epistemological scepticism

Given the primacy of common sense, Moore's objection decisively refutes Humean scepticism. The strengthened version of scepticism, however, can accept the primacy of common sense and reject Moore's objection by insisting on two distinctions.

The first is between scepticism about knowledge and scepticism about reasoning. Humean scepticism is directed against the possibility of knowledge. "Knowledge" is understood to be properly applicable only if the possibility of error has been excluded, and since error is possible in the case of all factual statements, Humean sceptics conclude that no factual statement can be known. The Moorean rejoinder is to point at the arbitrariness of this definition. As frequently as not we use "knowledge" to describe situations in which doubt would be unreasonable. So if the sceptic's point is merely to remind one that in the case of factual knowledge the logical possibility of error is ever present, then scepticism can be given its way. But the sceptic's gain is at the cost of triviality, for the issue is really whether or not there are good reasons for accepting any belief. And Humean scepticism leaves Moore free to assert that there are the best of reasons for accepting common sense beliefs. It is quite trivial to insist, as the sceptic does, on the inapplicability of the strict sense of "knowledge", for the inapplicability is based on an arbitrary verbal preference.

Scepticism, however, is much stronger than Moore allows for. The target of the sceptical attack is the process of reasoning and not any of its products. Sceptics attack the possibility of knowledge, true belief, or well-grounded opinion only indirectly. Their primary objection is against the lack of rational grounds for reasoning itself. If scepticism is understood in this way, then Moore's argument that we have the best reasons for accepting common sense beliefs and no reason at all to reject them needs to be supplemented by some account of what makes such reasons good ones.

Moore does attempt to provide this addition. The reason for accepting common sense beliefs is that their denial is inconsistent. The supposed inconsistency is not logical; the sceptic is not accused of formal self-contradiction. The charge against him, as we have seen, is that his philosophical beliefs are directly contradicted by his behavior. He says he doubts, but he does not act as if he doubted. And he does not act that way because he, like everyone else, accepts the primacy of common sense. The sceptic has fallen into the trap of supposing that his philosophical beliefs could be incompatible with his common sense beliefs, when in fact the former presupposes the latter. Moore conceives of his task to be to remind the sceptic that this is so.

But it is Moore that needs to be reminded of a second distinction, namely, between psychological and epistemological scepticism. Moore regards the sceptic as a neurotic who in one moment is gnawed by doubts and in the next acts as if his doubts did not exist. Hume, the sceptic, is rapped on the knuckles for lacking sound judgment and common sense, normatively interpreted. Hume, the billiard player, is praised for coming to his senses. In a word, Moore thinks of scepticism as if it were a psychological attitude. It may be that Moore is right about Hume, as well as about some other sceptics, but, as we have seen, the philosophically important kind of scepticism is epistemological. The sceptic's behavior can be indistinguishable from anybody else's, and the sceptic may accept all the common sense beliefs that Moore accepts. Epistemological scepticism is based on the argument that common sense beliefs, as indeed all others, lack rational ground, and Moore has not met this argument. The charge of inconsistency can be levelled only against the psychological sceptic. The epistemological sceptic accepts and acts on common sense beliefs, it is merely that he denies their rational warrant. Epistemological scepticism is not inconsistent.

## The positive argument: common sense is reasonable

In his celebrated "Proof of an External World" [10] Moore offers a proof of one common sense belief; it is, of course, easily applicable to very many others.

> I can prove now, for instance, that two human hands exist. How? By holding up my two hands, and saying, as I make a certain gesture with the right hand, 'Here is one hand', and adding, as I make a certain gesture with the left, 'and here is another'. . . . But did I prove just now that two human hands were then in existence? I do want to insist that I did; that the proof which I gave was a perfectly rigorous one; and that it is perhaps impossible to give a better or more rigorous proof of anything whatever. [11]

Moore insists on the proof being rigorous for it meets the necessary requirements: the premises are different from the conclusion, the premises are known to be true, and the conclusion follows from the premises.

The questionable part is the second requirement. Moore's argument in favor of having met it is:

> I certainly did at the moment *know* that which I expressed by the combination of certain gestures with saying the words 'There is one hand and here is another'. I *knew* that there was one hand . . . and that there was another. . . . How absurd it would be to suggest that I did not know it, but only believed it, and that perhaps it was not the case! [12]

Moore suspects that even after this clinching argument there may be some residue of dissatisfaction with his proof. He says:

> I am perfectly aware that . . . many philosophers will still feel that I have not given any satisfactory proof of the point in question . . . I can make an approach to explaining what they want by saying that if I had proved the propositions which I used as *premisses* in my proofs, then they would perhaps admit that I have proved the existence of external things, but, in the absence of such a proof . . . they will say that I have not given what they mean by a proof. . . . Of course, what they really want is . . . something like a general statement as to how any propositions of this sort may be proved. This, of course, I haven't given; and I do not believe it can be given. [13]

The dissatisfaction, Moore argues, is due to the mistaken belief of many philosophers that if a proposition is not proved, then it is unjustified to claim that one knows it. But Moore says:

> I can know things which I cannot prove; and among things which I certainly did know, even if . . . I could not prove them, were the premisses of my two proofs. [14]

Much of the apparent perversity of the argument disappears if the two senses of "proof" are recalled. In the first sense "proof" is what there is in favor of a conclusion that logically follows from premises which are themselves conclusively established. In the second sense, a conclusion may be "proven" if there are good reasons for accepting the premises from which it follows.

Moore's position is that there are good reasons for accepting the premises of his argument, but there are no conclusive reasons. He has proved the existence of his hands in the second, weaker sense, but he has not proved it, and it cannot be proved, in the first, stronger sense.

The ground for Moore's suspicion that proof in the strong sense cannot be given may be the following. If a conclusion is regarded as proven if and only if the premises from which it follows are also proven, then it is impossible to prove anything. For the premises in question are proven only if they are conclusions of arguments whose premises in turn are simularly proven. But these premises too require arguments with proven premises to back them up, and so infinite regress follows, for each proven premise requires a proven premise.

Sceptics, however, cannot gain any comfort from the impossibility of proof in the strong sense, for proof in the weak sense is possible. Good reasons can be given for many propositions that function as premises in arguments. There may be no conclusive proof of common sense beliefs, but it can be shown that there are good reasons for accepting them and no reasons for doubting them. The question is: what are these reasons?

The first is that everybody accepts common sense beliefs, and one cannot help accepting them. The primacy of common sense guarantees that all normal human beings start out by believing that common sense presents a true picture of the world. As we have seen, however, this is not a good reason, for the falsehood of common sense beliefs is quite compatible with their primacy. Furthermore, common sense is inadequate to deal with many anomalies, so there is reason for thinking that it needs to be improved.

The second reason for the truth of common sense beliefs is that their denial leads to inconsistency. But this, as we have seen, will not work either, for the distinction between psychological and epistemological scepticism allows the latter kind of sceptic to accept common sense beliefs, act on them, and simultaneously to deny there being any reasons for them.

So we come to the third and last hope for a rational defense of common sense, and this is that there is no reason to doubt the truth of common sense beliefs. Common sense may need to be improved by supplementing it with theoretical explanations; these, however, do not undermine common sense, but surpass it. The fact is that there is no alternative to common sense, and when philosophers propose such

55

theories as idealism or phenomenalism, then it is a simple matter to show that in their statement of the supposed alternative, they presuppose the truth of common sense. Their alleged refutation of common sense assumes the truth of what is to be refuted. This is not a strict proof of common sense beliefs, but it is a good reason for accepting their truth.

## Criticism of the positive argument: external and internal questions

A useful way of approaching Moore's argument is to put it in terms of the distinction between internal and external question—questions, that is, that arise within a theory and questions that are asked about a theory. The first step before applying this distinction to Moore's argument is the determination of whether or not common sense is a theory. "Theory" is sufficiently vague to allow widely different referents, so the question is not so much whether or not common sense is a theory, but rather how common sense differs from other ways of looking at the world. The primacy of common sense compels the view that the difference has to do with common sense being the necessary starting point and the background to all theories.

Moore's point then can be put by saying that the sceptical challenge to common sense may be posed either as an external or as an internal question. Moore's proof appears perverse because it rests on the assumption that the sceptic is asking an internal question. If it is an internal question, then Moore's proof is indeed rigorous and the best there is, for the proof consists in calling attention to the testing procedures and to the use of expressions of common sense. And given these, the sceptical challenge can easily be met.

But of course the sceptic would insist that he is asking an external question about common sense, so it is question-begging to evoke common sense in attempting to answer it. This Moore denies. There could be a question external to common sense only if there were a theoretical alternative to common sense from the point of view of which the question could be posed. Not only is there no such alternative, but also the sceptic in asking the question has accepted common sense beliefs. Furthermore, *any* candidate for being an alternative to common sense perforce accepts common sense, for common sense is primary, so there cannot be an external question about common sense. Consequently the sceptic is asking an internal question, and that Moore has answered.

The difficulty with Moore's argument is that one can accept the primacy of common sense, agree about the absence of alternative ways of looking at the world, and still ask quite sensible external questions about the rationality of common sense. There are at least three different types of external questions that a sceptic could be asking. None of these is directed at the acceptance of common sense—their target is the rationality of its acceptance.

The first type of question has to do with the *methods* employed within common sense for settling disputes. Some methods, such as induction and deduction, are accepted as reliable; others, such as appeal to the stars or consulting oracles are judged to be questionable. The skeptic may want to reflect on the ground or warrant of this distinction. In doing this, he demands a justification for standards of rationality the apeal to which permeates common sense. Moore, in response, must either offer a justification that appeals to considerations outside of common sense or simply stand firm and declare: this is what I do. In the first case, common sense, by itself, is inadequate to meet scepticism, in the second case, common sense judgments are admitted to lack rational justification.

The second type of question concerns the *goals* that are implicit in common sense. Here, of course, there are alternatives. Other goals are the pursuit of sainthood, self-destruction, the abnegation of the body, the transformation of the personality, the living of a desireless life, and the like. And these goals are competing with the common sense aspiration of coping with the environment so as to assure optimal physical and psychological well-being. But all these goals have been and are questioned, and the sceptic's question to Moore is about the reason there is for favoring one over the others.

The third type of question is about the *categories* of common sense. The classificatory scheme implicit in common sense dictates how one thinks about the world; such distinctions as between real and imagi-

nary, mental and physical, cause and effect, living and inorganic, in-
fuse common sense. A sceptic, without wishing to deny the validity
of these distinctions, might wonder about the justification of their
prominence. In the hierarchy of common sense categories some are
basic and others derivative. What is the reason for the organization of
the hierarchy? Moore would have to appeal either to considerations
external to common sense or admit his inability to offer the justification the sceptic demands.

Consequently Moore has failed to exclude the possibility of the
sceptic asking external questions about common sense, and he has
failed also to answer these questions within the self-imposed limitations of common sense.


## Summary and conclusion

The purpose of the sceptical challenge is to invite a rational justification of our beliefs and practices. The implication of the challenge is
that if the justification cannot be provided, then any set of beliefs and
any form of behavior has the same claim upon human acceptance as any
other. As a result, reason as a guide to human life must be regarded
as illusory. The danger in this is made obvious by the abundance of
unpalatable alternatives in existence.

The Moorean attempt to meet the sceptical challenge fails because
while it is true that common sense is primary, this does not guarantee
its rationality. Human beings cannot help holding common sense
beliefs, but the compulsion may lack rational warrant. Moore's arguments in favor of the rationality of common sense founder on two distinctions that the strengthened form of scepticism, although not its
Humean predecessor, can invoke against Moore with devastating results. Scepticism is not inconsistent, because epistemologcal scepticism is an attack on the rational grounds for accepting common
sense, and it is not an attack on the acceptance of common sense.
Common sense is not shown to be the only reasonable position, for
while it is true that there are no theoretical alternatives which do not
presuppose common sense, this does not make common sense reason-

able. The alternative to common sense being reasonable is that nothing is reasonable. And Moore has not excluded that possibility. The sceptic, the Moorean demurrer notwithstanding, can ask perfectly sensible external questions about the rationality of common sense. And these questions both require and lack answers.

The conclusion, however, is not just the negative one that the appeal to common sense fails to meet the sceptical challenge. The positive gain is the need to recognize the primacy of common sense. While this, in itself, does not refute the sceptic, it is an indispensable part of the coming refutation.

# 4 The implications of ordinary language: the paradigm case argument

"[O]rdinary language is *correct language.*"—Norman Malcolm, *"Moore and Ordinary Language"*

## Introduction

The paradigm case argument could—arguably—be derived from Moore's position.[1] The sceptic attacks common sense on the ground that one cannot be certain of any common sense belief. Moore, of course, asserts that one is certain of many of them. The sceptic, in Moore's possible view, is committed to arbitrary legislation of common linguistic usage. If "certain" were used to mean "the logical impossibility of being mistaken," then the sceptic would be right: no common sense belief is certain. But "certain" does not mean this. In everyday English the word is frequently used to mean that doubt is unreasonable. Thus it is perfectly proper to say that "I am certain that I have a head," although it is logically possible that I am mistaken. Moore thus simply juxtaposes ordinary usage to the sceptic's arbitrary departure from it and may be taken to argue on that ground that the scpetical challenge is illegitimate.

The most coherent statement of the nature and justification of the appeal to ordinary language is Malcolm's. The appeal has come to be known as the paradigm case argument (PCA). The PCA is best regarded as an attempt to weld three distinct philosophical theses into a powerful instrument for meeting the skeptical challenge. The first thesis is that philosophical arguments are not about facts, but about the correct ways of talking. The second thesis is that ordinary lan-

60

guage is correct language and philosophical arguments that go against it are fallacious. The third thesis is that it follows from the meaning of certain expressions that very frequently statements made by the use of these expressions are true. If all three theses were correct, then the PCA would not only be successful in meeting the sceptical challenge, but would also reveal the structure of philosophical attacks on common sense.

## The first thesis: philosophical arguments are not about facts, but about the proper ways of speaking.

Malcolm writes:

> When the philosopher asserts that we never know for certain *any* material-thing statements, he is not asserting this empirical fact. He is asserting that always in the past when a person said "I know for certain that p," where p is a material-thing statement, he has said something false. . . . If the philosopher's statements were an empirical statement, we can see how absurdly unreasonable it would be of him to make it. . . . The reason why he can be so cocksure, and not on empirical grounds, that it has never been and never will be right for any person to say "I know for certain that p," where p is a material-thing statement, is that he regards that *form of speech as improper.* [2]

What is it that distinguishes empirical and verbal disagreements? Argument about the correctness of the use of an expression may be due either to disagreement about facts or to disagreement about the meaning of the expression. Empirical disagreements can be settled if agreement is reached about the facts; verbal arguments are resolved if the disputants come to use the expression univocally.

Malcolm argues that the disagreement between philosophers, like Ayer [3] for instance, and common sense is verbal. A statement, according to Ayer, can be described as "certain" only if the logical possibility of it being proven false is excluded. This possibility, however, cannot be excluded in respect to any empirical statement, because it would require the logically impossible completion of an infinite series of verification. So the ordinary man's ascription of certainty to empirical statements rests on a misunderstanding of the meaning of "certain."

The correctness of this criticism of the ordinary use of "certain" need not concern us here. The relevant question is: is the disagreement really verbal? And we do not know what to say. It can be maintained with equal plausibility that the dispute is verbal, because it concerns the question of whether the *meaning* of "certain" makes its application to empirical statements possible, and that the dispute is empirical, because it is the *fact* of the impossibility of conclusive verification that prohibits the application of "certain" to empirical statements.

The antinomy arises because Malcolm's distinction between empirical and verbal arguments is too rigid. The dichotomy is supposed to be exhaustive, so that it could be deduced from an argument's not being verbal that it therefore must be empirical. Malcolm's argument that the philosopher's point is verbal rests on this distinction, for all that Malcolm does in support of his argument is to show that philosophers do not disagree about the facts of any given case. Only with the help of the exhaustively interpreted distinction can one conclude that the argument must be about "the proper form of speech."

Malcolm has fallen prey here to one of those "prejudices" that arise when a philosopher accepts "assumptions and narrow classifications" in which the history of his subject abounds—and which Malcolm, at another place, so convincingly exposes.[4] If it were true that a genuine problem must be capable of settlement by an appeal to facts, or be resolvable by an examination of the meaning of the expressions involved, then Malcolm's reliance on the empirical-verbal distinction as an exhaustive classification of philosophical problems would be justified. However, not only is this view mistaken, but also Malcolm and many critics of the PCA make common cause in repudiating it.[5] The curious fact is that while the consequences of abandoning an exhaustive empirical-verbal distinction are damaging to the PCA, just how the argument suffers has never been spelled out.

The PCA suffers because if the exhaustive dichotomy is abandoned, then the first thesis is only half right. Malcolm is clearly right when he insists that the disagreement between ordinary men and philosophers is not about what facts actually hold. For the argument to be of this kind the philosopher would have to be absurdly stupid: he should have to fail to notice facts that any human being routinely considers.[6] No, philosophers do not dispute about the facts, they dispute about something else. But the second half of the thesis does not follow. Malcolm is wrong in thinking that the "something else" they dispute about *must* be the proper forms of speech. The "must" stands or falls with the rigid empirical-verbal distinction. And since Malcolm abandons the latter, he cannot insist upon the former. Consequently, the philosophers Malcolm attacks for allegedly suggesting that the ordinary ways of talking about the facts are improper, can reply by accusing Malcolm of an *ignoratio elenchi* argument.

The question still remains, however, of what it is that philosophers are arguing about if it is neither about the facts, nor about the proper forms of speech. The answer is that when people classify, justify, or evaluate anything they do so by applying standards. When these standards are described, the classifications, justifications, and evaluations are understood. There is, however, this problem: are the standards justifiable and should these standards be used for classification and evaluation? This is a problem that concerns many philosophers. The first thesis of the PCA is correct in denying that this is a factual problem, it is incorrect, however, in asserting that the problem is about the correct ways of speaking.[7]

Insofar as Malcolm's argument in "Moore and Ordinary Language" is about the nature of philosophical arguments, it has serious faults. Philosophical arguments are not, or at least need not be about the proper forms of speech.[8] But of course there is much more to be found in Malcolm's version of the PCA. The next thesis may be thought of as offering a criticism of many philosophical arguments on the grounds that regardless of what they are about they err because they go against ordinary language.

# The second thesis: ordinary language is correct; philosophical arguments that go against it are fallacious

Malcolm argues for the view that ordinary language is correct by bringing out the absurdity of its denial:

Suppose a case where two people agree as to what the empirical facts are and yet disagree in their statements. For example, two people are looking at an animal. . . . Their descriptions of the animal are in perfect agreement. Yet one of them says it is a fox, the other says it is a wolf. Their disagreement could be called linguistic. . . . One of the other, or both of them, is using incorrect language. Now suppose that there were a case like the preceding with this exception: that the one who says it is a wolf, not only agrees with the other man as to what the characteristics of the animal are, but furthermore *agrees that that sort of animal is ordinarily called a fox.* If he were to continue to insist that it is a wolf, we can see how absurd would be his position. He would be saying that, although the other man was using an expression to describe a situation which was the expression ordinarily employed to describe that sort of situation, nevertheless the other man was using incorrect language. What makes his statement absurd is that ordinary language *is* correct language.[9]

Some of this argument's assumptions will become explicit if it is applied to the ordinary use of "certain." Suppose that a normal and healthy man, in optimal visual conditions, looks at the object in front of him, examines it carefully, and says in response to a question: "I know for certain that this is a book." This is a clear case of certainty; it is the sort of situation in which "he knows with certainty that . . ." can be properly used. If the situation is indeed as described, then further empirical investigation is out of place. If somebody still disagrees with the man's statement, then there are two options open. Either the disagreement is based on the suspicion that contrary to appearances, the situation is in some way abnormal, and then further empirical investigation is in order. Or, the disagreement is based on some difference in the way "certain" is used. In the first case, there can be eventual agreement about the appropriateness of what the man said—an agreement that depends upon settling the question of whether the situation is abnormal. In the second case, the disagreement will persist because it is based on the different senses of "certain." What makes this disagreement with the ordinary sense of "certain" absurd is that on the basis of a stipulated use the ordinary use of "certain" is criticized for being incorrect—not in fact, but linguistically. How could a man say in one breath that this is how the expression is ordinarily used, this is the use that is instrumental in achieving communication and description, and say also that it is incorrect to use the expression in this way? What standard of correct use does he have in mind if not successful communication? The best charge against the ordinary uses of expressions is that given these uses certain philosophical ends cannot be served. But this is a vacuous charge, since ordinary expressions were not meant to be used for the achievement of those ends.

When there is a perfectly clear case of the application of the expression "I know for certain that . . ." then, following Malcolm, we can say that it is a paradigm case of the application of the expression. A paradigm case is a standard; we appeal to it to judge the applicability of the expression to other cases. Our judgment will be based on the similarity or dissimilarity of the given case and a paradigm case. A paradigm case is not a formally defined or definable standard: it is not like the meter rod in Paris but more like having unanimous agreement among experts that a play is a tragedy, or a work is a classic. The difference is that all people who speak a language competently are agreed to be experts about paradigm cases. What makes this point so strong is that it is logical; to be a competent user *is* to know about paradigm cases.[10]

This then is behind Malcolm's dictum that ordinary language is correct language. The question is: can we go on from here and argue, as Malcolm does, that philosophical arguments that go against ordinary language are paradoxical and fallacious? It does not seem that we can.

For Malcolm's observation is too general; there are different ways of going against ordinary language. One is what Malcolm suggests: insisting on calling an animal "wolf" when it is ordinarily called "fox." The other is to remain within the rules of ordinary language and yet speak in an odd, paradoxical, eccentric way. When, for example, Russell says that all anyone sees is part of his own brain, he uses "see" in an odd way. The first way of going against ordinary language involves violations of grammatical and semantic rules. The second involves using expressions in unusual ways. The first is just a mistake; the second may not be a mistake and it may be justified. Malcolm's failure to draw this distinction enables him to criticize *all* cases of going against ordinary language on the grounds that they involve violation of grammatical and semantic rules.[11]

When philosophers use expressions that go against ordinary language, their use is usually odd, eccentric, paradoxical. It would be absurd to suggest that philosophers invariably forget the elementary rules of their language when they do philosophy. The question is: can the queer ways in which philosophers sometimes use language be justified? Why should they depart from ordinary uses and devise extraordinary uses, as Russell has done?

One way of answering this is to reflect upon the use of ordinary language. Most, if not all, ordinary language expressions lack precise definition. This is as it should be. For the looseness, the openendedness of the rules makes language a subtle, malleable, and useful instrument. Malcolm, Flew, Black, and other defenders of the PCA are quite right in insisting that the lack of precision is no fault, because for very many ordinary expressions there are clear, paradigmatic cases of their application. But not all cases are clear; expressions frequently acquire a metaphorical, analogical, extended sense, and so they become applicable to less-than-clear cases.

The metaphors, ambiguities, superficial grammatical similarities in which ordinary language abounds can be misleading. It is natural to think that since "he exists" and "he breathes" have similar grammatical structure, therefore predicating existence of him is like predicating breathing. Or one might be led on a wild-goose chase for the queerest things, because one supposes that since most of the time there is a real subject that may or may not have the property predicated of it, therefore whenever a property is predicated of something that something exists in some way. Again, it may be thought that since it is correct and true to say that "I know for certain that I am awake," and "I know for certain that all bachelors are unmarried," the certainty involved is the same.

A reason why philosophers go against ordinary language, in the sense of using ordinary expressions in paradoxical ways, is to call attention to and avoid the misleading implications of some ordinary expressions. The reason, for instance, why the paradoxical statement: "We do not know for certain the truth of any statement about material objects," may be used is to bring out that in one ordinary sense of "certain" this is true, while in another it is false. The paradoxical statement forces one to reflect on the meaning of "certainty."

The philosopher's reflection may take the form of trying to articulate criteria that guide the use of ordinary expressions. These criteria may well be imprecise; different senses of an expression may not be clearly distinguished. The philosopher may then adopt stricter criteria to guide his own use. He may suggest that one sense of "certain," in which it is logically impossible for counterevidence to appear, be distinguished from another sense, in which it is unreasonable to demand further evidence.

The philosopher's inclination to adopt stricter criteria is hardly objectionable. The difficulty arises when the philosopher criticizes ordinary use from the vantage point of his stricter criteria. This is what happens, according to Malcolm, when Ayer, for example, claims that we do not know for certain the truth of any statement about material objects. What is behind this claim is the adoption of a stricter-than-ordinary criterion of certainty: the logical impossibility of verification.

Malcolm regards what the philosopher says on the basis of stricter criteria as paradoxical and fallacious. What makes Malcolm think that this is so is the assimilation of the two ways of going against ordinary language. If the philosopher were like the man who accepts the characteristics of the animal and knows the ordinary sense of "fox," yet wants to use "wolf" to describe it, then his position would indeed be paradoxical and fallacious. But what the philosopher is really doing, if one must press this unfair analogy, is to point out that there may be cases in which we do not know what label to use, because the ordinary use is imprecise.

It is, of course, unlikely that this would happen with such clear cases as "fox" and "wolf." But it does happen in cases like "certain," "existence," "cause," "reason," "necessary," and so on. It may well appear paradoxical to deny that we know anything empirical with certainty, but if it is understood that "logical certainty" is meant, then the apparently paradoxical statement is not fallacious, but indisputably true. Malcolm is mistaken, therefore, in thinking that a philosophical statement cannot be paradoxical and true.[12]

But Malcolm may still be thought to have a point. If the philosopher, empowered by his stricter criteria, turns back onto the ordinary, less strict uses of the expression and declares them to be mistaken, he will be committing a "great absurdity." When the philosopher adopts stricter criteria, say of the use of "certain," he accepts at least part of the ordinary use of "certain," namely, the part where the ordinary and philosophical criteria coincide. Such coincidences must occur if the philosopher's claim that he is using the *same* expression, only more precisely, is to hold. But the philosopher can then engage in a wholesale condemnation of the ordinary uses of "certain" only at the price of declaring his own use, which overlaps with ordinary use, mistaken. If this is what the philosopher is doing, his case is self-refuting.

It is more likely, however, that a philosopher would argue that only certain uses are mistaken, in the sense of being misleading. The significant differences between the different uses of "certain," for example, obscure the relation between certainty, relevant evidence, and testability. The question here is: who is misled? Ordinary expressions used for ordinary purposes do not mislead ordinary people; ordinary expressions used for philosophical purposes, in accordance with stricter-than-ordinary criteria, do not mislead philosophers. Ordinary expressions can be misleading only if in their ordinary imprecise uses they are put to the achievement of philosophical purposes where precision is necessary. But nobody is likely to do that. This alleged complaint of philosophers would be like complaining that crowbars are inadequate for opening watches.

If philosophers insist that some ordinary expressions are misleading, they are mistaken, because neither the ordinary use, nor the philosophical use of ordinary expressions is misleading: each is suited to the achievement of its respective purpose. But Malcolm, insisting that philosophical statements are paradoxical and fallacious, is mistaken for the same reason. Malcolm takes philosophers to be criticizing the ordinary use of ordinary expressions; in fact, they are honing ordinary expressions for philosophical uses.

Perhaps the basic mistake Malcolm makes stems from the imprecision of the battle cry: ordinary language is correct language. The "is" is the "is" of predication, not of identity. It does not follow from the truth of the dictum that ordinary language is correct language that correct language is ordinary language. The correctness of ordinary language derives from its suitability for the achievement of ordinary purposes. The correctness of the philosophical use of refined ordinary language derives from its suitability for the achievement of philosophical purposes. The idea that these philosophical purposes are *always* illegitimate rests on the mistaken view that *all* philosophical arguments are about the proper forms of speech.

In sum, it appears that Malcolm's second thesis is also half correct. Ordinary language *is* correct language, but this does not mean that philosophical arguments that go against it are paradoxical and fallacious. They may be paradoxical and true; or they may seem paradoxical only until they are understood.

# The third thesis: it follows from the meaning of some ordinary descriptive expressions that frequently statements made by the use of these expressions are true.

This thesis involves the PCA in arguing for the connection between language and the external world by attempting to show that the necessary condition of the meaningfulness of some expressions is the existence of the external world. As Malcolm puts it:

> In the case of all expressions the meanings of which must be *shown* and can not be explained, as can the meaning of "ghost," it follows from the fact that they are ordinary expressions in the language, that there have been *many* situations of the kind which they describe; otherwise so many people could not have learned the correct use of these expressions.[13]

Perhaps the most sustained attack on the PCA comes from J. W. N. Watkins.[14] Although Watkins addresses his remarks to Flew's formulations of the argument,[15] on the crucial issue, expressed in the quotation above, Malcolm and Flew are in agreement. Watkins's objection is twofold: he charges that the PCA is committed to a mistaken theory of meaning, and that there is an unavoidable and fatally damaging dilemma facing the argument. It will be shown that both objections can be met, but not without having to reformulate the argument.

Watkins' first objection is directed against the theory of meaning allegedly presupposed by the PCA.

> The theory of meaning behind the Paradigm-Case Argument is that simple descriptive terms must be defined ostensively by pointing to paradigm instances. Thus the connotation of such terms is, if not exactly equivalent to, at any rate strictly dependent on, their denotation . . . to discover what such term means we must *first* look at those things in the world which it typically denotes: we cannot first learn what it means and then look around the world to discover whether or not anything exists which is denoted by it.[16]

This theory of meaning is mistaken because it "tends to blur the old distinction between connotation and denotation," and so one is led to suppose that since an expression has meaning, it follows that what it can be used to describe exists. As a result, the PCA "can be deployed against anyone who denies the existence in the world of a counterpart to any noncompound noun or adjective in the O.E.D." [17] If, however, connotation and denotation are distinguished, as they should be, then it does not follow from an expression having connotation that it also has denotation, and so the PCA fails.

One defence of the PCA rests on the recognition that the PCA can be made neutral between different theories of meaning. It is true that Malcolm and Flew explicitly say that it is the *meaning* of expressions that must be taught with reference to actual cases, and so it is perfectly proper to ask to what theory of meaning this commits them. But the PCA loses none of its force if it makes a much more modest claim. It should be argued that it is the *descriptive use* of some expressions that must be taught with reference to actual cases.

According to this proposal, the PCA can be taken to assert that it follows from an expression having a descriptive use that situations of the sort that it is used to describe exist. Whether or not this is true is beside the point for the moment. The point is that *if* it is true, it does not commit the PCA to any particular theory of meaning. For although it follows from an expression having use that it has meaning, it does not follow that meaning must be identified with use, or reference, or whatever. As a consequence, Malcolm's original statement has to be revised. This, however, can be done by simply substituting "descriptive use" for "meaning" in all relevant contexts.

Watkins's second objection poses a dilemma for the PCA. He assumes that even if the argument can somehow be saved from the first objection, this one will surely convict it. So the force of the second objection is not going to be mitigated by the substitution of "descriptive use" for "meaning."

The dilemma arises if it is supposed that it follows from an expression having a descriptive use that what it is used to describe at least sometimes exists. And the dilemma is this: of any expression to which the PCA is supposed to apply one can ask whether the connotation of the expression is prior to its denotation, or whether the denotation determines connotation. If connotation is prior to denotation, then it is always legitimate to ask whether or not anything exists that the expression can be used to denote. And since the question is legitimate, it cannot be held, as the PCA does, that it *follows* from an expression having a descriptive use that what it can be used to describe actually exists. If, on the other hand, the denotation of an expression is taken to determine its connotation, then it follows that whether or not something counts as a paradigm case of the descriptive use of an expression is a matter of definition. And so it becomes a tautology that there exist paradigm cases of the expression's application. The whole significance of the PCA rests on it being a contingently true claim that it follows from an expression having a descriptive use that there exist paradigm cases of its application.

Thus if Watkins's dilemma stands, then the PCA has either failed to prove that the existence of anything follows from an expression having a descriptive use, or it has been shown to make only a tautological claim. In either case, it has failed to prove the *existence* of paradigm cases.

Flew attempts to avoid the dilemma by arguing in his "Comment" that the claim made by the PCA is unnecessarily strong. There is no need to argue that the descriptive use of an expression *must* be taught with reference to actual instances. It is sufficient for the PCA if it is true that an expression's use *can* be taught in this way. For to prove

71

the existence of actual instances it is enough to show that the descriptive use of some expressions can be exemplified with reference to them. And so it is no longer tautologous to claim that an expression has paradigm cases corresponding to it, because the claim does not rest on the definition of the expression; the claim is grounded on the possibility of paradigm cases being used for exemplification. This possibility entails the existence of paradigm cases.

Watkins is ready to admit that Flew has escaped one horn of the dilemma, but only to be impaled on the other. For if an expression is not defined with reference to actual cases, denotatively, then it must be defined in terms of other expressions, connotatively. But, as Watkins argued, from the fact that an expression has connotation, it does not follow that it has denotation. Flew's argument that the expression does denote, because its use can be exemplified with reference to actual cases, is inconclusive, since the cases that are thought to be paradigmatic may not be so. It is possible, Watkins argues, that all cases are *mistakenly* identified as paradigmatic. The PCA needs to be supplemented by an argument establishing the genuineness of paradigm cases. Thus not even with Flew's modification can the PCA escape Watkins's dilemma.

The objection rests on the assumption that it is possible that when an ordinary descriptive expression is used for everyday purposes in normal situations, then its use could *always* be mistaken. The assumption is one that Malcolm, although not Flew, explicitly discusses. In reply to Watkins's objection, one needs to ask: is there a kind of mistake that could always be made when an ordinary expression is used for ordinary purposes? The mistake would not be about facts; Watkins does not suppose that when ordinary men assert, for instance, that the color of spilt blood is red, then they fail to notice, or are deceived by facts that philosophers take into consideration. There is agreement about the facts. Nor is it plausible to suppose that the mistake would stem from incorrect use of ordinary language to describe the facts; for the description is the ordinary description, and ordinary language used for ordinary purposes is correct language.

The argument between philosophers and ordinary men may be about presuppositions, justification, and evaluation. Philosophers should be taken as maintaining that it is better to evaluate facts in a way that is different from the ordinary. And philosophers may be right in this. Watkins's mistake is to suppose that it follows from this that ordinary men using ordinary language are mistaken. The reason why this does not follow is that they have different purposes. Given certain philosophical purposes, for instance, clarity, precision, justification, evaluation, it might be better to judge facts in nonordinary ways. But given the usual ordinary purposes, like communication, social intercourse, exchange of information, the present use of ordinary language is quite suitable. So while there may be much that a philosopher rejects in ordinary language when he pursues philosophical aims, it does not follow from even this perfectly justified rejection that ordinary language used for ordinary purposes is mistaken. Watkins's criticism that it is possible that the application of an ordinary expression is *always* mistaken therefore fails.

Thus provided, first, that the PCA is made neutral between different theories of meaning by restricting its application to the descriptive use of expressions; and second, that it is recognized that the connection between a descriptive expression and a paradigm case is a nonnecessary, nondefinitional exemplification, the objections raised by Watkins can be met.

In considering the third thesis, it has to be noted, however, that there is a presupposition the truth of which is essential for the PCA, and it has not yet been argued for. It is that there actually are expressions in the language to which the PCA can be applied. These expressions must be such that their descriptive use could be taught and learned with reference to actual cases. This is a revised formulation of a requirement that was previously much stronger. Watkins's objection forced the weaker requirement upon the defenders of the PCA. Teaching the meaning has had to be abandoned for teaching the use, to avoid being committed to a mistaken theory of meaning. And the necessity of teaching with reference to actual cases has been replaced by the possibility, so that the PCA would not be trivialized and thereby deprived of existential import. The reason why the PCA must require that the relevant expression be such that its descriptive use could be taught and learned with reference to actual cases is to avoid being committed to the absurd conclusion that by the use of the PCA the referents of all descriptive expressions could be proven to exist.

73

This requirement frees the PCA from automatic commitment to the existence of fictional, imaginary, mythical, abstract, nonempirical, and theoretical entities.

The presupposition of the PCA is that there are expressions in the language whose descriptive use can be taught and learned with reference to actual cases. The argument has established that *if* there are expressions of this sort, then it does follow that when they are used descriptively the resulting statements cannot always be false. In other words, if the antecedent is true, the third thesis of the PCA is correct. But is the antecedent true?

Malcolm, Flew, and Black can be interpreted as arguing for its truth by citing examples. Malcolm regards such spatial and temporal expressions as "to the left of," and "before," and expressions like "it is certain that," "it is probable that," as suitable examples. Flew's cases are "of his own freewill," "could have helped it," and the more prosaic "wet" and "yellow." Black makes out a detailed case for "making something happen."

A critic of the PCA would of course accept that these expressions have a descriptive use; he would merely deny that the PCA has shown that when they are used descriptively, then there ever is that situation in existence to which they are supposed to apply truly. Suppose someone critical of the PCA issued the challenge: "Nothing is really red." [18]

The PCA would be defended by holding that if nothing were red, then the descriptive use of "red" could not have been taught and learned. The existence of red things can be deduced from "red" having a descriptive use. But this does not follow. For all that is required by the PCA is to teach and learn the descriptive use of "red" with reference to cases of *apparent* redness. One can consistently accept the PCA's account of the use of "red" and deny that anything red exists.

The thrust of the objection, of course, is quite general. And when it is understood to apply to all descriptive expressions, than it becomes the sceptical challenge demanding a justification for the rationality of the belief that there really exist *any* situations to which descriptive expressions appear to apply truly. Directed specifically against the PCA, the sceptical challenge can be taken to deny that a distinction between real and imaginary cases can be drawn. It can be argued that no reason has been given by the PCA for holding that the cases with reference to which the descriptive use of any expression can be taught are anything but the product of the imagination of the person who may also fancy himself teaching others and generally interacting with some nonmind-dependent environment. The sceptical challenge shows that the PCA is compatible with solipsism.

The reply, on behalf of the PCA, that if what the sceptic claimed were true there could not be any descriptively used expressions is inadequate. The sceptic accounts for there being such expressions by the possibility that their use has been taught and learned with reference to apparent, not actual, cases. The argument that for a situation to be apparent, there must *be* some situation, and so something actual must exist is easily countered. For the sceptic can agree that appearance is parasitic on reality and argue that for all the PCA shows, the reality may be entirely mental, the product of the only thing that exists: a solitary mind.

## Conclusion

It must be admitted that the PCA fails to carry the burden that was placed on it. As an analysis of philosophical arguments and as a criticism of departures from ordinary language it has serious defects. Insofar as it is an argument purporting to justify inferences from language to reality it does not succeed, because it has not excluded the possibility of solipsism.

The reason for the PCA's failure is that not one of its three theses is wholly correct. It is true that philosophical arguments are not about facts, but it does not follow that therefore they must be about correct language. Ordinary language is correct language, but philosophical arguments need not be fallacious just because they violate it. Even if the PCA is correct in the analysis of the meaningfulness of certain expressions, the leap to ontological conclusions still remains open to the sceptical challenge.

# 5 Science as a touchstone of rationality: Popper

*"Science is one of the few human activities—perhaps the only one—in which errors are systematically criticized and fairly often, in time, corrected. This is why we can . . . speak clearly and sensibly about making progress there."*—Karl R. Popper, *"Truth, Rationality, and the Growth of Knowledge"*

## Fallibilism and the sceptical challenge

Popper's view is that science is the paradigm of rational inquiry and that the success of science is the answer to the sceptical challenge. Against this, it will be urged that science, understood in Popper's way, rests upon presuppositions which themselves need to be rationally defended. But this defense can be scientific only if the question is begged. There is, therefore, a prior enterprise, the defense of presuppositions, upon whose success the rationality of science rests. If this enterprise is successful, it, and not science, is the paradigm of rationality, while if it is unsuccessful, not only does science fail as a paradigm of rationality, but it also fails to be rational.

The philosophical position that occasions these doubts is fallibilism. According to the fallibilist, human beings are doomed to error. Not even the most secure, the best supported belief is free from the possibility of mistake. Certainty is an illusion, proofs are deceptive, knowledge, understood as justified true belief, is an impossible ideal. Fallibilism challenges the epistemological orthodoxy that regards knowledge as the attainable product of a reliable process of reasoning. It denies the authority of reasoning, and consequently declares knowledge, regardless of its source, to be unattainable.

Two forms of fallibilism need to be distinguished. Weak fallibilism is the view that it is logically impossible to exclude the possibility of error in the case of any conclusion arrived at by reasoning. It allows, however, that even though reasoning is inevitably prone to error, some beliefs may be rational and ought, therefore, to be accepted. Strong fallibilism goes further and denies that any belief can

76

have rational warrant. While weak fallibilism cautions against error and advises that all beliefs be tentatively held, strong fallibilism denies that reasoning can provide grounds for the acceptance of any belief. Reasoning, on this view, is a blind alley, an illusion, a vain pretense. Strong fallibilism, thus, is another name for the sceptical challenge.

The weak fallibilist accepts that reasoning is untrustworthy and beliefs should be tentatively held, but he stops short of scepticism. He holds that we can learn from our mistakes, a process which is the hallmark of rationality, which makes the growth of knowledge, understood as the acquisition of rationality supportable beliefs, possible. The most notable champion of this position is Popper.

The great merit of Popper's position is that while it rejects the faulty analyses of rationality offered by previous theories, it does not draw an antirationalist conclusion. Instead, Popper proposes his own account: critical rationalism. The fact is, however, that the combination of weak fallibilism and critical rationalism leads to strong fallibilism, that is, to scepticism, and Popper has not managed to stop this progression.

## Popper's critical rationalism [1]

Popper takes rationality to be characterized by the critical attitude, and the natural sciences as the field where the critical attitude is most typically exemplified. He sets about to reconstruct the logic of science and thereby answer questions about rationality, truth, knowledge, and similar epistemic notions.[2]

Consider the development of science. In the prescientific stage there are a large number of myths, practices, beliefs, assumptions about reality. These form the background against which problems occur. Science starts with problems. Problems reveal that there is a tension between various traditional assumptions, or that the traditional assumptions conflict with observation. A solution is demanded by the necessity of coping with the environment, and this requires having an accurate picture of it.[3]

77

Forming an accurate picture of the environment calls for a conjecture. A conjecture is a guess about the nature of reality. The purpose of the conjecture is to bring the traditional assumptions into harmony with observation in such a way that what was previously problematic will become understandable. The conjecture gives a picture of reality; its role is to depict how reality may be so that one's assumptions would fit it. The fact that a problem has occurred shows that the old assumptions do not quite fit reality and need to be revised. The conjecture is a possible revision.[4]

Given the background and the problem there are, of course, a great many conjectures possible. All successful conjectures reconcile traditional assumptions with existing observations and offer a solution by proposing a new picture of a segment of reality. But not all successful conjectures are rational. What makes a conjecture worthy of scientific attention is that it is criticizable or falsifiable.

A criticizable conjecture is a rational scientific theory; an unfalsifiable conjecture is pseudoscientific, metaphysical. The criticizability or falsifiability of a scientific theory consists in it being specifiable what would have to happen for the theory to be shown to be mistaken.[5]

Popper's break with verificationism, that is, with the view that the rationality of a scientific theory depends on the evidence available for it, is closely connected with the asymmetry of verification and falsification. A counterinstance to a theory tells much more decisively against it, then does a verifying instance tell for it. This feature follows from the nature of theories, for if a theory is a conjecture composed in part of traditional assumptions and past observations, then theory has some verifying instances built into it due to the possibility of repeating those observations which it supposedly explains. The uselessness of evaluating a scientific theory on the basis of successful verifications can be easily seen by noticing how simple a matter it is to generate successful verifications from scientific theories that are known to be mistaken.[6]

Instead of looking for observations that bear out the picture of a segment of reality formed by a scientific theory, one should then, according to Popper, look for observations that could not obtain if reality was as the theory depicted it. Scientific theories issue prohibitions: such-and-such could not happen. The testing of scientific theories comes to cajoling reality into yielding up those features, which, according to theory, are not there. To test a theory is to try to refute it. If a theory withstands testing, if one has tried hard to refute it and failed, then the theory is acceptable and can be reasonably held until either it is refuted by some more ingenious test, or some new problem occurs that the theory cannot handle.[7]

A theory that is known to be mistaken presents clear evidence about the nature of reality: it tells us that reality is not as the theory depicted it. Some theories resist refutation, at least temporarily, and these are accepted, but not of course proven. For theories cannot be known to be true with any certainty; at best, they can be known to have survived sophisticated critical attempts and have presented a solution to our problems. This is the reason why they should be accepted. There is, however, nothing final or certain about surviving theories. Their day of reckoning is merely put off until the problems they inevitably generate they can no longer solve.

Knowledge grows, but this must not be thought of as a process whereby an increasingly larger number of truths are discovered. The growth of knowledge consists in making bolder and bolder conjectures; conjectures that are exposed to criticism, survive it, and lead to the solution of increasingly more difficult problems.[8]

The growth of knowledge is motivated not only by the need to solve problems, but also by an ideal: truth. The purpose of theories is not to solve problems, but to solve them in such a way that the theory gives a true picture of reality. Truth is the regulative ideal of the growth of knowledge; it is the ideal limit toward which theories tend. Truth, however, is unattainable; the ideal can be approximated, but it can never be achieved. That this is so follows from what has been said up to now, for to claim that a theory is true requires that it be provable, and to prove a theory requires the elimination of the possibility of error. Not only is it impossible to eliminate all sources of error, but also even if this were accomplished, nobody could know that it had been done.

Theories must be judged on the basis of their problem-solving capacity, their boldness of conjecture, and their survival of criticism. But it does not follow that if a theory passes these tests, then it is true. All that follows is that it is closer to being true, that it has

79

greater verisimilitude than do theories that failed the tests. Verisimilitude is a relative concept; it must always be expressed as the property
of a theory vis-a-vis another theory. We know that a true theory
would be a picture of a segment of reality that corresponds exactly to
reality. But we also know that one can never know that a theory is
true; all that can be known is that it is the best, the boldest, most informative solution to a problem and that while observations might be
found which would tell against it, none have. We have all the reason
for accepting such a theory even though we do not and cannot know
that it is true.[9]

If the quixotic quest for certainty is abandoned, if it is realized that
truth is an unattainable ideal, then the failure to achieve it need not
be counted as a failure of reason. The function of reasoning is to solve
problems, to provide conjectures about the nature of reality, and to
submit these conjectures to criticism. Though reason is fallible, this
fallibility can be turned to good advantage by the method of conjectures and refutations, a method exemplified by scientific inquiry.
Mistakes are unavoidable, but we can learn from them. Weak fallibilism, therefore, does not lead to strong fallibilism.

## Criticism of critical rationalism: the metaphysical presuppositions of science

Critical rationalism fails because it has *not* avoided strong fallibilism.
The view that scientific inquiry is the paradigmatic rational activity
and as such it is the remedy against scepticism is open to serious objections. The point of these objections is not that the rationality of
the scientific enterprise *per se* is in doubt, but rather that the assumption that scientific inquiry is rational needs also to be rationally supported and Popper's attempts to do so are unsuccessful. The alleged
progress of science is not an obstacle in the way of strong fallibilism.

The distinction between the context of justification and the context
of discovery is essential to the rational appraisal of scientific inquiry.
The circumstances surrounding a man's formulation of a theory are
judged to be irrelevant to the justification of the theory. The psychol-

ogical, sociological, and fortuitous factors influencing a problem situation bear no relation to the rational appraisal of the problem's solution. What leads a man to say something is independent of the truth or falsehood of what he says.

Popper explicitly accepts this distinction:

> This question of how it happens that a new idea occurs to a man . . . may be of great interest to empirical psychology; but it is irrelevant to the logical analysis of scientific knowledge. This latter is concerned not with *questions of fact* . . . but only with questions of *justification or validity*. . . . The task of the logic of knowledge . . . consists solely in investigating the methods employed in those systematic tests to which every new idea must be subjected if it is to be seriously entertained.[10]

The rationality of scientific inquiry, or indeed of any inquiry, would be fatally undermined if questions of justification could not be answered in a satisfactory way. To acknowledge that this happens is tantamount to admitting that the inquiry cannot be rationally appraised; that this unavoidably happens is one of the main contentions of strong fallibilism.

One attack on the distinction between the contexts of discovery and justification is based on the idea that the standards by which theories are appraised are themselves theory-bound, part of the fundamental assumptions of the domain in which the theory occurs. Hence appraisal is either question-begging, or it must occur with reference to context-independent standards. It is very difficult to see, to say the least, what such standards could be.

Suppose, for instance, that the standard by which a theory is judged to be rational is that it has been reached by following a certain method. Two methods that enjoy widespread acceptance among philosophers and practitioners of science are intersubjective testability and quantifiability. Goethe's theory of colors is unquantifiable, Piaget's studies of the development of individual children are intersubjectively untestable.

Intolerantly it may be said that since these cases contradict methods of scientific inquiry, they are irrational. Guided by a more liberal spirit, they could be declared merely unscientific, and the possibility of favorable judgment of their rationality with reference to

81

some nonscientific standard may be allowed. But this is a very peculiar way of dealing with counterexamples. Clearly both Goethe and Piaget thought that they were doing science, and it is unlikely that they were unacquainted with the scientific methods. They seem, however, to reject the methods that most scientists accept. Those and indeed any methods can thus be legitimately questioned, and consequently adherence to them requires justification. The justification cannot merely be that this is how scientists do things, because scientists are prepared to criticize practice that conflicts with their own. Is this criticism rational, or is it just a flaunting of prejudice?

The argument in favor of accepting such methodological requirements as intersubjective testability and quantifiability is that with their aid scientific problems can be solved. It would not do at all, of course, to identify scientific problems as problems tractable by the application of scientific methods, for then the whole scientific enterprise would become self-guaranteeing. Since problems not amenable to scientific treatment would not be considered, and *simpliciter,* would not be considered unsuccessfully, science could not fail.

It might be suggested that problems do not come hallmarked as scientific; problems just occur and as it happens science is an excellent device for solving many of them. But this will not do either, for problems do not just occur. There are, as it were, no problems in nature. Events, occurrences, processes appear problematic only against a background of presuppositions which shapes expectations. If the expectations urge scientific solution, the employment of scientific methods is no doubt amply warranted. But perhaps a man who refuses to follow the accepted methods does so because his expectations have been shaped by different presuppositions, and hence different things strike him as problematic. To judge the adequacy of his solutions by the scientific yardstick is like commenting adversely on a pointillist painter for not using straight lines.

The reply might be that not all problems arise against presuppositions. There are universal problems that stem from the physiological needs of human beings and from the nature of the environment which has to be forced to yield up the satisfaction of these needs. This is no doubt true, but its truth presents no argument in favor of those presuppositions which form the foundation of science. For there are and have been many civilizations that solved these basic problems without the application of scientific methods. The scientific solution is *a* solution, not *the* solution. To judge other, nonscientific, approaches by applying to them scientific standards is of course question-begging. A successful argument for science being the paradigm of rationality must be based on a demonstration that those presuppositions upon which science is based are rationally preferable to other presuppositions.

If a grand label is wanted, these presuppositions might be called "metaphysical." At any rate, they express *a priori* beliefs about the nature of reality. They are the organizing principles of experience: the devices we employ to make sense out of the data that continually bombard each human being. The presuppositions are certainly not necessary, they are not supposed to be true by definition. At the same time, they are not empirical either, since they would not be refuted by experience that seems to conflict with them. Experience cannot be used to appraise these presuppositions, for it is the role of these presuppositions that they be used to appraise experience. Kant called them synthetic *a priori* principles, Collingwood referred to them as absolute presuppositions, and Popper, no doubt, would include them into the "background" against which problems arise. *A priori* presuppositions may be ontological, such as, "There is a spiritual element in reality," or "Everything is made of matter," or "There exists a life force"; or they may be dichotomies in terms of which experience should be classified, for instance, "cause and effect," "mental and physical," "real and apparent," "transcendental and sensible"; or the presuppositons may be about how nature works and how best to understand it, for example, "Nature allows no exceptions," "Nature is orderly," "God's will be done," "God does not play dice," "There is purpose in nature," and so on.

The acceptance of scientific inquiry as a paradigm of rationality requires a demonstration of the presuppositions upon which scientific inquiry rests. But such a demonstration cannot come from within science, since it would already presuppose what requires to be proven, namely, the presuppositions of science.

Naturally, Popper is aware of these pitfalls and attempts to avoid them. For him, what makes the scientific enterprise preferable to other attempts at problem-solving is the cumulative, progressive nature of science. Popper writes:

> I assert that continued growth is essential to the rational and empirical character of scientific knowledge; that if science ceases to grow it must lose that character. . . . Science is one of the very few human activities—perhaps the only one—in which errors are systematically criticized and fairly often, in time corrected. This is why we can say that, in science, we often learn from our mistakes, and why we can speak clearly and sensibly about making progress there. In most fields of human endeavour there is change, but rarely progress . . . for almost every gain is balanced, or more than balanced by some loss. And in most fields we do not even know how to evaluate change.[11]

This view of science has been contested by Kuhn.[12] Central to Kuhn's thesis is the distinction between normal and revolutionary science. The distinction rests on the notion of paradigm. A paradigm performs three main functions. First, it is a scientific achievement that has come to be regarded as a model or ideal of scientific research in a given period. It is an achievement that opens up new avenues of research, new ways of tackling problems; it establishes the foundations of a new way of looking at reality. The work of Newton or Darwin, for instance, constitute paradigms in this sense. Another aspect of the paradigm is that it determines type of questions that scientists ask. If certain observations suggest problems, it is because they are at odds with expectations based upon the paradigm. So the paradigm acts as a regulative ideal prompting some questions, judging others as irrelevant or uninteresting, prescribing methods of research that are likely to be successful. In its third role, the paradigm is a textbook or an actual piece of research: a concrete scientific achievement that functions as an educational tool for the training of future scientists. It is a showcase of good science.[13]

Normal science refers to a period of scientific research when there is an agreed-upon paradigm; revolutionary science occurs when scientists for one reason or another become dissatisfied with the existing paradigm and replace it by another. Normal science, as the adjective suggests, is what science largely is. The overwhelming majority of scientists spend all of their professional time pursuing normal science, that is, research more or less determined by a paradigm. Scientific

84

revolutions, the replacement of one paradigm by another, are very rare. When they occur, they determine for generations to come what normal science is to be.

Kuhn agrees with Popper that science starts with problems, but he disagrees about the nature of the problems. The paradigm, according to Kuhn, imposes something like a grid upon nature. The grid has large gaps and it is not clear how to fill them. The paradigm gives an outline of nature; the task of normal science is to complete the outline, to fill in the gaps, to transform the loose grid into a finely meshed one. Scientific problems, then, are the difficulties encountered in the way of completing the task of normal science. Scientists doing normal science, in a sense, already know what nature is like: it is as the paradigm depicts it. Their problem is the application of the big picture to the particular case. Normal scientists are given the general answers, the rules by which the answers can be reached, and an excellent example of reaching the answer—they are given all this by the paradigm—and their problem is to reconcile a particular observation with the dictates of the paradigm. Their activity, Kuhn suggests, is better described as puzzle-solving, rather than problem-solving. The solution of a problem of normal science is not the discovery of some new truth about nature, it is a successful reconciliation of an observation with the expectations created by the paradigm.

But what happens if the reconciliation is not achieved? Is it not then that there is a refutation of the paradigm? Do scientists have to admit then that nature has said "No!" to their paradigm? Not at all. If a scientist fails to reconcile an observation with the paradigm, there are two options open. It may be concluded that the scientist failed to solve the puzzle, or the paradigm may be rejected. Normal science is characterized by the adoption of the first option. Only if the paradigm is already suspect would a conflict between it and an observation be interpreted as a criticism of the paradigm.

The role of criticism is thus profoundly different for Popper and Kuhn. The task of criticism, according to Popper, is that of getting nearer to the truth, of increasing the verisimilitude of our theories by eliminating mistakes. Mistakes are built into theories, and it is thus theories that suffer as a result of criticism. On Kuhn's view, criticism may well leave theories intact and reflect adversely only on the skill, intelligence, or ingenuity of the scientist. As a result, criticism does not bring one closer to truth, it merely spurs the normal scientist toward more ingenious attempts at reconciliation. Popper regards science as an unceasing attempt to overthrow the paradigm; Kuhn sees science as increasingly sophisticated attempts at defending the paradigm. Popper thinks that normal science is atypical, Kuhn thinks that revolutionary science is atypical. Neither denies that the phase the other regards as important occurs, each denies that the other has correctly gauged its importance.

If Kuhn's view of science is correct, then Popper's critical rationalism fails. Science, then, would not be distinguished from other areas of human endeavor by its capacity for progress. Progress in science is filling in the gaps left by the paradigm. But such progress is possible in any field that has a paradigm. If an historian accepts, say, dialectical materialism, his paradigm is provided by Marx and progress consists in explaining more and more historical events in dialectical terms. If a jurist accepts the codification of social behavior as the legal ideal, then progress will be recognized as the extension of the legal system to increasingly greater areas of social life. Paradigms breed progress, and scientific progress has no special place.

The disagreement between Popper and Kuhn is a family quarrel. They disagree about the nature of science, but they do not disagree about science being the rational enterprise *par excellence*. Kuhn in reply to the charge that he defends irrationality in science writes:

> To describe the argument as defence of irrationality in science seems to me not only absurd but vaguely obscene. I would describe it . . . as an attempt to show that existing theories of rationality are not quite right and that we must readjust or change them to explain why science works as it does. To suppose instead, that we possess criteria of rationality which are independent of our understanding of the essentials of the scientific process is to open the door to cloud-cockoo land.[14]

This is a pure expression of one of the presuppositions that need defending. Popper and Kuhn agree in making it, and they are at one in failing to defend it. The point of the sceptical challenge is that unless the presupposition is defended, strong fallibilism prevails. For strong fallibilism need not deny that there is progress in Kuhn's sense; it needs merely to deny that the paradigm is rationally defensible. Strong fallibilism detects no substantive difference between working on a paradigm, scientific or otherwise, and completing a jigsaw puzzle.

Kuhn's endorsement of science as the touchstone of rationality is a semantic decision. It amounts to advocating that we should use "rational" to refer, in its primary sense, to scientific inquiry. But definitions, as we have seen in criticism of analytic rationalism, will not assuage the strong fallibilist. Rationality, for it to be worth anything, must have something to do with truth, where truth is understood as correspondence between statements or theories and the world. Popper endorses this conception of truth and rationality, Kuhn denies it. In characterizing the difference between himself and other philosophers of science, including Popper, Kuhn writes:

> There is another step . . . which many philosophers of science wish to take and which I refuse. They wish, that is, to compare theories as representations of nature, as statements about "what is really out there" . . . I believe nothing of that sort can be found. . . . If I am right, then "truth" may, like "proof," be a term with only intratheoretic application.[15]

The disagreement between Kuhn and Popper is, thus, partly over the question of whether or not a correspondence theory of truth is possible. Kuhn argues that it is not possible, and we must rest content with a coherence theory: truth is an intratheoretical term. But if this is the case, then any theory, domain, or field of human endeavor can be judged rational and true provided it has a paradigm, a method of working on the paradigm, and is internally consistent. Rationality and truth, then, become ideals the satisfaction of which rests upon the prior acceptance of those presuppositions that form the foundations of a domain. And when the strong fallibilist demands rational support for the presuppositions themselves, champions of the coherence theory are helpless. They have to resort to the kind of *ex cathedra* pronouncements that Kuhn provides, namely, that if science is not rational, then nothing is. The strong fallibilist rejoinder, of course, is to endorse the consequent of that dubious conditional.

Can Popper avoid this conclusion? If problems, the methods for solving them, and criticism are merely ways of getting from prescientific presuppositions to paradigms, then the ideal of objective truth recedes. The paradigm, it is true, may be approximated, but what is the guarantee that it is truth thereby which is brought closer? How can it be determined whether or not a paradigm corresponds to reality? How could Popper avoid the possibility that a paradigm is an arbitrary way of looking at nature whose adequacy is judged by its internal coherence and the capacity to solve problems that arise only because scientists subscribe to prescientific presuppositions?

A possible, albeit unsatisfactory, answer is provided by Popper's follower Lakatos, who frames his discussion in terms of research programs. Lakatos writes:

> One must never allow a research programme to become a *Weltanschauung* . . . setting itself up as an arbiter between explanation and non-explanation. . . . Unfortunately this is the position that Kuhn tends to advocate: indeed, what he calls "normal science" is nothing but a research programme that has achieved monopoly. But, as a matter of fact, research programmes have achieved monopoly only rarely and then only for relatively short periods . . . *The history of science has been and should be a history of competing research programmes (or, if you wish, "paradigms"), but it has not been and must not become a succession of periods of normal science: the sooner competition starts, the better for progress.*[16]

The guarantee that a paradigm does approximate nature, according to Lakatos, is that there are competing paradigms. The success of a research program means that it is a better model, a more accurate representation of nature than its competitor is. But how is the success of a paradigm or of a research program to be judged? One of Lakatos's examples of a research program is the mechanistic view of nature. Suppose it is contrasted with a teleological research program. According to one paradigm, nature is like a clock; according to the other, nature is like a growing acorn. Clearly, testing and prediction will not show what nature is like. If a scientist cannot find the causal law explaining the occurrence of an event, the mechanistic view of nature will not be abandoned. It will be assumed that the scientist has not found the law. Similarly, if the discovery of a fact seems to contradict the design that was thought to exist in nature, the conclusion will not be that nature has no design, it will be assumed that the design is other than what it was thought to be.

Research programs can be judged vis-a-vis the problems which they attempt to solve. Success consists in problem-solving, failure in the lack of it. As we have seen, however, problems that prompt research programs occur only against the background of expectations created by prescientific presuppositions. Hence the adequacy of the research program must be judged against the rationality of those pre-scientific presuppositions upon which it is based. And it is the rationality of these presuppositions that the strong fallibilist calls into question. Lakatos recommends that scientists should build competing castles on air, and he ably reconstructs the architectural problems involved. The strong fallibilist is right in demanding something firmer.

If the arguments offered thus far are correct, then there follows an old, but neglected problem: in order to maintain the rationality of science and in order to avoid strong fallibilism, the presuppositions upon which scientific inquiry rests must be rationally supported. It does not seem to be questionable that there are at least some ontological, methodological, and classificatory presuppositions underlying scientific inquiry, and there may be axiological presuppositions as well. It is only fitting that these presuppositions be brought out into the open, examined, and given a chance to prove, as Popper would say, their mettle. The merit of fallibilism is in calling attention to the problem. Popper attempts to deal with the problem by acknowledging that the presuppositions are there and insisting that they can, all the same, be subjected to rational appraisal by the use of the method of conjectures and refutations. But Popper fails; for scientific inquiry, the practice of conjectures and refutations, owes its problems, methods, and ideals to the acceptance of those presuppositions that it is now trying to make respectable. Unless independent, non-scientific, arguments are provided for the presuppositions, science must be hopelessly question-begging. What could such independent arguments be? The answer is clear, although perhaps a little surprising: metaphysical. The conclusion seems to follow that the rationality of science and the possibility of metaphysics stand or fall together.

89

## Conclusion

Critical rationalism, postulating science as the paradigm of rationality, fails to counter the sceptical challenge. The very general reason for its failure is that science itself rests on presuppositions whose rationality is under sceptical attack, so the issue of rationality arises at a point that is logically prior to the possibility of offering science as a touchstone of rationality. What makes this state of affairs especially significant for the rationalist is the fact that the human orientation towards the environment need not be based on science. Popper is probably right in insisting that science is characterized by the critical attitude. But it needs to be argued, and it has not been successfully argued, that rationality is characterized by the scientific attitude. After all, there are enduring, highly civilized cultures, such as prenineteenth-century Chinese culture, which seem to allow for perfectly rational beliefs and actions without science playing an appreciable role in them.

Nevertheless, the examination of critical rationalism has yielded three important results. Each of these will occupy a crucial role in the subsequent argument. The first is that meeting the sceptical challenge depends upon the defense of presuppositions that underlie not just science but all domains of inquiry. The traditional name for that defensive enterprise is metaphysics. So the sceptical challenge forces rationalists to engage in metaphysics. This presents the considerable problem of how a rationalist can have any traffic with metaphysics in the light of extremely damaging contemporary criticisms of it.

The second result is that whatever account of rationality one ends up with, the critical attitude must somehow figure in it, for the critical attitude is simply the opposite of dogmatism, of the blind adherence to authority. If rationality is to have any meaning at all, the willingness to consider arguments against one's position must be part of it. Popper's error is that he has made too much of the part, to the detriment of its other components.

In the dispute between sceptics and rationalists, it is illuminating to discuss Popper's contribution to the debate in terms of what has been called "Ramsey's Maxim." [17] Considering a dispute about a fundamental question that does not seem to be capable of decisive settlement, Ramsey writes:

> In such cases it is a heuristic maxim that the truth lies not in one of the two disputed views but in some third possibility which has not yet been thought of, which we can only discover by rejecting something assumed as obvious by both the disputants.[18]

Sceptics and rationalists have assumed as obvious that rationality depends on finding reasons for one's beliefs. Popper rejects their assumption and thereby gives a new direction to this age-old debate.

The third result is that the extremely important role that problem-solving plays in rationality must be recognized. In fact, problem-solving will be argued to be the most important standard of rationality.

# 6 The illegitimacy of the sceptical challenge: Winch

"[C]riteria of logic are not a direct gift of God, but arise out of, and are only intelligible in the context of, ways of living. . . . It follows that one can not apply criteria of logic to modes of social life as such. For instance, science is one such mode and religion another; and each has criteria of intelligibility peculiar to itself. So within science or religion actions can be logical or illogical. . . . But we cannot sensibly say that either the practice of science itself or that of religion is either logical or illogical; both are non-logical."—Peter Winch, The Idea of a Social Science

## Introduction

Theories of rationality face an initial hurdle: if rational defense is taken to consist of a successful appeal to standards of rationality, then standards of rationality cannot be rationally defended.

The traditional—Cartesian—starting point for theories of rationality is to search for some principle or belief that cannot reasonably be doubted and then attempt to deduce other principles or beliefs from the allegedly indubitable one. There are two decisive objections to this approach. The first is that whether or not a potential fundamental principle can reasonably be doubted must be settled, according to this view, with reference to some standard or another. But the sceptic, questioning the rationality of all standards, will also question the particular one used to render the first principle "indubitable." So to meet the sceptical challenge it is necessary to go beyond the Cartesian tradition. The second objection is that even though assiduous attempts have been made throughout the history of philosophy no standard has been found that both guarantees the rationality of theories or beliefs which conform to it and at the same time is itself rationally defensible. The obstacle in the way of finding such a standard is logical.

If the sceptical challenge is to be met a different starting point must be adopted. It is far more fruitful to begin with the observation that language affords the distinction between rational and irrational systems of beliefs. The sceptic does not deny that the distinction is drawn, he merely objects to the idea that the distinction is well-founded. He grants that there are standards of rationality implicit in everyday practice, but, the sceptic argues, the standards are arbitrary. By this he means that no acceptable reason has been given for them.

One way of meeting this challenge is to argue for its illegitimacy. It is meaningless, so the rejoinder goes, to ask for reasons in support of standards of rationality, for what counts as reason is determined by these standards. What one can do is to show how "rationality" functions within a system of beliefs and then point at the descriptive account and say: this is what we do, this is what "rationality" means. For the sceptic to want anything more is to misunderstand the meaning of "rationality."

We have seen that this is the strategy of analytic rationalism and that it fails to meet the sceptical challenge, for the sceptic points out that to call something "rational" is not only to describe it but also to evaluate it. And it is perfectly legitimate to ask for some reasoned explanation for one's preference. What makes the reply to this question important is that fundamentally different and profoundly objectionable evaluations are readily available with no way of choosing between them.

In this age of analysis, however, analytic rationalism has a fundamental appeal. If one version is refuted, another invariably makes its appearance. The most recent and probably the most sophisticated candidate is the theory of rationality in Peter Winch's *The Idea of a Social Science* and in "Understanding a Primitive Society." [1]

Winch's theory is Wittgensteinian. He develops and expands the suggestions Wittgenstein made in *Philosophical Investigations* and *On Certainty*. [2] The justification for examining Winch's theory rather than Wittgenstein's is that Wittgenstein has offered no theory of rationality. The clues, pointers, brief discussions and examples of his that touch on this point require systematic development and Winch has provided it. Perhaps there are theories of rationality other than Winch's that can be derived from Wittgenstein's writings. The fact

93

is, however, that only one—Winch's—is publicly available, and that is the one to be examined here.

Winch sets out a coherence theory of rationality. His view is that "rational," "irrational," and their cognates have meaning only within a form of life. Thus it is improper for the sceptic to demand and for the rationalist to try to supply a context-independent account of rationality. The inquiry into the rationality of what exists within a form of life is legitimate, but it is illegitimate to question the rationality or irrationality of a form of life itself.

Part of the significance of this theory lies in the fact that it licenses the rationality of anything that is a rule-conforming part of any *bona fide* form of life. Thus if religion and magic, for instance, qualify as forms of life, then both they and any conventional religious or magical practice would, for that reason, become automatically immune to rational appraisal.

The disagreement between coherence theories of rationality and scepticism is only a matter of emphasis, for it makes no substantive difference whether their common point is expressed by the claim that "rationality" has application only within a system of beliefs or by the assertion that no system of beliefs can legitimately be called "rational." Both views deny the possibility of a context-independent account of rationality.

The reason for examining Winch's coherence theory of rationality here is to prepare the ground for a theory of rationality that will be capable of meeting the sceptical challenge. Winch's theory will be used as a foil. By offering increasingly general criticisms of it the beginnings of an acceptable theory of rationality will eventually emerge.

## A coherence theory of rationality

The expression, "form of life," comes from Wittgenstein,[3] but neither he nor Winch offers a straightforward account of its meaning. Winch helps by giving examples of forms of life,[4] by using synonyms,[5] and by offering some general remarks.

These remarks suggest the idea that a form of life is a manner or a style of social living characterized by an identifiable way of expression and governed by its own rules of communication. But a form of life is also a way of acting. Living a form of life and engaging in practices characteristic of it are inseparable.

Forms of life essentially involve social interaction whose main vehicle is language. Words in a language have meaning if they are used in the same way on the same kinds of occasion. But "the same" is systematically ambiguous: whether or not two things count as the same depends on the context of the question. A rule is needed to give specific sense to "the same." Meaningfulness thus depends on rule-following, upon acting in the same way on the same kinds of occasion; but it is only in terms of a rule that "the same" acquires a definite sense. Hence Wittgenstein's remark: "The use of the word 'rule' and the use of the word 'same' are interwoven." [6]

A person can be said to follow a rule only if two requirements are met: it makes sense to suppose that somebody else could in principle discover the rule which is being followed, and it makes sense to ask whether or not he is doing what he does correctly.

The rules of a form of life are shared by the participants through their being engaged in similar types of behavior, an engagement prompted by having similar interests and aims. Participation in a form of life implies a fundamental, enduring commitment that need be neither conscious, nor chosen, yet endowing one with a way of life. [7]

Winch emphasizes the central importance the notions "form of life" and "rule" have for his thesis. Having quoted Wittgenstein's pointer: "What has to be accepted, the given, is—so one could say— forms of life," [8] Winch goes on:

> The philosophies of science, of art, of history, etc., will have the task of elucidating the peculiar natures of those forms of life called 'science', 'art', etc., epistemology will try to elucidate what is involved in the notion of a form of life as such. Wittgenstein's analysis of the concept of following a rule. . . . is a contribution to that epistemological elucidation. [9]

To participate in a form of life is to have accepted, *inter alia,* a set of concepts and rules. These concepts settle for us the form of the expe-

95

rience we have of the world. There is no way to get outside these concepts and compare them with the world. "The world *is* for us what is presented through these concepts." [10] Nor do rules or criteria that guide the use of concepts have an independent status:

> [C]riteria of logic are not a direct gift of God, but arise out of, and are only intelligible in the context of, ways of living or modes of social life. It follows that one cannot apply criteria of logic to modes of social life as such. For instance, science is one such mode and religion another; and each has criteria of intelligibility peculiar to itself. So within science and religion actions can be logical or illogical. . . . But we cannot sensibly say that either the practice of science itself or that of religion is either logical or illogical; both are nonlogical. [11]

In consequence it is "crucially wrong. . . . to characterize the scientific in terms of that which is 'in accord with objective reality'." [12] For,

> reality is not what gives language sense. What is real and what is unreal shows itself in the sense language has. . . . Both the distinction between the real and the unreal and the concept of agreement with reality themselves belong to our language. . . . To understand the significance of these concepts, we must examine the use they actually do have. [13]

A form of life must correspond to reality, but what is "real" and what is not is decided within the form of life. The check of the independently real is not peculiar to science. The scientific way of testing has been mistakenly elevated into a paradigm for other modes of discourse. God's reality, for instance, is independent of what men think. But what it amounts to can be seen only from the religious tradition in which the concept of God is used. Within the religious form of life the conception of God's reality has its place. [14]

Rationality involves conformity to norms. The difference between forms of life is not that some do and others do not conform to norms, but that different norms are being followed within them. [15]

> Rationality is not *just* a concept *in* language like any other; it is this too. . . . But I think it is not a concept which a language may, as a matter of fact, have and equally well may not have. . . . It is a concept necessary to the existence of any language. . . . Where there is a lan-

guage it must make a difference what is said and this is only possible where the saying of one thing rules out . . . the saying of something else. . . . This, however, is so far to say nothing about what in particular constitutes rational behaviour; that would require more particular knowledge about the norms they appeal to in living their lives.[16]

It is thus a necessary condition of rationality that there be norms, but the existence of any system of norms is sufficient for rationality.

## Two internal criticisms

The first criticism of Winch's theory of rationality is that it requires that there be different forms of life and, at the same time, makes it impossible to differentiate them. The fundamental idea of Winch's theory is that each form of life has its own standards of rationality and hence the rationality of a form of life cannot be legitimately criticized by applying to it an alien standard. The possibility of distinguishing between different forms of life is thus essential to Winch.

But how can this distinction be drawn? How can it be found out whether two candidates for being forms of life are the same or different? Since "the use of the word 'rule' and the use of the word 'same' are interwoven" [17] the possibility of drawing the distinction depends upon having a rule. Given the rule, the sameness and difference of forms of life can be judged; without the rule, the judgment cannot be made.

The difficulty Winch faces is that of accounting for the relation between the rule used for distinguishing forms of life and forms of life themselves. If the rule is said to be part of a form of life, then the question is merely postponed. For how is that form of life distinguished from other forms of life? No doubt by appealing to a rule. But is that rule, too, part of a form of life? The individuation of any form of life depends on having the rule, but having the rule depends on there already being an individuated form of life. This circularity makes it impossible to distinguish one form of life from another. Consequently, it is impossible to know by what standard of rationality a form of life can properly be judged. If religion and science are not different forms of life, then criticizing religion by scientific standards may not be inappropriate.

Suppose, however, it is denied that the rule used for distinguishing forms of life is part of a form of life; the rule may be said to be independent of any form of life. This answer, however, vitiates Winch's whole enterprise whose purpose is to show that there are no rules, and *simpliciter,* no rules of rationality outside of forms of life.

Winch's theory of rationality succumbs to the following problem: a rule is needed for distinguishing between different forms of life. If the rule is part of a form of life, then circularity makes the individuation of forms of life impossible. If the rule is independent of all forms of life, then Winch has provided a counterexample to his own theory.

It might be supposed that the objection can be avoided on the assumption that the rule for distinguishing different forms of life occurs within a form of life, but it is self-referential. The rule may be said to contain a description of some important features of the form of life within which it occurs. Other forms of life can then be distinguished by noting whether or not they lack some of the specified features. But this will not do for the following reason.

The point of having such a self-referential rule is to distinguish a given form of life from another. This, however, assumes what the rule is supposed to establish: namely, that there are different forms of life. Of course, the existence of different forms of life is vital to Winch's view of rationality, but their existence must be shown, it cannot just be assumed.

The supposed self-referential rule cannot show it because it disguises the difference between a candidate for another form of life being in fact another form of life and it being a poor example of the form of life in which the rule is stated. Suppose, for instance, that the self-referential rule occurs in science; it specifies some of the important features that science has. The rule is then applied to religion, and naturally religion is found to lack some of the features that science has. There are two conclusions derivable from this: first, science and religion are different forms of life; second, religion is an inferior kind of science. The first conclusion supports Winch's case that religion and science cannot be criticized from each other's point of view. The second conclusion, however, shows that religion can be criticized from a scientific vantage point. The employment of the self-referential rule could not lead to the distinction between these two cases. All the rule could do is to help to note that there are differences between a form of life and something that may or may not be one. But whether the differences are signs of inferiority or manifestations of an alternative way of looking at things remains undecidable. It is precisely this decision that Winch's supporters must find a way of making.

The second criticism is that while Winch needs to show that it is impossible to rationally justify the practice of criticizing one form of life from the point of view of another, his theory of rationality renders such justification possible. Winch's argument is that a form of life embodies certain beliefs and practices, rules are to be extracted from them, and rationality or irrationality is to be judged by determining whether or not the appropriate rule is being followed. Beliefs and activities that are part of one form of life cannot be appraised from the point of view of another form of life, for this involves judging them by reference to rules to which they were not meant to conform. To offer such criticism is "nonsensical," "absurd," to be guilty of "philistinism," and to commit a "category-mistake." [18]

In exorcising this error, Winch traces part of its pedigree; he writes: "I start with John Stuart Mill. . . . because Mill states naively a position which underlies the pronouncements of a large proportion of contemporary social scientists," [19] and again, "It will not do simply to dismiss Mill as antediluvian, for his approach flourishes still at the present time." [20] Evans-Pritchard and other anthropologists, as well as MacIntyre, are all castigated in "Understanding a Primitive Society" for the same error. In fact, one could help Winch by pointing at the immense literature where religious beliefs and practices are criticized from a nonreligious point of view, where one political way of life is criticized from the point of view of another, and where a historical period, say, the "Dark Ages" is criticized from the vantage point of another, the Enlightenment for instance.

The fact is that criticizing one form of life from the point of view of another is something people do. Anthropologists, sociologists, historians, politicians, and ordinary men frequently engage in the practice. Rules could be extracted, and reasonable and unreasonable ways of doing it could be distinguished. There is nothing to stop one from thinking of this absurd, nonsensical, philistine activity as being a form of life.

And this presents another problem: either forms of life can be criticized from the point of view of other forms of life, or they cannot be. In the former case, magic and religion can be argued to be irrational without absurdity. In the latter case, Winch's criticism of the form of life involving external criticism of other forms of life is illegitimate. In either case, Winch's position collapses.

## External criticism: forms of life and common sense

"Form of life" is a characteristically Wittgensteinian notion, but the idea expressed by it has invited acceptance by philosophers who are at various distances from that tradition. Carnap's conception of a linguistic framework, Kuhn's idea of research centered around a paradigm, D. Z. Phillips's work on religion [21] all share with Winch the following basic conception. Language can be divided into distinct spheres which operate more or less autonomously. Within these areas there are rules that settle what is problematic, relevant, and what counts as evidence. The cohesion of each autonomous enterprise is guaranteed by the goals, purposes, and interests that the participants share. Various philosophers disagree about what should be recognized as a discrete system of this sort, but there is widespread agreement about their existence.

It is very convenient to refer to religion and science as different forms of life, to say that phenomenalism and physics are different linguistic frameworks, that art and business are different universes of discourse, or belong to different categories. The usefulness of these expressions, however, is seriously jeopardized if they are treated too rigidly by making too much of their supposed autonomy and by emphasizing the difference between their referents at the expense of similarities.

What underlies many coherence theories of rationality is just this misplaced emphasis. For only if forms of life, linguistic frameworks, or whatnot, are entirely distinct does it become plausible that each has its own conception of reality, rationality, and proof. And only then could it be a mistake to criticize one from the point of view of another. For if they share some terms and procedures, then their points of view may not be so far apart as the coherence theories would have it.

A brief reflection on the relation between common sense and forms of life will illuminate this point. It will be remembered that Moorean arguments for the primacy of common sense have been accepted. These arguments, of course, fall short of establishing the rationality of common sense, but for the present purposes it is sufficient to note that the acceptance of and action in accordance with common sense beliefs is criterial for being a normal human being. Their acceptance comes to the fact that the vast majority of human beings in all cultures acts in accordance with them, and they do so even if they avow beliefs that contradict the common sense ones. If someone acts contrary to common sense beliefs it is proper to suspect him of sickness, insanity, or more remotely, of not being human.

Common sense is the picture of the world that human beings cannot help having due to their physiological make-up. It is the basis we all start with but there is no guarantee of its truth. Common sense is given in that it is the starting point of all inquiry, but this does not mean that it reveals the structure of reality. Common sense is simply the most secure and widely accepted part of the view human beings form of the world.

What then is the relation between common sense and forms of life? There are several reasons for thinking that common sense is not a form of life. It is optional whether or not a person participates in the activities proper to a form of life, but it is not optional, at least not in the same sense, whether or not a person behaves in accordance with common sense beliefs. A religious man may abandon his faith, an artist may give up art, and in so doing they cease to participate in a *form* of life. But if someone were to abandon behavior in accordance with common sense, he would be giving up *life*.

The second reason for not thinking of common sense as a form of life is that it permeates all forms of life. There could not be a form of life whose participants systematically ignored common sense beliefs in their behavior, for it simply is a fact about human beings that they perceive the world in terms of five sense modalities—that sounds are heard as having varying pitch and intensity, that sights are made up of colors, shapes, and the like. A human being shares with all others his senses and in consequence the type of information he has. Furthermore, he shares also the type of response he is capable of giving because human beings have similarly equipped bodies. These form the boundaries of human possibility, and common sense simply marks the limits. Of course within the limits enormous variations are possible, but the variations are all departures from the physiologically given.

All the various forms of life start with common sense. They may emphasize different parts of it, study in detail some aspects and neglect others, they may come to explain features of it that appear puzzling and offer different interpretations of its significance, meaning, or purpose. Forms of life may even yield beliefs that conflict with common sense beliefs; but not even forms of life can produce systematic behavior that goes against common sense. The reason is that such behavior goes against human nature and is consequently destructive of it. A human being, of course, can choose to destroy himself, but self-destruction is not a form of *life*. Common sense is the ground of forms of life, it is not itself a form of life.

The third reason has to do with language.[22] Forms of life are social, requiring language as a medium of communication. It is customary to talk about religious and scientific language, but "language" used in this way is a metaphor. English, Hindi, and Hopi are languages in the primary sense. The technical vocabulary that forms of life may develop are languages, at best, in a secondary, derivative sense. It may be that a scientist and a religious man cannot understand each other, but that is not because they do not speak the same language. For they both speak one natural language or another. Their failure is due to their unfamiliarity with each other's technical vocabulary. Just as common sense is the ground of forms of life, so also is an ordinary, natural language the ground of various specialized languages developed within forms of life.

If, say, English did not occupy something like a substratum of religious and scientific and other derivative languages, then it would be impossible to explain how communication could take place. Winch emphatically endorses the public and social nature of language,[23] because he recognizes that communication requires a shared referent. People can talk to each other only if they are capable of identifying and reidentifying the same features of reality. This, however, is possible only if they have a common conception of reality and of truth and falsehood. Unless they had it to some extent, communication could not begin; if there were no shared conceptions, there would be no agreement about what counts as successful identification of some feature of reality, and thus it could not be known to what anybody was referring. The possibility of communication, therefore, requires that there be a shared ground between the languages of various forms of life.

It should be noted that the force of these remarks about the primacy of common sense and the dependence of forms of life upon it are not meant to claim that common sense is rational. The arguments aim at the conclusion that regardless of whether or not common sense is rational, forms of life presuppose it. Common sense and ordinary language are not themselves a form of life, but the starting point of all forms of life. And this conclusion has disastrous consequences for the coherence theory of rationality and for Winch's version of it. For participants in different forms of life can no longer be regarded as creatures totally alien to each other; they share common sense beliefs and also a language. It may be that within science and religion such terms as "rationality," "proof," and the like acquire a technical sense; and so when a man talks, *qua* scientist, he means something quite different by "rationality" than when another man, *qua* religious believer, talks about it. But whatever they mean when they use the terms in their derivative, technical sense, men do mean the same when they use the terms in their ordinary senses, and those senses they share, The significance of this is that shared beliefs and language provide precisely the standard, independent of forms of life, that Winch is committed to denying.

Suppose that two alter egos of Winch, Rench participating in the religious and Sinch in the scientific mode of existence, wish to talk to each other about the rationality of their respective beliefs and practices. Rench is rational because his relevant behavior reflects the

Thirty-nine Articles and Sinch is rational because he follows the hypothetico-deductive method. Each acknowledges that the other's behavior does indeed conform to norms, and hence, it is rational. But Sinch, in his heart of hearts, says: maybe Rench's behavior is in accordance with the Thirty-nine Articles, but I do not think that accepting the Thirty-nine Articles is rational. If Sinch is right, then Rench may turn out to be irrational after all.

In order to put this disagreement with precision two senses of rationality need to be distinguished. A person is weakly rational if his behavior is in accordance with some norm, while a person is strongly rational if his behavior is in accordance with a rational norm. Sinch's point is that Rench may be weakly rational, but he is not strongly rational.[24] And Sinch may make this view known and Rench may contest it. Such arguments occur with frequency and not just about religion and science.

The interesting, and for Winch the troublesome, question is about the medium in which such arguments are conducted. Sinch clearly does not use religious discourse to state his point, and if Rench answers in religious terms, he begs the question. Nor is the argument conducted in scientific discourse, for Sinch is not a fool and he does not expect Rench to understand mathematical formulas or to be giving an experimental justification for accepting the Thirty-nine Articles. How, then, do Sinch and Rench talk to each other?

The reasonable answer is that they do so in English. Expressions like "religious language" and "religious mode of discourse" are, as we have seen, metaphors. Users of religious and scientific languages do not need a translator, at least not in the way in which a translator would be needed if one spoke English and the other German. The fact is that both religious and scientific discourses are derivative; they are conducted in a natural language upon which they superimpose a technical vocabulary. It may be that "rational" acquires one technical sense in religious discourse and another in scientific discourse. Both technical senses, however, derive from the original, nontechnical uses of "rational." The usual procedure for conducting such arguments as that between Sinch and Rench is to show how the contested sense of "rational" is related to, how it derives from the original, nontechnical senses of "rational." And these senses Sinch and Rench both understand merely by virtue of being competent users of English. Rench's answer to Sinch should be to attempt to trace step by step how the ordinary senses of "rational" came to be employed in religious discourse. Sinch, if he wishes to object, may do so by trying to make the case that the religious use of "rational" constitutes too radical a departure from the ordinary uses; he may say that religious apologetics have no right to use the word because its technical sense is separated by an abyss from its ordinary senses.

The fact is, however, that this answer to the question of how Sinch and Rench communicate is not available to Winch. For his case rests on the assumption that there are no standards independent of forms of life with reference to which judgments about the rationality of actions and beliefs can be evaluated: "we cannot sensibly say that either the practice of science itself or that of religion is either illogical or logical; both are nonlogical." [25]

Winch's theory faces the following problem: if common sense and ordinary language do form a substratum of forms of life, then there is a ready-made, context-independent standard with reference to which claims made within different forms of life can be appraised; if, on the other hand, common sense and ordinary language are regarded as one form of life among many, then it becomes impossible to explain how communication is possible in the absence of a shared conception of reality.

The fundamental difficulty in holding a coherence theory of rationality is that its adherents must take the existence of discrete systems or forms of life seriously and, at the same time, they cannot do so. There must be different, nonoverlapping forms of life, otherwise there would be no reason for thinking that there are different, mutually exclusive norms of rationality. But the compulsion to recognize discrete forms of life makes it impossible to account for communication between participants in them, for communication requires a shared medium, and if forms of life are really discrete, then there could not be any. On the other hand, if there was a shared medium, then forms of life would have to be related to it, and through it to each other; consequently they would not be really discrete, and criticism of one from the point of view of another would be possible.

## Conclusion

There is something essentially illuminating and something fundamentally mistaken in Winch's attempt to meet the sceptical challenge. Winch is very much on the right track in trying to overcome scepticism by a close analysis of rationality. The best hope of answering the sceptic is to provide a theory of rationality that is immune to his attack.

The great difficulty that Winch's defense of rationality encounters arises on account of the assumption that a satisfactory theory of rationality could be provided by describing what is done in various forms of life. The notion of a form of life is incoherent when it is transformed from a convenient metaphor into the cornerstone of rationality. But the idea that a satisfactory account of rationality need be only descriptive is also defective. For a sceptic will accept the description and challenge the prescription implicit in judgments of rationality. And no amount of description can meet that challenge. So, to put it plainly, a theory of rationality must not only say what rationality is but also why it is good.

The coherence theory of rationality is not new: Hegel and Bradley held versions of it. Traditional coherence theories of rationality, however, were held in conjunction with monism. It was thought that rationality is system-bound, but there is only one possible system. Winch departs from the tradition and combines the theory with radical pluralism; he allows the possibility of an indefinite number of systems, each with a peculiar notion of rationality. The arguments so far have been directed only against those versions of the coherence theory that are committed to the Balkanization of natural languages.

The next step is to develop a theory of rationality. It has a critical and a constructive task. The latter is to offer a theory of rationality which is not completely system-bound. The completion of this task, however, also completes the critical one. For if rationality is not completely system-bound, then both monistic and pluralistic coherence theories of rationality, as well as scepticism, are shown to be mistaken, for they are all committed to denying that such a theory of rationality is possible.

# The state of
the argument:
the sceptical
challenge and
the gains from
unsuccessful
attempts to
meet it

The purpose of these remarks is to ease the transition from the statement of the problem and from the consideration of some unsuccessful attempts at solving it to a more promising line of attack.

The discussion of the attempts to use success in action, common sense, ordinary language, science, or a coherence theory of rationality as a bulwark against the sceptical challenge has not been merely a critical enterprise. There has emerged, after criticism, from each of these approaches some ideas that the rationalist neglects at his own peril. Pragmatism bequeaths us the view that rationality, to be worth anything, must present a more successful policy of action than do any of its rivals. And it supplies the methodological tool of distinguishing between external and internal questions. The appeals to common sense and ordinary language establish the unavoidable starting point of all inquiry. The primacy of common sense supplies some of the facts with which any theory, including a theory of rationality must start. And ordinary language is the medium in which the problem must be stated and in which, if it can be, it must be solved. The examination of critical rationalism has yielded the idea that a theory of rationality must be capable of defending those presuppositions upon which science, and all other inquiries, rest. On the positive side, critical rationalism attempts to explicate rationality in terms of the critical attitude; this is undoubtedly part of rationality, but seeing that it is not the decisive part leads to the all-important connection between rationality and problem-solving.

These ideas, severally, are too weak to counter the sceptical challenge, but if they are welded together into an acceptable theory of rationality, then the sceptical challenge can finally be met. For the construction of an acceptable theory of rationality, as Winch has seen, is the crucial step in refuting scepticism. What the sceptic challenges is the possibility of rationality and a successful theory of rationality establishes that possibility. Of course, having a theory of rationality is not sufficient; it has to be shown also that some beliefs are actually rational in that they conform to the theory. If this were not done, the sceptic's claim, that there are no rationally defensible beliefs, would remain unchallenged.

These considerations determine the structure of the argument to come. First, the theory of rationality needs to be constructed, and then it must be applied.

# PART 3
# RATIONALITY

# 7 The requirements of the theory of rationality

*"The concept of reason plays an extremely important part . . . in philosophy. It also plays an important role in all the social sciences, particularly political science, sociology, and psychology. It is of crucial significance in psychiatry. It is therefore surprising that there has been relatively little work on this concept. Philosophers and others have generally used the concept of reason, and the related concept of justification, as if these concepts were understood by all. But, as it will become evident, these concepts are almost universally misunderstood. The general low esteem into which reason has fallen in many circles is due primarily to this misunderstanding."*
—Bernard Gert, *The Moral Rules*

Before a theory of rationality is presented it should be clear what its aims are. This makes it possible to criticize the theory if it fails to achieve its objectives. The primary aim, of course, is to defend a conception of rationality that escapes sceptical objections. The theory of rationality, however, could fail in this task either by not meeting its requirements—to be set out below—or by having defective requirements.

## External and internal accounts of rationality

It will be remembered that a suitably altered version of the distinction between external and internal questions has been previously accepted. Internal questions arise within a theory. A successful theory ought to be able to provide at least possible answers to all internal questions. A failure to do so signals the failure of the theory. External questions are about a theory and they concern such matters as the reasons for the theory, the relation of the theory to its rivals, the methodology employed by the theory, and the like. A theory of rationality must be able to answer both external and internal questions. The external and internal accounts are answers to these questions.

Internal accounts of rationality aim to subject the concept to philosophical analysis. The results will be a description of the criteria guiding its employment and an account of the type of circumstance in which it is proper to ascribe or withhold the term. There is a clear sense in which it must be possible to give an internal account, since "rationality" is an English word in usage.[1]

The sceptic has no quarrel with internal accounts. His point is not that "rationality" is not or should not be used in ordinary discourse. The sceptic objects not to the employment of the term, but to the belief that the assumptions underlying the employment are justifiable. And by that he means that there is no reason for thinking that beliefs which have been awarded the epithet "rational" are more likely to be true, provide accurate information, or lead to a successful course of action, than beliefs from which this adjective is withheld.

The sceptic's contention rests on the point, by now familiar, that the standards by which the supposed excellence of beliefs is judged are themselves arbitrary, for they are rationally unjustified. The *ad hominem* rejoinder that the sceptic himself engages in the practice whose arbitrariness he asserts carries no weight. For the sceptic's very point is that all beliefs, including his own, are arbitrary in that they lack rational warrant. The form of the sceptic's argument is *reductio ad absurdum:* he reaches the conclusion damaging to his target by assuming, but only for the sake of argument, his opponents' premises.

No amount of analysis or description of how "rationality" is used within a system, or way of life, or domain can answer the sceptical question, for it is a question *about* rationality: an external question. This is the fundamental reason why the standard refutations of scepticism fail to make even a dent in the attack upon rationality.

The theory of rationality, therefore, must provide an external account of rationality in reply to the external question. The external account must show that there is a rational way of supporting even a theory of rationality. The charge of arbitrariness can be met only by finding a standard that is rationally acceptable without the support of

yet a further standard and one that renders the theory of rationality itself rationally justifiable.


# Explanation of preanalytic facts

Some of the facts that the theory of rationality sets out to explain by
providing the internal account are the linguistic habits of competent
users of the language when they employ or withhold the term "rational" and its cognates. Thus, for instance, science and history are ordinarily recognized as rational; witchcraft, astrology, and phrenology,
when practiced in these days by educated people of the Western civilization are irrational; psychoanalysis and extrasensory perception are
debatable cases. Caligula, especially as Camus portrayed him, was irrational, while Hume and Spinoza were rational. It is irrational to cut
off one's foot because one's toe hurts, but it is rational to consult a
physician in such a case.

The theory of rationality begins with such common judgments and
it should be able to explain what justification they are ordinarily
thought to have. Such an explanation goes part of the way toward
meeting the charge of arbitrariness, for the more understandable a
judgment is the less arbitrary it appears to be. The sceptical
challenge, however, is not met merely by exhibiting the reasons
behind ordinary judgments of rationality. For the sceptic will deny
that the reasons are any good. Nevertheless, the theory of rationality
must begin by discovering these reasons so that argument about their
acceptability can begin.

The observance of this requirement ought to make it possible to
avoid a common pitfall. Philosophers are prone to begin with a problem that arises out of a set of facts and offer a solution that results in
the reinterpretation of the facts which gave rise to the problem in the
first place. Thus they solve a problem different from the one they
meant to solve. The theory is intended to justify judgments of rationality as they are commonly made and understood; these judgments comprise some of the facts to which the theory must do justice.

## Rationality and logic

Rational arguments must conform to the rules of formal logic and to the less well articulated informal conventions that guide the use of language. The theory of rationality faces two problems on this account. The first is to argue for the rationality of relying upon logic. Logic, after all, is composed of a collection of rules and some reason must be given for their acceptance. The second problem is to show that while rationality is tied to logic, conformity to logical rules is not sufficient for rationality. Failing this, any logical practice, regardless of the substance of its beliefs, would have to be declared rational. Rationality, it must be shown, has to do not just with the form of one's beliefs, but with their content as well.

## Rationality and success in action

The strongest *prima facie* case for rationality rests on the claim that it is the most promising policy for action. Pragmatism elevates this into the fundamental requirement of rationality. Even though the pragmatic argument failed, it is clear that the theory of rationality would be defective if it did not explain why following a rational course of action will tend to be more rewarding than rival policies. But just as with logic, the theory must guard against the identification of rationality with only one of its requirements. The equivocation would lead to the absurd conclusion that just so long as a belief resulted in a successful course of action it was rational. At the same time, it must be shown why it is that rationality is the most promising policy.

## Rationality and criticism

The postulation of criticism as a standard of rationality is Popper's great contribution. But just as other standards of rationality, criticism, too, needs to be rationally supported. And when the arguments

114

are given, criticism loses its supposedly privileged place among other, rationally defensible, standards of rationality. Criticism is a necessary requirement of rationality, but only in certain circumstances, and it is not sufficient for rationality. The theory of rationality must explain both the necessity and the lack of sufficiency.

## Defense of presuppositions

One of the reasons for the failure of science as a paradigm of rationality is the existence of presuppositions whose acceptability science assumes but does not support. The rationality of science, and indeed of any inquiry, depends upon the possibility of rationally supporting the presuppositions upon which it rests. The enterprise of defending presuppositions is metaphysics. The theory of rationality, therefore, should not only leave room for, but must actively encourage, the practice of metaphysics. For the failure or impossibility of metaphysics would mean that the sceptical challenge cannot be met. In consequence, it is necessary to reflect upon the nature of metaphysics and upon the question of how it is possible to defend the rationality of presuppositions without appealing to further presuppositions which, like their predecessors, require rational warrant.

## The rationality of theories

The primary question concerns the rationality of theories, for the rationality of persons depends on the rationality of their actions and beliefs, and the rationality of actions, in all but the most primitive situations, depends upon the rationality of the beliefs upon which they are based. But beliefs do not occur in isolation: they are part of a system. Individual beliefs have presuppositions and implications; their truth or falsity is essentially influenced by the truth or falsity of other beliefs; their acceptance or rejection depends on assumptions about methods that can be used for testing them; and the way in which the beliefs are expressed is determined by the classificatory or categorial assumptions implicit in the language. The natural starting point for a theory of rationality is therefore at the rationality of theories; actions, persons, individual beliefs derive their rationality from the context of theories.

## Psychological, formal, and philosophical accounts of rationality

The theory of rationality must avoid two tempting ways of handling the problem. One is to treat rationality as a character trait possessed by people who have a disposition to make decisions and accept beliefs by weighing reasons. To develop a theory of rationality based on this assumption is a psychological task, and can, perhaps, be discharged by empirical psychologists. But having a psychological theory of rationality will not silence the sceptic, for his point is that rational behavior is just one kind among others and it is as much lacking in rational defense as are types of behavior that are incompatible with it. The psychological theory of rationality helps to identify instances of rationality, but it does nothing to establish their preferability.

The other temptation is to account for rationality entirely in formal terms. This would require the postulation of some criteria and rationality would simply be judged by conformity to the criteria. Rationality, then, would be treated much like validity: a timeless property of arguments. The formal approach is closer to what a philosophical account of rationality should be, but it still has a great defect. It ought to be recognized that a belief or theory may be rational in one situation and fail to be rational in another. If the theory of rationality were entirely formal, then the nature of the situation could have as little relevance to judgments of rationality as the content of propositions has to the validity of the arguments of which they form parts.

One question to which the theory of rationality ought to provide an answer is: given such-and-such standards of rationality and such-

and-such situation, is a particular theory rational? Of course, another task is to provide standards that withstand sceptical objections.

## Conformity to standards of rationality

The purpose of setting out these requirements of the theory of rationality is to provide a way of evaluating it. It has already been noted that two grounds upon which the theory could fail are nonfulfillment of the listed requirements and the inadequacy of the requirements. The third ground is that the theory could fail to be rational. But since finding a way of determining whether or not any theory is rational is the very purpose of the construction of the theory of rationality, the rationality of the theory of rationality depends upon its capacity to conform to its own standards. It is natural to suppose that this requirement gives rise to complex logical tangles. The fact is, however, that this is not so. The theory of rationality to be defended can be shown to be rational with surprising ease.

# 8 A theory of rationality: the external account

*"For man . . . the life according to reason is best and pleasantest, since reason more than anything else is man. This life therefore is also the happiest."*—Aristotle, *Ethica Nicomachea*

## Introduction

The fundamental requirement in meeting the sceptical challenge is a defense of the prescriptions implicit in judgments of rationality. Both rationalists and sceptics are, or ought to be, prepared to accept that rationality involves conformity to standards. It might even be possible for them to reach agreement about what these standards are. But critics of rationality are unwilling to regard these standards as anything but conventional, arbitrary norms that we happen to have accepted. A satisfactory theory of rationality must confront this problem.

The theory of rationality to be defended in this and the next two chapters offers an internal and an external account of rationality. The internal account supplies the internal standards of rationality: logical consistency, conceptual coherence, explanatory power, and criticizability. The external account provides the one external standard: problem-solving. The internal account adumbrates four standards, the external account provides the fifth standard upon which the other four rest.[1]

The theory of rationality must account for two features of our preanalytic notion of rationality. The first is that a rational theory affords a better way of getting on in the world than an irrational one. The second is that the reason why a rational theory is likely to be better in this respect is that it has a better chance of being true, of corresponding to what there is than an irrational one. The external account constitutes an analysis of the first preanalytic feature of rationality by defending problem-solving as the external standard of rationality. The internal account is an analysis of the second preanalytic feature: truth-directedness. The four internal standards make it possible to eliminate theories which are successful solutions of problems yet whose success is not due to their verisimilitude. Thus the external and internal standards together guarantee that if a theory conforms to them, then that theory presents a successful solution to the problem that prompted it and that its success is due to the theory's accurate representation of the relevant portion of reality.

Before embarking on the exposition and defense of the theory of rationality, two questions need to be distinguished. First: what makes a theory rational? And second: what makes the acceptance of a theory rational? The significance of this distinction is enormous for it permits the separation of the epistemological merits of a theory from the psychological attitude one adopts toward that theory.[2] A theory is rational or not independently of whether anyone accepts it. A rational theory may be rejected by everyone without impairment of its rationality, and an irrational theory may be accepted by everybody without producing a change in the epistemological worth of the theory. Rationality of theories is an objective property.

The consequence of this distinction is that defenders of rationality must recognize two radically different challenges. One is expressible as: what could legitimately show that a theory is either rational or irrational? The other is: why should a person accept a rational theory rather than an irrational one?

The general answer to the first challenge is that a theory is rational if it conforms to the four internal and one external standards of rationality and it is irrational if it fails to conform to one or more of the standards. The general answer, however, will be satisfactory only if the standards are justified. In this chpater the external standard will be discussed and justified; in the next chapter, the four internal standards will be examined and it will be shown how they are grounded upon and justified by the external standard.

The general answer to the second challenge is that a person should accept a rational theory rather than an irrational one, because it is in his interest to do so, whatever his interest happens to be. The task of Chapter Ten will be the explanation and defense of this answer to the second challenge.

## Problem-solving

Theories are held against a background. The background may include beliefs, prejudices, expectations, other theories, value judgments, myths, rituals, practices, and countless other cultural phenomena. Generally speaking, the background is the culture, the tradition, or the way of life in which the theory occurs. The most important feature of the background, from the present point of view, is a problem. Many things may count as problems. On the simplest level, a person may want to do something that he regards as desirable, but the culture does not have the means to do it. For instance, he might wish to cure cancer, but is incapable of doing so. The problem may arise, however, because surprises, anomalies, "inexplicable" events occur. The problematic nature of anomalies stems from the traditional assumptions and expectations that are part of the background. For an event is anomalous only if it contradicts previous standards of normalcy. Speed greater than the speed of light, telepathic communication, the discovery of an insect species with intelligence comparable to ours would be anomalous occurrences given the present Western tradition. But problems may arise without anomalies. They may be due to the discovery that the background comprises mutually exclusive elements. Theories, expectations, practices may be so related that adherence to one amounts to repudiation of the other. The practice of Christianity may be incompatible with the practice of war; the ideal of mental health may conflict with the ideal of creativity; high living standards provided by efficiently organized industrial societies may greatly diminish personal liberty. Problems may occur in many ways and the different types of problems form an endless list. This is why it is unprofitable to attempt a definition of "problem."

Problems, however, do have a common feature: they stand in need of solution. The role of theories is to provide solutions. To understand a theory, therefore, is to understand also the problem to which the theory offers a solution. The problem, the theory, and the solution provided by the theory jointly explain the point of holding the theory.[3]

Theories solve problems by offering an imaginative account of the nature of things in the relevant domain. What prompts the adoption of a theory is the recognition that if things were as depicted, then what was previously problematic would no longer be so. Theories aim to reconcile the tradition and the anomaly; or they attempt to confront the problem by bringing out what is implicit in the tradition; sometimes theories are turned critically upon their own background and result, usually in a revision, and occasionally in a wholesale replacement of the tradition.

Problems show that our understanding of the world is deficient. We may want to do something, but given what we think we know, we cannot do it. Or something happens which in our existing view should not or could not happen. Or we may have ideals and the means we have for achieving them actually frustrate their realization. In all such cases, we need an explanation to reconcile what we take to be the case with what is the case. Theories offer these manifold reconciliations.

From the point of view of the theory of rationality, our interest should center on a particular aspect of the connection between problems and theories: the aspect of explanation. Theories aim to replace deficient with improved understanding, and, as their result, what was previously problematic is no longer so. It is easy, but nevertheless misguided to confuse the psychological and explanatory aspects of the connection between problems and theories. Theories are proposed by people, and it is people who are bothered by and need to solve problems. But the question of whether and how well a particular theory solves a problem is totally independent of whether or why anybody holds the theory and of what he thinks or feels. The psychological aspect of theorizing is one thing, the explanatory aspect is another. It is, therefore, not part of the theory of rationality defended here that whenever a person is committed to a theory, he is then able to provide an account of the problem-situation. Frequently, people are unaware of their commitments, and even if they are aware of them, they may be at a loss to explain their commitments's point. The important question, in the present context, is whether or not the explanation can be provided.

The crucial claim being made here is that the problem-solving feature of theories must constitute the foundation of a successful theory of rationality. The reason for this is that problems constitute the fundamental link between theories and the world. Problems occur when people bump, as it were, into reality. Problems signify that what we take to be or would like to be the case is not the case. Since the point of theories is to solve problems, naturally the ultimate test of their adequacy is whether or not the problems are solved. A theory offering a possible solution is worthy of serious consideration; one providing a successful solution goes a long way toward becoming worthy of acceptance. So the proposal is to regard problem-solving as the external standard of rationality. It is not the only standard, but it is the only one that is capable of providing the link between what we think and what there is.

All other standards are human inventions and critics have no trouble showing that whatever standards human beings accept are internal to some form of life, tradition, or theory. Rationality is regarded by them as an exercise in conformity to norms, rules, procedures, and as such no better than conformity to any other set of requirements. And though critics may grant that it is necessary to conform, they maintain that it is quite as warranted to conform to one class of standards as to any other. Standards of rationality have no special place, hence it is illegitimate to try to appraise conformity to other standards on rational grounds.

The adoption of problem-solving shows a way out of this morass of relativism, for it affords a way of rationally evaluating different sets of standards. What needs to be asked, then, is which of these alternative sets affords a better solution of one's problems.

## Problems of life and problems of reflection

There is a difficulty in this account of problem-solving. It might be argued that to judge the rationality of a theory by determining whether or not it presents a possible solution to the problem that prompted it is a hopelessly question-begging enterprise. For what counts as a problem depends on the theory. The existence of evil is problematic only to someone who believes that there is a good God. The accidental nature of some historical events requires explanation only if it is supposed that there are historical laws. Generally speaking, there are no problems in nature; problems occur when facts disappoint one's expectations. And expectations, as well as what is to count as fact, are shaped by the theories whose rationality one is endeavoring to determine. Problem-solving, it may be argued, is no more external than anything else.[4]

The reply to this objection will take the form of distinguishing different problem-areas and then showing that within each of these areas human beings encounter some of the same problems regardless of what theories they hold. There are, of course, problems that could arise only against a specific theoretical background. The objection, however, rests on the mistaken assumption that all problems are theory-generated.

People are confronted with problem-areas. A considerable portion of their activities arises out of the need to solve problems within these areas. One not altogether satisfactory classification of these problem-areas is to divide them into problems concerning a person's response to nature or his physical environment, to other people and society, and to himself.

Within each of these problem-areas there occur problems that people have merely by virtue of being human. Such problems are not the by-products of any particular theory. They occur because the species has evolved in a particular way and because the environment is what it is. I shall call these "problems of life." If problems of life are not solved, the agent is damaged. The damage may be fatal, or merely destructive. At any rate, solving problems of life is required for the survival and well-being of people. Problems of life are common to all members of the species, but their solutions, of course, are extremely varied. Because there are different and occasionally conflicting ways of dealing with problems of life, it is necessary to choose between alternative solutions. Making such choices requires reflection and this yields another type of problem: those of reflection. The fundamental problem of reflection is to find a method of choosing the most suitable among many solutions to problems of life without actually trying out the rival candidates in practice. The point of reflection is to minimize the risks involved in acting inappropriately.

The first problem-area, having to do with the human response to nature, comprises such problems of life as the satisfaction of various physiological needs, health, shelter, and protection; generally speaking, the problem is to safeguard one's physical security and well-being. Evolution from primitivism affords the luxury of choosing between different solutions to such problems of life. The choice requires understanding, and science and technology are born out of the need to choose well. Problems of science and technology, then, are the corresponding problems of reflection.

The second problem-area concern's one's relation with other people and society. These problems arise because man is a social being. The typical problems of life that occur in this connection have to do with one's attitude to family, sex, authority, and violence. The source of these problems is the inevitable conflict between the satisfaction of one's desires and their frustration by the rules of whatever society a person lives in. The associated problems of reflection are those with which we are familiar under the labels of "politics," "morality," and "the law."

The third problem-area has to do with people's attitude to themselves. Put simply, it is about being happy; expressed more analytically, it concerns the pursuit of a rich and interesting internal life, self-knowledge, and self-acceptance. Characteristic problems of life in this area are the conflict between long- and short-range satisfaction, the attitude to one's death, pain, suffering, and learning one's physical and psychological limitations and capacities. The appropriate problems of reflection arise out of the need to imaginatively expand one's horizons so that new options may be discovered. It is in accordance with these that people shape themselves, and it is by comparing their own with other people's lives that they come to a better understanding of themselves. One great importance of literature is that it is likely to be helpful in this endeavor.[5]

The objection noted before arises out of a failure to distinguish between problems of life and reflection. Problems of reflection are indeed theory-generated, but problems of life are not. Problems of reflection arise because problems of life have competing solutions. So while it is true that problems of reflection presuppose a theory, it is no less true that the theory is held because it is expected to provide solutions to problems of life.[6]

Theories presuppose problems of life. We come by problems of life and the necessity of solving them by virtue of being human, and not because we are ensnared by this or that theory.[7]

It is difficult to argue this point. The best argument perhaps is to repeat what seems obvious: protecting one's physical well-being and security, resolving the conflict between one's desires and the rules of society, finding a way to be happy are universal human problems that do not come from theoretical commitments, but from the human condition. The thesis is falsifiable: it needs merely to be shown that contrary to its claim, these problems do presuppose a theoretical background, but it is extremely doubtful that this falsification could be provided.

If this argument is successful, then solving problems of life is an external, context-independent standard of rationality. The rationality of a theory depends, in part, on its presenting a solution immediately, or more usually at some remove, to a problem of life. It is necessary, but not sufficient, for the rationality of a theory that directly or indirectly it contributes to the solution of some problems of life.

The difficulty that besets much of the contemporary discussion of rationality is that the various standards offered all presuppose an already established theoretical framework. Conformity to logic, Popper's criticizability, the Wittgensteinian notion of rule-following in a form of life, the positivistic appeal to verifiability, various justifications of induction, and many others, are equally vitiated by the devastating attack of critics. For the critics' strategy is to acknowledge that what is claimed to be rational is indeed rational in a given framework and then go on to question the rationality of the framework. And, of course, so long as the standards offered are internal, the critics' questions cannot be answered. The merit of the standard of solving problems of life is that with its help the critics' challenge can be met. A framework is rational, *inter alia,* if it contributes a possible solution to a problem of life. Since problems of life are independent of theoretical frameworks, so is the standard based upon them.

The standards of rationality canvassed in much philosophical literature aim at providing a method for solving problems of reflection. And, of course, they need to be solved. But such problems ring hollow and appear contrived unless connected with some problem of life. This is why at the foundation of a theory of rationality there must be a way of determining whether or not the proposed theory provides a solution, immediately or later, to a problem of life. Only an affirmative answer allows one to proceed, for only such an answer gives point to the theory in question.

When we proceed we usually encounter conflicting solutions to problems of life. But not even this is necessary. Primitive people may not be able to afford the luxury of debating the merits of alternative solutions, for their problems are pressing. They may have to be satisfied with the first solution they find, and this may be turned into a sacred edifice, the questioning of which is a taboo jealously observed by all. Standards of rationality, other than problem-solving, have nothing to say to such people. Yet their outlook may be rational. For they have problems the solution of which is a matter of survival, and with the help of their beliefs the problems are solved. Of course, their outlook would not be rational if they were aware of and ignored alternatives to it. If there are alternatives, and only then, will internal standards occupy their rightful place in legislating competing answers to problems of reflection. This is why it may be rational to believe in magic and witchcraft in a primitive culture, while it would be irrational to hold the same belief in ours.[8]

## Removable problems and enduring problems

There is a widely shared mistaken assumption that bedevils the exploration of the relation between rationality and problems of life. The assumption is that if a problem is solved, then it ceases to exist; its corollary is that nothing counts as a solution unless it leads to the disappearance of the problem that it was meant to solve. The root of this mistaken assumption is the unjustifiable application of the model of much scientific problem-solving to problems of an entirely different kind.

The model has the following features. We begin by encountering an obstacle; we want to do something and cannot do it. This is followed in cases of successful problem-solving by an explanation. The explanation enables us to understand how things are and we come to see both why the obstacle arose and how to overcome it. The last component is the actual removing of the problem. So the sequence is: obstacle, explanation, understanding, removal of obstacle. If a problem is seen as an obstacle, then it is solved only if the obstacle is removed. Problem-solving, according to this model, leads to changing some aspect of the world.

One explicit statement of this view is Dewey's, but the assumption, of course, goes far beyond pragmatism. Dewey argues that inquiry starts with a "felt difficulty" and its purpose is "the controlled or directed transformation of an indeterminate situation." [9] Implicit in Dewey's view is the positivistic assumption that genuine problems are either factual or verbal. Verbal problems yield to clarification, while factual problems are solvable scientifically. "All real problems," says Schlick, "are scientific questions, there are no others." [10] And even such a consistent opponent of positivism as Popper echoes this fallacy when he talks about philosophical problems: "Genuine philosophical problems are always rooted in urgent problems outside philosophy, and they die if these roots decay." The context makes it clear that the root of genuine philosophical problems is in science. [11] Scientific problems are created by lack of understanding, and if a successful explanation is provided, then the problem no longer exists. Pragmatists, positivists, and at least some Popperians agree in thinking of problems in these terms.

The consequence, of course, is that nothing counts as problem-solving unless it leads to the cessation of the problem it meant to solve. So theories that are offered as solutions of problems without resulting in the disappearance of their problems cannot be successful candidates for rationality.

It is a mistake, however, to suppose that finding a solution to a problem of life or reflection necessarily implies that the problem has ceased to exist. Some problems endure, endlessly persist, and solving them consists in making a continued effort of coping. Such problems will be called "enduring." Other problems are merely short-term obstacles and solving them does indeed result in their disappearance; these will be called "removable."

As an initial illustration of this distinction consider a man wanting to drive a nail in the wall. He may have the problems of not having a hammer and a nail. But once he finds them, he no longer has this kind of problem. Suppose, however, that he is also shortsighted and clumsy. These problems are enduring features in his life and he cannot make them disappear. What he must do is to learn to cope with them, to do as well as he can with these handicaps. Solution, in this case, consists in finding a way to live with problems and not in getting them to disappear. The solution does not produce a change in the world, it results in a *modus vivendi*.

Some problems endure because human beings and the world are what they are; it is not lack of effort, ignorance, or stupidity that makes them persist, but the scheme of things. Scaling a mountain, understanding a joke, proving a theorem, discovering the cause of an event are problems only until a solution to them is found. But respecting other people's dignity, distributing permanently scarce resources, controlling one's temper are not problems capable of removal. They endure because there is a conflict and the conflicting elements are not easily changed. Solution consists in developing a policy which minimizes the undesirable consequences of the conflict.

Generally speaking, the solution of removable problems demands a specific action in a specific situation, while the solution of enduring problems consists in developing a policy in accordance with which one can act in problematic situations. The development of a policy is not always necessary. It is important only when frequently recurring problems are faced and when these problems stem from the same persisting conflict. But the problem that is solved by the development of a policy is an enduring one only if the underlying conflict cannot easily be resolved.

Consider, for example, the problem of what attitude a person should have toward his illness. If I find myself ill, my course of action is obvious. I consult a physician and do as he says. My problem is removable, provided my illness is not serious. But suppose that a person is frequently beset by illness, and infirmity is a constant feature of his life. He, then, has to develop a policy. He may become closely attentive to his health, spend much of his life monitoring danger signals, and live a cautious, moderate life. Alternatively, he may try to ignore as much as possible his illness and endeavor to live as normally as he can. Or he may become resentful, bitter, and treat each symptom as yet a further sign of the unfair scheme of things. The problem of what policy to develop, and, once developed, to maintain it is what is meant by an "enduring" problem.

The distinction between removable and enduring problems applies within the problem-areas discussed before. For regardless of whether a person's problems arise in connection with his physical environment, society, or himself, the distinction between specific problems calling for specific solutions and patterns of recurring problems calling for a policy of action persists.

The relation, however, between problems of life and reflection, on the one hand, and removable and enduring problems, on the other, is less clear. It will not do to identify problems of life with removable problems and problems of reflection with enduring problems. For many removable problems are problems of reflection and many problems of life are enduring problems. Testing a theory by experimentation, proving guilt or innocence in a law court, interpreting the symbolism or allegory in a novel are problems of reflection, yet removable. One's attitude to sex, authority, family are problems of life but also enduring problems.

Yet there is a relation between these two sets of problems. The difference between problems of life and reflection is that the former are necessarily nontheoretical, while the latter must occur against the background of a theory. What establishes the connection is not the logical necessity but the fact that removable problems are more frequently solvable without appealing to a theory, while the solution of enduring problems, having to do with choice of policies, usually require theoretical considerations. Hence it can be said that enduring problems tend to be problems of reflection and problems of life tend to be removable. These connections, however, are empirical and not logical.

The difficulty caused by the mistaken assumption that solving a problem of life leads to the disappearance of the problem is that problem-solving comes to be regarded as a technological question. It is viewed as an exercise in removing obstacles from the way of doing what one wants. It should be clear by now that while many problems are indeed solvable in this way, not all are. And this has an important consequence for the theory of rationality.

It is a necessary condition of a theory's rationality that it should offer a possible solution to the problem that prompted it. In the light of the previous discussion, problem-solving must be understood as including both removable and enduring problems. However, the prevailing view is that even if rationality has to do with problem-solving, the problem must be removable. And since by far the most effective way of solving removable problems is through science and technology, science and technology have become the ideals of rationality.

That logical positivists and pragmatists share this view requires no demonstration. But it is interesting to note that many of their critics do so as well. Popper, for instance, writes: "[T]he natural sciences with their critical methods of problem-solving. . . . have represented for quite a long time our best efforts in problem-solving." [12] Kuhn, at least on this point, agrees: "To suppose. . . . that we possess criteria of rationality which are independent of our understanding of the essentials of the scientific process is to open the door to cloud-cuckoo land." [13]

The result of regarding science as the paradigm of rationality is that nonscientific theories suffer in comparison with them. It is, of course, true that science is the best way of solving removable problems. But nonscientific theories attempting to solve enduring problems should not be adversely judged because they fail in this misguided comparison. The solution of enduring problems calls for policy decisions and an adequate theory of rationality must be capable of accounting for the rationality of such decisions as well. The prevailing feeling of hopelessness in the face of enduring political, moral, and aesthetic conflicts is traceable to the belief that these affairs are noncognitive, emotive, rather than rationally decidable. And that belief comes from regarding science as *the* paradigm of rationality. It is true that enduring political, moral, and aesthetic problems are not scientifically solvable. But it does not follow that these problems cannot be solved or that their solutions cannot be rational.

## Conclusion

The external account of the theory of rationality is based on the idea that the context-independent, objective standard of rationality is problem-solving. The context-independence and objectivity of the standard is guaranteed by the existence of problems that occur naturally, without the mediation of theories and without being by-products of theories. These problems have been called "problems of life" and they stem from the nature of human beings and the exigencies of the environment. The primary purpose of theories is to solve them and the basic standard for judging the rationality of theories is their success in solving problems of life.

In most actual situations, the simple picture of there being a problem of life and a theory intended to solve it does not hold. Usually, problems arise against the background of theories and are thus not problems of life but problems of reflection. Problems of reflection occur in the context of theories, but the primary role of theories is to solve problems of life. The justification of the important role assigned to problems of life in the theory of rationality is not the frequency of their occurrence, but that they constitute the fundamental link between theories and the world. Problems of life guarantee both the objectivity and the relevance of the theoretical superstructures erected in response to them. These superstructures consist of theories intended to solve problems of life, problems of reflection arising out of these theories, further theories intended to solve problems of reflection, and more problems and more theories.

Problem-solving is the key to the rationality of theories and for this reason it is crucial not to have a simpleminded interpretation of what counts as problem-solving. The distinction between removable and enduring problems is made to guard against the widespread and false belief that solving problems means that the problem ceases to exist. Many problems are removable, but many others are not. The solution of enduring problems consists in finding a theory that enables one to cope with the problems. Such theories offer policies for living with permanent and problematic situations, they are not blueprints for changing some aspect of the world.

The external standard of rationality is thus problem-solving, and what problem-solving is is elucidated with reference to the distinction between problems of life and reflection and the distinction between removable and enduring problems.

There are two reasons, however, why the external account does not, in itself, provide a satisfactory theory of rationality. The first is that it is rarely the case that the problem-situation affords only two choices: to solve or to fail to solve the problem. In normal situations one has a choice between several competing solutions. An adequate theory of rationality, therefore, has to offer some way of deciding between conflicting solutions. The internal account is proposed to accomplish this task.

The second reason is that the identification of the rationality of theories with successful problem-solving produces a purely pragmatic theory of rationality. The great weakness of this approach is that it severs the connection between rationality and truth. What makes a theory rational is that it gives a possible account of how things are; a theory is successful because it accurately depicts the facts. However, a theory of rationality that equates rationality with success cannot exclude a mistaken but successful theory from serious consideration. Consequently, it may recommend as rational policy to act on a theory that is known to be mistaken. But success may be due to luck or to inability to see the dire long-range consequences of short-term problem-solving. One wants theories to succeed, but only for a special reason: for having provided an accurate picture of the world. Problem-solving guarantees that only successful theories will be thought to be rational, but it fails to guarantee that a conforming theory succeeds for the right reason. The internal standards of rationality will help to distinguish between fortuitous success and success due to verisimilitude.

# 9 A theory of rationality: the internal account

*"A man demonstrates his rationality, not by a commitment to fixed ideas, stereotyped procedures, or immutable concepts, but by the manner in which, and the occasions on which, he changes these ideas, procedures, and concepts."*—Stephen Toulmin, *Human Understanding*

## Introduction

The complete theory of rationality consists of both the external and the internal accounts. The argument in the previous chapter aimed to establish problem-solving as the context-independent and objective standard of rationality. In this chapter, the internal account will be presented. That account is concerned with discussing and justifying the four internal standards of rationality: logical consistency, conceptual coherence, explanatory power, and criticizability. The internal standards of rationality rest upon the external standard in two different ways. First, the internal standards are justified by the external one. That is, the reason why the four internal standards should be accepted is that conformity to them leads to successful problem-solving. The second way in which the internal standards are dependent on the external one is that the appeal to them logically presupposes that a successful appeal has been made to the external standard. That this is so can be seen by reflecting on some of the implications of the distinction between problems of life and problems of reflection.

As we have seen, problems of life require solutions, but the solutions need not be theoretical. Urgent problems frequently have to be solved urgently and there is no time left for theorizing. In such situations, the only standard of rationality is that of solving the pressing problem of life. Civilization, however, makes the occurrence of these situations rare. Normally, there is time not only for the interposition of one theory between the problem and its solution, but for the consideration of several competing theoretical solutions. Problems of reflection arise when competing solutions have to be decided upon.

133

The internal standards of rationality are appealed to only in these contexts. This is why the appeal to internal standards is logically secondary to the successful appeal to the external standard.

Thus the internal standards depend upon the external one because the latter justifies the former, and because the former do not become relevant until the latter are satisfied.

The dependence of the internal standards upon the external one requires amplification of the previous claim that conformity to the five standards of rationality is severally necessary and jointly sufficient for the rationality of a theory. The situation in which this continues to be true is the one in which the task is to decide between competing theoretical solutions directly of problems of reflection and indirectly of problems of life. Such are the situations that confront us in the overwhelming majority of cases. There are, however, also situations in which a theory may have to be judged rational even though it satisfied only the external standard of rationality. These are the situations in which there is only one solution to an urgent problem of life. The occurrence of this kind of situation establishes that conformity to the internal standards is not a necessary condition of the rationality of a theory in all possible contexts. The amplification required is that conformity to the external and internal standards is severally necessary and jointly sufficient for the rationality of a theory, provided the theory is a candidate for solving problems of reflection.

This necessary amplification, however, presents a possibility which many would regard as paradoxical. It may be that a theory is rightly adjudged rational and yet it fails to conform to such standards as, for instance, logical consistency. How could a theory be rational and not be logically consistent? Considerable discussion will be devoted to this question.

The accounts of the internal standards of rationality must, therefore, discharge the following tasks. First, there has to be an explanation of what the standard is. Second, the standard must be justified by showing how it contributes to problem-solving. Third, it must be shown both why it is that the standard is a necessary condition of the rationality of a theory, if the theory is a solution-candidate of a problem of reflection, and how it is possible that a theory could be rational in some contexts even though it fails to conform to the internal standard in question.

There is a final comment—a reminder—before turning to the discussion of the internal standards. A justification of rationality needs to answer, as we have seen, two questions: first, what makes a theory rational? and second, what makes the acceptance of a theory rational? or, why should a person accept a rational theory? In the last chapter and in the present one, the discussion was and still is aimed at answering the first question. In the next chapter, the second question will be answered.

## Logical consistency

A rational theory must be logically consistent. It must not happen that a conclusion entailed by an essential part of the theory formally contradicts a conclusion that follows from another essential part of the same theory. The standard of logical consistency requires that the logical consequences of a theory should harmoniously coexist and should not exclude each other.

The reason why a theory should be logically consistent is that theories are attempts to provide a possible way of thinking about a segment of reality and a formal contradiction conclusively demonstrates that it is logically impossible for reality to be in that way. A theory committed to logical impossibility is self-defeating. For the purpose of the theory, the formulation of a possible way of thinking, is rendered unattainable by the theory itself if it results in an impossible way of thinking.

There is, however, a difficulty here. It might be accepted that though the account provided by a theory must be logically possible, what does and does not count as logically possible depends upon the particular logical system that one accepts. The difficulty is that there are alternative logical systems.

This claim can be interpreted in at least two ways. The logical system we do have is concerned with establishing the formal relations among propositions. There may be alternatives to it in that logical systems could be constructed whose aims are different; dialectical logic, for instance, is an alternative in this sense. This problem is easily handled, however, for the two logical systems are not rivals, and consistency can be treated as a purely formal relation within mathematical logic. Dialectical and mathematical logic do not conflict if it is realized that the latter is not supposed to have any existential presuppositions.

The more acute form of the difficulty, however, is if it is argued that there are alternative logical systems, where each system presents a rival account of the formal relations among propositions. If the competing logical systems yield identical propositions as consistent, and differ only in their *modus operandi,* then once again there is no threat to this standard of the rationality of theories.

But what if the two systems give conflicting analyses of consistency? What if some of the things that are logically possible in one system are logically impossible in the other? The resolution in that case must be practical. If there are no detectable errors in either of the systems and if they do issue in conflicting accounts of logical possibility, then it must be ascertained whether or not what each claims to be logically impossible is indeed so. And that can be done by the empirical testing of propositions that one system treats as referring to a logically possible state of affairs and which the other regards as asserting a logical impossibility. Those who are reluctant to decide the merits of conflicting logical systems on practical grounds may find solace in two considerations. One is the absence of any strong reason for thinking that there actually are such conflicting systems. The other is put very well by Winch: [1] "Criteria of logic are not direct gift of God, but arise out of, and are intelligible only in the context of, ways of living." In other words, the rules of logic are formalized procedures extracted from successful practice involved in day-to-day living. It is perfectly natural to determine which of several conflicting logical systems is better by checking them against the practice out of which they supposedly grow.

But what if a sceptic agrees that logical consistency is indeed a requirement for having a possible way of thinking about some segment of reality and disagrees with the aspiration of having such a way of thinking. What can a rationalist say to someone who disavows interest in having theories?

The answer is to reflect on the nature and purpose of theories. If our lives are disrupted, if expectations are disappointed, if traditional practice breaks down, then one is forced to ask: how can things be put right, how can the problem be solved? And the construction of a theory must be the first step in solving the problem. For the theory provides a possible picture of the relevant segment of the environment. The restriction on the possibilities is that they must all provide a scheme such that if things were as depicted, then what was previously problematic or puzzling would no longer be so, the purpose of theories being to solve problems.

It would be a mistake, however, to think that logical consistency being a requirement means that it is a necessary condition of the rationality of any and all theories. The relation between rationality and logic is much more tenuous than it is commonly supposed to be. There are rational theories that violate fundamental rules of logic and are thus illogical, but are not thereby irrational. Consequently, logical consistency is not a necessary condition of the rationality of theories.

By "logic" *our* logic is meant: the rules contained by and large in Aristotle's *Organon* and in *Principia Mathematica.* It is what one can find in any reasonably competent textbook of logic. Conformity to logic, of course, does not require knowledge or awareness of the rules, it requires only their observance. "Logic" may be used in many other senses. But when it is claimed here that a theory may be illogical and rational, the sense of "logic" just mentioned is meant.

It is more difficult to be clear about the meaning of "rationality." One way of characterizing the enterprise of Chapters Seven, Eight, Nine, and Ten is that it is an attempt to clarify the meaning of "rationality." So until the enterprise is completed, the clarification cannot be provided. Yet something must be said at this stage to indicate the sense of "rationality" in the claim that a theory may be illogical and rational. The best that can be said now is that rationality, for the purposes of this discussion, is problem-solving. So the claim to be defended is that a theory may be rational, in that it is a successful solution to a problem, and yet be illogical, in that it violates fundamental rules of logic.

The argument proceeds by the examination of anthropological evidence for the existence for the existence of a tribe whose members accept an illogical theory which occupies a position of crucial importance in their lives. Yet this illogical theory is rational. Following this, the anthropological evidence will be interpreted and its significance indicated. The next step will be the discussion of two objections. One is based on the Quinean view of analyticity and the indeterminacy of translation. The other assumes the analyticity of logical principles.

The source of the anthropological evidence is an influential study by Evans-Pritchard.[2] It appears that Nuer frequently make identity-claims which seem to contradict the principle of identity. That principle is that two individuals are identical if and only if neither has a characteristic that the other lacks. Nuer make four different types of identity-claims. The first three only seem to contradict the principle of identity, the fourth, however, really does. That will be the required example.

Nuer say that cucumbers are oxen; that twins are birds; that crocodiles are Spirit; and that swamp light is Spirit. Evans-Pritchard reports that it is clear from the context of these utterances that Nuer mean to identify the items connected by the copula. They behave toward them as if they were the same, they insist on talking about them in terms of identity, and they treat with incomprehension the suggestion that they are different. Yet when the identified items do not appear in the context of the identity, Nuer treat them just as we would. Thus they value oxen more than cucumbers, they do not expect twins to fly, and they have a suitably cautious attitude toward crocodiles. But when these pairs do occur in the context of identity, the previous recognition of their differences seems to disappear.

There are two features that characterize these identity-claims. The first is that each embodies the assumption that even though a thing is what it is, it is also something more. Thus Nuer do not deny, indeed they insist, that cucumbers are cucumbers, but they also hold that cucumbers are oxen. And they mean by "oxen" what we mean. Crocodiles, Nuer believe, are the beasts with the dangerous jaws, but they are also Spirit. The logically troublesome element is this belief that a thing is what it is, yet it may also be something else.

The second common feature is that all four cases seem to involve the illogical claim that two things are identical even though they have different characteristics. There is also a third feature, but that characterizes only those cases in which one term of identity is "Spirit." And this is that while Nuer insist that crocodiles and swamp light are Spirit, they deny that Spirit is either crocodiles or swamp light. Thus they seem to believe both that two things are identical and that the identity is asymmetrical.

Let us begin reflecting on these cases by noticing that Evans-Pritchard writes against the background of a theoretical controversy of great importance. Levy-Bruhl [3] argues that primitive people, like Nuer, are characterized by prelogical mentality. They have not reached the stage of development where they can think logically. So it is not surprising that they violate the principle of identity. Primitive thinking is characterized by "participation." This means that even the most routine, everyday events are seen as having significance beyond their occurrence, because spirits participate in everything that happens. Nuer believe that there is something more to swamp light and to crocodiles and this is the participation of Spirit. Evans-Pritchard repudiates the idea of primitive mentality and he sets out to show that Nuer mentality is not prelogical. If we just go beyond superficial appearances, we shall see how what Nuer believe can be represented in logical terms.

The position defended here is in disagreement with the interpretations of both Levy-Bruhl and Evans-Pritchard. The former denies, as it is done here, that Nuer beliefs are logical, but he insists that they are, therefore, irrational—a conclusion disputed here. The latter argues that Nuer beliefs are logical. If that were so, then the position defended here would be almost (but not quite, as it will be shown) deprived of the evidence upon which it rests.

The question to ask is, then, how does Evans-Pritchard attempt to show that Nuer beliefs are logical? He proceeds by a painstaking examination of the four types of identity-claims, and he succeeds in three cases. The first is the cucumber-ox identity. The context in which they are treated as the same is that of sacrifice. Frequently, cucumbers are sacrificed in place of oxen, and when this occurs Nuer say that and behave as if the cucumber about to be sacrificed were an ox. Cucumbers come to function as oxen in certain contexts just as IOUs come to function as money in certain contexts. There is nothing illogical in this.

This second case is the identification of twins with birds. Here the identity-claim rests on the Nuer religious belief that birds and twins occupy the same privileged position in their relation to Spirit. Thus birds are twins because they have identical relations to a third thing. When Proudhon says that property is theft, he means that property and theft are the same because they are alike in relation to morality. Neither Proudhon nor Nuer violate logic.

The third case is the identity of crocodiles and Spirit. Nuer believe that the lineage of each family is under the protection of Spirit. The protection is represented in different forms and the material representation—the totem—of one lineage is crocodile; lion is the totem of another lineage. The identity between crocodiles and Spirit is thus symbolic. Nuer of the appropriate lineage respond to crocodiles as to Spirit, because they believe that one symbolizes the other. But the material representation of Spirit can fall into disfavor even though the symbolic relation is retained. Thus a Nuer whose totem was lion came to hate lions because they destroyed his livestock. It was not thought, however, that he was thereby disrespectful of Spirit. Nuer think of crocodiles and lions as Christians think of the Bible. One might wish to contest the truth of their beliefs, but not on account of logical errors.

The fourth identity-claim, however, does not yield to this sort of elucidation. Nuer say that swamp light is Spirit. One difference between this case and the previous three is that here there is no independent description available for swamp light. Swamp light is known by Nuer only under one description and that description makes it identical with Spirit. Swamp light is *bieli* and *bieli* are Spirit. It might be supposed that if this is true, then no identity-claim is being made here. Nuer simply believe that what we call "swamp light" is in fact Spirit. But this would be a mistake. For while *bieli* is Spirit, Spirit is not *bieli*. Nuer for "is Spirit" is *"e kwoth."* So they say:

*"bieli e kwoth,"* but not that *"kwoth e bieli."* They mean to identify swamp light with Spirit and they intend the identity to be asymmetrical.

It is important to realize that the "swamp light is Spirit" claim is not meant to ascribe a property. What is meant is not that Spirit enters into swamp light. Whenever there is swamp light, there is Spirit; swamp light *is* Spirit; it is not the subject of which Spirit is predicated. Furthermore, the identity is not functional, since swamp light is Spirit in all conceivable contexts; it is not relational, because there is no third thing to which swamp light and Spirit stand in the same relation; nor is it symbolic, for there is not supposed to be one thing representing another thing; there is only one thing.

As a final piece of evidence, a feature of Nuer religion should be described. Nuer believe that there are Spirits of the above and of the below. The higher a Spirit is, the more symbolic is its material representation; and conversely, the lower it is, the more closely the Spirit is fused with its material form. So as one descends in the hierarchy of Spirits, the notion of representation has less and less application. *Bieli,* our swamp light, is a very low Spirit indeed.[4]

We would still want to say here that *bieli* must involve representation, because Spirit is immaterial and swamp light is material. There is a substantial difference between them, so how could they be thought of as the same. Nuer, however, think differently. Theirs is a dualistic religion, but the duality is not between material and immaterial but between created and noncreated ("self-existent" as we would say). *Bieli* are created, and so they are in the same category as our swamp light. There is no substantial difference to stand in the way of nonrepresentational identity.

Thus Nuer mean to say, and they seem to think, that two things are identical in the sense that there exists only one thing, and that the identity is not functional, relational, or symbolic. They use metaphors, but this identity-claim is literal. Yet, while one thing is said to be identical with the other thing, the other thing is not identical with the first thing. Swamp light is Spirit, but Spirit is not swamp light.

It will not be contested that provided the theory implicit in Nuer religion is correctly translated, it is illogical. The question is whether it is also irrational. And that question is to be answered by trying to see whether or not the theory solves some problem that Nuer have. The theory is what might be called the theology of Nuer religion. Nuer who accept the religion are committed to the theology, although they may not realize that they are so committed, nor what it is to which they are committed. The theology is illogical because it involves the violation of the principle of identity.

What is the problem that Nuer religion solves? Nuer, like other people, have feelings about the scheme of things. They feel fear and terror and they hope for comfort. These feelings are not directed at particular objects. Of course, Nuer do fear and hope for particular things, but they also have feelings about things in general. These generalized feelings constitute the substance of their attitudes toward reality, their lives, what the future might bring, whether things are likely to go well or badly for them. By and large, Nuer fear things and because they fear them, they are concerned with allleviating their fear. Their religion is concerned with bringing them hope and comfort. It tells them how Spirit, the object of fear and the source of hope, can be placated by sarifices. Their religion teaches them a way, the only way they know, of living in peace with the world.

It should not be thought that Nuer religion has the role of providing a procedure which, if followed, will bring the supplicant a particular benefit, such as a cow. One role at least of the religion is to assuage the feelings that Nuer have. And that task is accomplished by teaching Nuer a way of being and acting that will make it possible for them to accept what they take to be the scheme of things. Evans-Pritchard's remarks on this subject are profoundly illuminating.[5]

Nuer thinking about *bieli* is intimately linked with this general account. *Bieli* is one kind of Spirit of the below. It appears in swamps and elsewhere, such as on meteorites and hippopotamuses. But the objects on which they appear always have a special significance for Nuer. These objects, for instance, are frequently totemic representations of Spirit and different Nuer families stand under the protection of different totems.[6]

The rationality of the illogical theology to which Nuer are committed derives from the successful way in which this theology enables Nuer to live relatively happily in a world which they see as being fraught with terror. Their position is not that they have a number of alternative theologies or philosophies to choose from and, perversely, they opt for an illogical one. They know only of one religious belief-system. The choice they have is not between competing *Weltanschauungen,* but between one that gives them comfort and the absence of any: an absence that guarantees terror. It is for this reason that Nuer are rational in accepting an illogical theory. And it is because such cases occur that logical consistency is not a necessary condition of the rationality of theories in all contexts.

Let us now examine some problems of interpretation that arise out of this consideration of Nuer religion. It has been mentioned before that if it turned out that the evidence provided by Evans-Pritchard did not support the interpretation offered here, then the present thesis would remain unimpaired. Suppose that the thesis does rest on a misunderstanding of Evans-Pritchard or that Evans-Pritchard misreported Nuer behavior. Either, of course, would mean that false things were said of Nuer, and so we do not really know how Nuer behave. But the thesis is not concerned with making an anthropological point: its interest is philosophical, in that it attacks the belief that conformity to logic is a necessary condition of rationality. One way of arguing against this belief is by supplying counterexamples which show that a theory may be both rational and illogical. The counterexample must depict this possibility. No more is needed, for to show that something is logically possible (that a theory may be illogical and rational) is sufficient to refute the claim that that sort of thing is logically impossible (that a theory can not be both illogical and rational). So if it turns out that a mistake has been been made about Nuer, the argument can simply be changed to concern an imaginary tribe.

Suppose that the argument is taken to show not that Nuer beliefs are illogical but that Nuer have a different logic, and their beliefs conform to their logic, just as ours do to our logic. So Nuer beliefs are, after all, both logical and rational. This point can be taken in a number of different ways and in some there is no need to disagree with it.

The first thing to notice is that even if it were true that Nuer conform to a logic different from our own, the point would still stand.

For it was concerned with showing that given *our* logic, a belief may be rational even though it is illogical. Secondly, as we have seen, it is extremely unclear what an alternative logic would be like. There is a sense in which there are many alternative logics. If by "logic" "rule-following" is meant, then different clusters of rules yield different logics, and clearly Nuer, then, have a different logic. Anybody can use "logic" in any way he likes. The claim is that given one of these uses—ours—Nuer violate it.

Suppose, however, that there is an attempt to minimize the force of the argument by placing it in the larger context of Nuer life. It might be said that Nuer appear illogical only in some contexts, while in others they conform to logic as well as anyone. And, it may be continued, the contexts in which they appear to be illogical are not truth-functional. Thus the troublesome identity-claim is made by Nuer not with the intention of describing some aspect of reality, but as an evocative, ritualistic, or emotive claim. To accuse them of illogicality on this ground is like accusing members of our society of being illogical because they make puns, write poetry, or portray illogical people on stage. The trouble with the account, it might be said, is that it mistakes a nonlogical context for an illogical one. In consequence the claim that illogical theories may be rational fails, for, at best, an example is provided only of a nonlogical theory that is rational.

But this is a misplaced charge. Nuer do believe that there exists swamp light and when they say of it that it is Spirit, they mean to say something true about the world. When they say that something is a swamp light, they recognize the possibility of misperception and optical illusion. So, since they recognize that they may err, we must suppose that they aim to tell the truth as they see it.

If it is acknowledged that the context from which the example is taken is truth-functional, it may still be argued that it is a small isolated case of illogicality that has no effect on Nuer life as a whole. It is just a pocket of illogicality, not unlike the Monte Carlo fallacy, or, as some would say, belief in the triune nature of God. By and large, conformity to logic and rationality go together in Nuer society, just as in ours; the argument makes too much of an aberrant case.

Once again, however, this defense fails, for religion occupies a central place in Nuer life. Spirits exert their influence upon the world in their beliefs, as laws of nature are believed by us to determine what happens. And the Spirits with which Nuer are in most intimate, daily contact are just those spirits of the lower realm of which swamp light is an example. Giving up the illogical identity-claim would be for them as giving up the belief that there is a natural explanation for electricity would be for us.

It does not seem that any of these possibilities help to avoid the need to recognize that conformity to logic and rationality need to go together.

Let us now consider two strategies for attempting to criticize the thesis that the Nuer's theory is illogical and rational. The first is to deny that the theory is illogical and the second is to deny that it is rational.

The first strategy derives from Quine's view about analyticity and the indeterminacy of translation. The criticism may grant that *if* Evans-Pritchard succeeded in providing a correct translation from Nuer to English, then the relevant Nuer theory is indeed illogical. The question, however, is whether the translation is correct. And the very thing that has been taken as evidence for the illogicality of their theory these Quinean critics take as evidence for the incorrectness of the translation.

The first step in the criticism is to provide various candidates for logical relations that could underlie Nuer beliefs that swamp light is Spirit. One possibility is that it is a part-whole relation. A possible translation of Nuer *"bieli e kwoth"* is "swamp light is a part of Spirit." Spirit is a whole composed of many parts and one of these parts is swamp light. This explains why Nuer think of swamp light as Spirit and refuse to identify Spirit with swamp light. But this will not do. Nuer believe in the existence of many different Spirits, and *bieli* is one of them. *Bieli* is not part of anything: it is a discrete, independent entity and it is identical with what we think of as swamp light.

A different possibility is that the logical relation is class-inclusion. Swamp lights are to Spirit what dogs are to animals. The class of Spirit and the class of animals includes swamp light and dogs as members. And that is why it is correct to assert that "swamp lights are Spirit" and "dogs are animals" and yet to deny that "spirits are swamp light" and "animals are dogs." This, however, is another mis-understanding. For such class terms as "Spirit" and "animal" are ab-stract. There exists no spirit or animal apart from particular Spirits and animals. And if all Spirits and animals disappeared, the class of Spirits and animals would be empty and "Spirit" and "animal" would refer to nothing. Nuer think of Spirits as existing in their own right; there are many different Spirits and *bieli* is one of them. It is not an abstraction, but an individual existing in their midst.

Nor is it accurate to try to think of Nuer beliefs on the model, say, of how we think of the various physical forms water could take. "Swamp light is Spirit" is not like "ice is water," because while ice is a form of water swamp light is not a form of Spirit. Spirit of that kind comes in one form only: swamp light. And if, *per impossibile,* it changes form, it becomes a different Spirit.

But the failure to find a logical relation that would account for the apparent violation of the principle of identity by Nuer does not stop these Quinean critics. The second step in their criticism is to note that the failure can be explained either by there not being a logical relation to be found or by the lack of ingenuity or acuity of the searchers. Accordingly, the critics' stance is that all the evidence available about Nuer beliefs is consonant with two possibilities: either Nuer are illogical or our translations are poor. The objection is that no matter what additional evidence one may gather the disjunction will persist, so the inference that Nuer are illogical is illegitimate.

The second step in the criticism fails for two reasons. The first is that actually there is evidence that could rule out one of the disjuncts, and the second is that the objection is inconsistent. The evidence that could determine whether or not Evans-Pritchard's translation is accu-rate, and so Nuer beliefs are illogical, is the testimony of Nuer who have been raised in their native environment, but who, as adults, have learned to speak English very well and are now bilingual. Sup-pose that bilingual Nuer are unanimous in claiming that *"bieli e kwoth"* does indeed violate the principle of identity and that no En-glish translation that does not take the violation into account is accu-rate.

The usual Quinean rejoinder is that bilingual natives are in no bet-ter position than anthropologists, for the way in which people think about the world is inseparable from the language they speak. And if they speak two languages, then they have two ways of thinking which may not be identical. The conviction of a bilingual person that expressions in different languages mean the same is unverifiable, for all the facts that could yield a decision appear entombed in the expressions themselves. The fact is that Nuer respond to swamp light as if it was Spirit. But the interpretation we put on this fact cannot be supported by Nuer behavior. The interpretation depends on accurate representation of the way Nuer think and that can be done only in Nuer language.

This rejoinder, however, is weak. What one can do is to postulate a hypothesis that a Nuer expression is to be translated in a certain way and then invite objections to it. This is clearly a possible procedure, for it has been followed here. It was conjectured that *"bieli e kwoth"* violates the principle of identity, and then it has been shown why such competing interpretations as part-whole relation, class-inclusion, and being different forms of the same thing fail. This is not a conclusive proof of the hypothesis, but until an objection is presented that the hypothesis cannot meet, the hypothesis stands. There are reasons for the hypothesis: it explains the facts, and there are no reasons against it: alternative explanations have been refuted, so it is reasonable to accept it.

Another reason for the failure of the second step of the Quinean criticism is that it is inconsistent. The statements of the criticism presuppose the incoherence of analyticity. If this were not so, then one could suppose that there are logically neccessary principles shared by all languages and so at least the formal conditions for translation must exist. The Quinean thesis about analyticity and the thesis about the indeterminacy of translation are thus logically connected. But if such logical principles as identity are not analytic, then it should be possible to conceive of situations in which they do not obtain. Yet when one such situation is proposed, the objection is that there could never be a determination of whether or not it is indeed that sort of a situation. This is just wrong. Either principles of logic are analytic, or they could fail to obtain in certain situations. In the former case, the Quinean rejection of analyticity fails. In the latter case, the counterexample to the principle of identity cannot be ruled out by an appeal to the supposed indeterminacy of translation. The criticism is inconsistent because it attempts to combine the rejection of analyticity with the logical indeterminacy of translation. Consistency can easily be achieved by interpreting the supposed indeterminacy of translation in practical terms. But so interpreted it is not an objection to the thesis defended here. For the strongest claim it can support is that it is very difficult to find out what Nuer mean. That can be accepted without any damage to the claim that the relevant theory is illogical and rational.

It is inconsistent to reject the analyticity of logical principles and yet fail to accept the thesis that a theory may be rational even if it is illogical. For if logical principles are not analytic, then they are revisable. And if they are revisable, then there must be situations in which something rational is said and yet the unrevised principle does not and should cover it. That there are such situations is what gives impetus for the revision of the logical principle.

The second general strategy leads one to object to the thesis on the grounds that while Nuer beliefs are indeed illogical, they are also ir-rational. The argument is that if Nuer mean by *"bieli e kwoth"* what has been maintained here, then what Nuer say is necessarily false. They make an asymmetrical identity-claim and there could no more be such an identity than there could be a round square. "Asymmet-rical identity" is a contradiction in terms and it is not practically or empirically, but logically impossible that anything corresponding to the phrase could exist. The illusion that what Nuer say is rational comes from two sources. One is that their translated words are in-telligible and they form a grammatically correct sentence. The other is that we assimilate the sentence to a logical model, such as class-inclusion, that is rational. But, of course, intelligible words and grammatical accuracy are not sufficient for rationality, and the assimi-lation is an error.

The first thing to notice about this objection is that it rests on the analyticity of logical principles. If Quine's criticisms are correct, then this objection fails. But since the success of the argument should not be made to depend on Quine's criticisms of analyticity, an indepen-dent argument will be offered to meet this objection.

The argument is that conformity to logic is not a necessary condi-tion of rationality because there are theories that are both illogical and rational. This objection juxtaposes the opposing claims that there could not be an expression that is both illogical and rational. The question that needs now to be asked is why this is supposed to be so. Clearly, to argue that conformity to logic is a logically necessary condition of rationality and then to rule out possible counterexamples as irrational is question-begging. So the thesis must be understood as being that conformity to logic is an empirically necessary condition of rationality. But on this reading the objection fails because it rests on the claim that there could not be a counterexample. And if the objection is revised to the claim that no counterexample has been given, then Nuer beliefs can be cited and thereby refute the objection.

These two objections have it in common that they invoke their respective analyses of analyticity against the claim that conformity to logic is not a necessary condition of rationality. The rejoinder is that if the analyticity of logical principles is given up, then there must be possible theories that violate a logical principle and are rational, while if logical principles are taken to be analytic, then the dismissal of the possibility of counterexamples is question-begging.

The conclusion of this discussion of logical consistency as an internal standard of rationality is that logical consistency is a necessary condition of the rationality of a theory in all situations where competing theories offer various solutions to problems. Logical consistency, however, is not a condition of rationality in problem-situations where there is an urgent problem and only one solution. These kinds of cases, however, occur only rarely. For all practical purposes, logic and rationality go together.

It would be a mistake, however, to equate rationality with problem-solving and logical consistency. For logical consistency does not guarantee that a theory that conforms to it does in fact solve a problem. All it guarantees is that the theory is a logically possible solution. It is necessary to go on, therefore, in search of additional standards that can be used to decide between competing logically possible solutions.

## Conceptual coherence

The use of language is guided not only by formal logical requirements, but also by informal rules. If formal logic can be compared to the legal system binding upon the citizens of a country, then informal

149

rules of language are like the unwritten customs, mores, and traditions that dictate behavior. And since the construction of theories is part of human activity, it too must be bound by the rules, or its practitioners must resign themselves to propagating "conceptual absurdity," as this offspring of irrationality will be called.

In normal circumstances, the use of a sentence has a purpose. The point of using a sentence results from the belief that by its use the purpose is likely to be achieved. If a person wanted to achieve something, but does not believe that language will help him, he will, of course, not use it. Hence it is possible to draw certain inferences about the beliefs of a person by observing his normal use of language. For instance, a person addressing someone implies that he believes that there is another person, that he can be heard, that they speak the same language, and so on. These inferences will be said to be "contextually implied" by the use of language.

The standard of conceptual coherence is based on the recognition that the use of a sentence has a point only if the contextual implications are true. If a sentence is used in normal circumstances and the contextual implications are false, then conceptual absurdity results.

Conceptual absurdity is closely related to pragmatic paradoxes.[7] Pragmatic paradoxes occur when the use of a sentence contradicts some of the assumptions upon which the use is based. Grant gives two splendid examples: "Clichés must be avoided like the plague," and "Prepositions are not for ending sentences with." Such sentences, if meant seriously, are self-defeating. If the assumptions contradicted by the use of the sentence are necessary for the use of *any* sentence, then, and only then, conceptual absurdity results.

Conceptual absurdity does not derive from the fact that a speaker makes a very obvious mistake, like saying: "I am walking," when he is sincere, a competent user of the language, normal and healthy, and he is sitting. Nor does the absurdity result from a self-contradiction, like saying: "I can stay for an hour, but I cannot stay for sixty minutes." The absurdity derives from a person using a sentence to deny that a condition necessary for the use of any sentence obtains, and the act of using the sentence naturally demonstrates the contrary of what is being denied. For instance, a person who says, "No language exists," commits this type of absurdity.

Conceptual absurdity is a danger signal; its occurrence indicates that in normal circumstances the contextual implications of the use of a sentence are false. But why should the falsity of contextual implications lead to any kind of absurdity? The reason is that contextually implied statements are necessarily true. This does not mean that their denial leads to self-contradiction, or that they are true by virtue of the meaning of the words occurring in them. This means that *if* there is to be a language, then contextually implied statements *must* be true.

Contextual implications are noncontingent, nonanalytic necessary truths. They are noncontingent because given the contingent fact that there is a language, contextual implications must be true. The force of the "must" is that it would be logically impossible for there to be *our* language if the contextual implications were not true. They are nonanalytic, because it is a contingent fact that there is our language; there might be none at all, or an entirely different kind.

The truth of contextual implications, in normal circumstances, guarantees conceptual coherence, while the occurrence of conceptual absurdity makes conceptual coherence impossible. Conceptual coherence, or the avoidance of conceptual absurdity, is thus the second internal standard of rationality.

It may be objected, however, that this account of conceptual coherence is faulty because it is unfalsifiable. A possible way of objecting to the account would be to show that language may be used quite well even if contextual implications are false. But, the objection runs, the argument is so constructed that this could never be done, because the argument is supposed to apply to normal situations only, and all possible counterexamples could simply be dismissed as abnormal cases. If each counterexample is disregarded, then the argument has a built-in criticism-deflecting device. What, then, would count against the claim that in normal circumstances the contextual implications of the use of a sentence are either true or conceptual absurdity results? What follows is an attempt to answer this question in three steps.

The first step is to notice that in at least one sense of "normal circumstances," normal circumstances occur in the majority of cases. It is, of course, in this sense that the phrase has been used. "Normal circumstance" means the standard situation, the expected, that which happens if nothing special takes place, the usual situation. And the usual, the standard, the expected, occur most frequently—in the majority of cases.

The second step is to recognize that it is not a happy coincidence elevated to the stature of an empirical generalization that normal circumstances do indeed occur in the majority of cases. It is not as if we could wake up one morning and be forced by our environment to conclude that normal circumstances occur in the minority of cases only. What counts as normal depends on what we believe occurs in the majority of cases. If what we believe happens in the majority of cases does not in fact happen, or does no longer happen, then we either confess to an error as to what we previously regarded as normal, or come to the conclusion that what used to count as normal does so no longer. In either case, we revise our idea of normalcy. Therefore, the situations that are correctly described as "normal" are the situations that are correctly described as "occurring in the majority of cases."

There are two reasons why one may be reluctant to accept this point. The first is that "normal" is used not just descriptively, but also evaluatively. "Normal person" may mean not just "average person," but also "reliable, dependable, sane person." If "normal" is used evaluatively, it makes good sense to say "only a minority is normal," but if "normal" is used descriptively, then "only a minority is normal" is self-contradictory. It is always in the descriptive sense that "normal" is used here.

Another reason for the possible reluctance to accept that normal circumstances occur in the majority of cases is that one may be unclear about what happens in the majority of cases. Naturally, when there is doubt about that, there is doubt about what happens normally. The point that is being made, however, is that if one has no doubt about what happens in the majority of cases, then one has no doubt about what happens normally.

The third step in meeting the charge of unfalsifiability is to remember that "the normal," "the majority of cases," "the usual," do not refer to specific types of situations. What is normal changes with the context and with time and place. The result of the shifting references of "the normal" is that while one can argue *prima facie* that if something is normal, then it occurs most of the time, one cannot argue on the same ground that specific types of situations are normal.

The argument for the claim that it is normal that specific types of contextual implication must be true or conceptual absurdity results is based on a particular analysis of what is involved in our linguistic practices. The argument is falsifiable by providing an alternative analysis from which the above disjunction does not follow.

Can a sceptic refuse to accept conceptual coherence as a standard of rationality? It does not seem that he can. For the sceptic is a language user and the use of language can accomplish the goals for which it is used only if it conforms to the standard of conceptual coherence. A sceptic, wishing to reject this standard, has two options. He can refrain from the use of language, at the price of depriving himself from one of the best problem-solving tools. This would exempt him from the acceptance of conceptual coherence, but it would still not be an objection to it, for the standard applies only to the use of language. The second option is to continue to use language but violate the standard. In this case, the sceptic's use of language becomes incoherent. For, as we have seen, the purposes for which language is used can be achieved only if conceptual coherence is preserved. Therefore the sceptic's disregard of it would lead him to engage in an activity in order to achieve an end that he believes cannot be achieved by so doing.

Conceptual coherence combined with logical consistency are necessary but not sufficient for the rationality of theories. The necessity holds in situations where competing theories present options. And the lack of sufficiency obtains because the two internal standards so far discussed merely assure that a theory that conforms to them is capable of providing a possible solution to whatever problem prompted it. These two standards guarantee the coherence of a theory, but they do not provide a method for choosing the best among conflicting coherent solutions.

## Explanatory power

The third requirement of rationality is that a theory must offer a possible solution to the problem that prompted it. The solution is an explanation which provides a possible way of thinking about a segment of reality. The explanation is successful if it in fact solves the problem. Explanations can be thought of as issuing a conditional: if you think of reality in this way, then what was previously problematic will no longer be so.

The obvious difficulty is that for each problem there are many possible explanations, and each may be logically consistent and conceptually coherent. Rival explanations, therefore, have to be evaluated. This can be done by determining, first, whether all the relevant facts are explained, and second, whether the explanation could, in principle, be disproved. The first requirement will be discussed here, while the second requirement will be considered as the fourth internal standard of rationality.

The difficulty in deciding whether or not a theory explains all the relevant facts is that it is not clear what is to count as fact. It seems indisputable that the clear distinction between facts provided by "pure" observation and interpretation provided by theory cannot be maintained. There is no "pure" observation; the problem-situation, one's previous knowledge and experience, expectations, a sense of relevance and irrelevance inevitably affect whether something is observed and also the manner in which it is observed. There always lurks in the background the interpretation proffered by a theory. It is ready to be imposed, and the senses obligingly provide already packaged data to suit the preexisting bias. The theoretical background crucially influences the judgment of whether something is to be seen as a discrete unit or as part of a whole, of whether it functions as evidence or as part of the problem to be explained, or even whether it is important, noteworthy, or relevant.

The sceptic has a ready-made objection here. A theory is rational, he might argue, if it explains all the relevant facts. But what counts as a relevant fact depends on the theory. Two or more rival theories could thus each legitimately claim to have explained all the relevant facts. Each may explain the facts rendered relevant by its own presuppositions and yet be explaining different sets of facts. As a result, the merits of rival theories cannot be adjudicated on the ground of their different explanatory power.

To counter this objection consider some examples. There was a strange and abnormal behavioral pattern described during the late

154

medieval witchcraze as possession by the Devil. Nowadays the same behavior is described as a form of psychopathology. The descriptions come from different theoretical backgrounds. If the sceptical objection were correct, it ought to be impossible to say that these different theories attempted to explain the same set of facts. If what counts as fact were determined by particular theories, then there could not be a shared factual ground between late-medieval demonology and contemporary psychoanalysis. Actually, there is common ground, as there is also between a Marxist and a Toynbean explanation of the decline of the Roman Empire, between a biochemical and demographic account of the spread of an epidemic, and between a physical and an aesthetic explanation of how a painting's color-effects were achieved. The fact is that explanations offered from the vantage point of different theories frequently are recognizably explanations of the same facts. Contrary to this possible sceptical objection, rival theories typically agree about what the facts are and dispute about the correct explanation.

This state of affairs is made possible by the primacy of the common sense view of the world. Just as forms of life must be grounded on common sense, so also must theories. The reason for the necessity is the limitation imposed upon human beings by their constitution. Theories are constructed by human beings to solve problems. And while it is true, of course, that many problems would not arise or be solved if one had only the common sense view, it is no less true that even the most abstruse problems emerge in the context of one theory or another. Problems may occur as epiphenomena of theories, but theories have a point if they are possible solutions to problems. The sequence of problem-theory-new problem-new theory, and so on, may be unending as far as the future is concerned, but it does have a beginning in the past. Given human nature, the starting point must be what has been called a problem of life.

Problems of life demand a solution and theories provide the evolutionarily most successful method of problem-solving. For, to echo Popper,[8] in pretheoretical, primitive times we died if our solutions failed, nowadays, given civilization, our theories die in our stead. The purpose of theories is to solve problems, and they do so by providing an explanation. The problems theories usually solve are problems of reflection, but problems of reflection occur only because problems of life give rise to the method of solving them by constructing theories. The context in which problems of life arise is that of the common sense view of the world. Theories may supersede it, but that is where they must start. The common ground between theories is guaranteed by their common starting point.

The answer to the sceptic who calls into question this standard of rationality is to trace for him the connection between the explanatory power of a theory and its capacity to solve problems of life. The better an explanation a theory offers, the more likely it is to solve problems. And solving problems is in the interest of the sceptic too. To disclaim interest in the solution of problems of reflection can be due only to myopia, for problems of reflection arise because problems of life need to be solved. The sceptic, being human, cannot avoid having and needing to solve problems of life.

The discussion of this standard of rationality, however, is too general. It is true that the rationality of a theory depends, *inter alia,* upon its explanatory power. But what counts as a good or poor explanation varies with the type of theory. Theories of literary criticism, science, history, and morality are likely to have different kinds of explanations. So while the need for explanatory power is common to all theories with rational pretensions, there is need also for subsidiary standards of what counts as an adequate explanation in various contexts. The exploration of what these subsidiary standards are or ought to be in the context of various types of theories is a complex and important task, but it will not be undertaken here. There are two excuses for this. The first is that if the five standards of rationality are successfully defended, then the main purpose of the book, meeting the sceptical challenge, is partially accomplished, and the adumbration of subsidiary standards is irrelevant to that task. The second is that, as it has been argued, particular types of theory rest upon presuppositions whose rationality can be defended only upon metaphysical grounds. So actually we must discuss one kind of subsidiary standard—that kind which determines what counts as a rational explanation in metaphysics. The rationality of other types of explanation depends upon the successful completion of that task.

156

## Criticizability

The fourth internal standard of rationality is, with some important changes, the Popperian notion of criticizability. The fundamental idea here is that the rationality of a theory depends, in addition to conformity to the other standards, upon its openness to criticism, by which is meant the logical possibility of specifying what would show that a theory is mistaken. The point, of course, is not that rationality demands that a theory be mistaken, but that it requires the *possibility* of its being mistaken.

The basis for this standard follows from the nature of theories. A theory is a possible explanation of some part of reality. The explanation is incompatible with other possible explanations. The absence of anything that could be incompatible with the explanation is conclusive evidence of its inadequacy, for to explain is to commit the theory to reality being such-and-such. But a commitment always entails the denial of countless other options, and each of the denied options is a potential criticism of the theory in question. If the denial of nothing is entailed by the theory, then the commitment of the theory is completely vacuous. Vacuity, of course, signals the absence of explanation. The possibility of criticism, therefore, is a necessary condition of the adequacy of the explanation.

The criterion of criticizability restricts the explanatory power of theories in two ways. First, it prescribes the limits within which a rational explanation must fall: it must exclude many states of affairs. The more a theory excludes, the more criticizable it is. A high degree of criticizability indicates that the theory offers a great deal of precision and specificity, and conversely, the relative absence of vagueness and generality. Thus, the more criticizable a theory is the better is the potential of the explanation it offers. Second, the criterion makes it possible to decide rationally among rival theories that conform to the previous standards. The decision rests not merely upon noting that the competing theories are criticizable, but upon actually criticizing them. Severe and ingenious criticism is bound to weed out weaklings. The criticism proceeds by attempting to show that what the theory excluded, in fact, obtains. It aims to show that what the

157

theory is committed to denying is actually so. Thus the explanation offered by the theory is shown to be mistaken.

The surviving theory becomes the solution of the problem. A criticizable theory, which also conforms to the other standards, is rational. A theory that survives serious criticism and wins out against competition is not only rational, but also acceptable. An acceptable theory is stronger than a merely rational one. For it is not only open to criticism, but it has also withstood it. The conclusion warranted by critical attention to an acceptable theory is that what it is committed to excluding stays excluded, that what it says is so is really so. But finding a theory acceptable does not involve the right to claim that it is true. For an acceptable theory has merely survived the criticisms of which one could think; it was victorious only over presently available rivals. A true theory would have to survive all possible criticisms and be preferable to all possible rivals. It is logically impossible to know what all possible criticisms and rivals are, and even if a putative list were available, it would be impossible to determine whether or not it was complete.

It is thus a consequence of this standard that theories cannot be known to be true. However, once it is understood how little this limitation actually means, its harmlessness becomes patent. First of all, it does not affect the claim that certain theories are eminently reasonable and should, most certainly, be accepted. For if a theory offers a solution to the problem that it was supposed to solve, if the solution is rational, in the terms discussed, and if it both survives criticisms and prevails over its rivals, then one has all the reasons for accepting it and no reason at all for doubting it. Secondly, to say that a theory cannot be known to be true is merely to recognize the fact that one may not have thought of all possible criticisms, or that a better, not yet invented, rival explanation may be produced. This is the background of the injunction not to have a dogmatic attitude toward what one believes. Thirdly, "truth" is far from being a univocal notion. If one has a right to call something true only if the logical possibility of error has been excluded, then theories should not be said to be true. But "truth" may be used to describe a theory that one has a right to accept and then theories may be said to be true. Furthermore, not even purists are prevented from applying the term, for such locutions as "I believe that it is true," or "there is no reason for doubting its truth" are readily available. Only the dogmatic claim is proscribed.

A closely related but much less widely recognized consequence of this standard is that theories cannot be known to be false either. A theory would be false if what it was committed to asserting was shown not to be so. The theory says that reality is such-and-such and if it is established that reality is not such-and-such, then the theory would be false. But just as conclusive verification of a theory founders on the unavailability of all possible rivals, so also conclusive falsification is made impossible. For how can one determine that there *could be* no legitimate ways for the theory to handle a criticism? And how can one determine that the criticism itself cannot *possibly* be shown to be faulty? The best that can be done is to accept the criticism, because, as things are, it cannot be met, and to give up the theory because nobody can think of a legitimate way of defending it. There is a point beyond which a theory should be rejected, just as there is a point beyond which it should be accepted, but these points do not coincide with the truth and falsity of the theory.

There is a gap between the truth or falsity of theories and it being rational to accept or to reject them. The gap is created by human fallibility. Truth and falsity are the ideal limits between which the appraisal of theories must fall. The ideal limits are unattainable, because there cannot be a demonstration that all possibility of error has been eliminated. But the implications of this cannot comfort the sceptic, for it does not follow that the acceptance or rejection of a theory cannot be supported by excellent reasons. Indubitability and conclusive demonstration are indeed impossible, but the realization that theories deal with contingent matters should render otiose these unreasonable expectations.

The recognition of this gap between the ideals and their reasoned approximations makes it possible to explain a frequent occurrence in the history of ideas which could not be accounted for by anyone denying its existence. There are many theories which were reasonable to accept at one time and were shown to be mistaken later. Similarly, theories have sometimes been rightly rejected as unreasonable, where subsequent considerations have shown them to be perfectly viable options. The obvious thing to say about such cases is that a theory we have good grounds for regarding as false now was in fact acceptable in the past, and a theory which is now reasonably thought to be true should have been rejected at another time. Truth and falsity are timeless but unattainable ideals. Reasonable acceptance and rejection vary with time but they are within our grasp. If, however, reasoned acceptance is said to be possible only if the theory is true, and reasoned rejection deserved only by theories whose falsity is demonstrated, then the acceptance of all false theories would have to be declared irrational and only true theories could be said to be rational to accept. As a result, most of our predecessors would have to be suspected of being irrational and most of our contemporaries be regarded as prime candidates for being rational. This is a disturbingly anthistorical attitude whose intolerance is matched only by its implausibility. The attitude, one must note in passing, characterizes too much of what is thought of as the scientific outlook. It might be mitigated if people realized that the same attitude might render us irrational in the eyes of our intellectual offspring.

The standard of criticizability grows out of verificationism, the view that the rationality of theories depends on there being evidence in their favor. Criticizability is based on the recognition that the mere existence of evidence for a theory contributes very little towards its rationality. For any theory, even one known to be irrational, can have evidence in its favor. Astrological predictions are sometimes verified, people recover after the ministrations of witchdoctors, palmists do sometimes correctly foretell the future, and some criminals and geniuses have just the sort of bumps on their skulls that phrenologists say they should have. Evidence for a theory may establish the initial plausibility of the explanation by showing that it applies to some cases. But one counterinstance is far more important than any number of verifications, for verifications show only that some things actually are as the theory suggests; they cannot establish that all things are that way. A single counterinstance, however, is sufficient to demonstrate that not everything is as the theory asserts.

Criticizability is sometimes identified with the attempt to find empirical observations that would refute a theory. This is an unnecessarily and erroneously restrictive interpretation. No doubt theories, especially scientific ones, can be criticized on the basis of empirical observation. But not all theories are scientific, and not all possible criticisms are observational. Theories of literary criticism, explanations of historical events, legal reconstructions, political, moral, aesthetic theories can rarely, if ever, be criticized by empirical observation. Yet they can be criticized.

Once again, however, we must guard against the error of making criticizability a necessary condition of the rationality of theories in all contexts. The root of this error is the belief that the rational attitude toward anomaly is to welcome it. For the anomaly is a criticism and the critical attitude, according to this erroneous view, is an essential component of the rational attitude. Anomaly shows that one's present beliefs are not adequate: the anomalous instance stands as a criticism of them. The systematic search for the anomalous is thus taken to be an essential feature of the critical, and hence of the rational attitude, for anomaly prompts one to change and thereby improve one's beliefs. The constant tension between belief and anomaly is what guarantees the growth of knowledge.[9]

It appears, however, that there is a large class of behavior, reported by anthropologists, that goes directly counter to the critical attitude:

> Taboo reactions are often given to occurrences that are radically strange or new; for these too (almost by definition) fail to fit into the established category system. A good example is furnished by a Kalabari story of the coming of the Europeans. The first white man, it is said, was seen by a fisherman who had gone down to the mouth of the estuary in his canoe. Panic-stricken, he raced home and told his people what he had seen: whereupon he and the rest of them set out to purify themselves—that is, rid themselves of the influence of the strange and monstrous thing that had intruded into their world.[10]

There are two diametrically opposed attitudes possible when an anomalous occurrence threatens one's system of beliefs: one is to change the system so that expectations are brought into harmony with the anomaly; the other is to protect the system by attempting to get rid of the anomaly. The first attitude is supposed to be paradigmatically rational, and the second, by implication, irrational. But surely, this judgment is too hasty.

Consider two different situations in which a system of beliefs encounters an anomaly. In the first situation, the question is which of several competing systems one should accept. The anomaly shows that the subject had opted for one that will not do, so he abandons it in favor of another system. In the second situation, there is only one system, it has prevailed since times immemorial, there is no known alternative to it. In facing the anomaly, the choice is between having a way of comprehending the world and not having any, between chaos and order, between the ability to cope and being lost.

There is some reason for thinking that the first situation is typically Western, while the second characterizes many primitive societies. Writing about the differences between them Horton says:

> What I take to be the key difference is a very simple one. It is that in traditional cultures there is no developed awareness of alternatives to the established body of theoretical tenets; whereas in scientifically oriented cultures, such awareness is highly developed . . . absence of any awareness of alternatives makes for an absolute acceptance of the established theoretical tenets, and removes the possibility of questioning them. . . . A second important consequence . . . is that any challenge to established tenets is a threat of chaos, of the cosmic abyss, and therefore evokes intense anxiety.[11]

The critical attitude may well be rational in scientifically oriented cultures, but it is clearly not so in societies where its consequence would be disintegration. Hence the critical attitude is not essential to rationality in *all* situations.

What has gone wrong is that the problem-situation in which a system of beliefs is held is underemphasized by the champions of the critical attitude. Sometimes the rational attitude is to hold fast to a set of beliefs in the face of counterevidence.

The sceptic may raise two objections against criticizability as a standard of rationality. The first is that given the standard, no theory can be acceptable, for all theories succumb to criticism. One of the main contentions in this book is that the most serious criticism of theories, including scientific ones, is upon metaphysical grounds. Theories rest upon presuppositions and, if rational, the presuppositions must be criticizable. Now the argument of the sceptic is that these presuppositions do not survive criticism. Hence all theories are in the same position: they rest upon undefended presuppositions. Consequently the choice between different theories is arbitrary. The sceptic does not deny that one scientific theory may be better than another. He denies that a scientific solution to a problem can be rationally preferred to a religious, mystical, or political solution because their presuppositions are equally weak. In reply, it has to be argued that presuppositions can be defended. This argument will be the subject-matter of Part Four.

The second objection is that criticizability is arbitrary as a standard of rationality. The answer, however, is the same as it was in the case of the same objection against the other standards. Criticizability is not arbitrary because it helps in solving problems that human beings have. Having a way of deciding which of several theoretical solutions is likely to be the best is in everybody's interest. And this is the task that criticizability is meant to perform.

## Conclusion

The strategic value of the theory of rationality in the battle with scepticism is that the sceptic can no longer claim that rationality is arbitrary, in that it is just one way of being and acting among many others. If the sceptic wishes to continue to challenge rationality, it is necessary for him to provide some ground for his challenge. He might try to argue that while rationality is desirable, it is unattainable, for, as a matter of fact, no theory can be shown to be rational or acceptable. Or he might argue that while rationality is not arbitrary, it is undesirable. Rationality, the sceptic might say, is a possible way of life, but it is a mistake to live one's life that way. These and other objections to rationality will be considered in the next chapter. But from now on the burden of stating a *prima facie* case falls upon the critics of rationality, because the case for it has made out. If there is some argument against acting to try to solve one's problems, or, if there is a better way than the rational, or if there is some harm in pursuing a rational policy, then the alternative must be stated. The *prima facie* case for rationality establishes a defeasible connection between action and rationality. If there is no reason not to, then one ought (prudentially) to accept a rational theory and act on it.

163

# 10 The value of rationality

*"The irrationalist insists that emotions and passions rather than reason are the mainsprings of human action. To the rationalist's reply that, though this may be so, we should do what we can to remedy it . . . the irrationalist would rejoin that this attitude is hopelessly unrealistic. . . . It is my firm conviction that this irrational emphasis upon emotion and passion leads ultimately to what I can only describe as crime. One reason for this opinion is that this attitude. . . . must lead to an appeal to violence and brutal force as the ultimate arbiter in any dispute."*—Karl R. Popper, The Open Society and Its Enemies

The purpose of this chapter is to argue for the value of rationality. The argument will proceed in three phases. The first phase will take up the second of two questions that have been distinguished in Chapter Eight and reiterated in Chapter Nine. The first question is: what makes a theory rational? That question has been answered by the theory of rationality. The second question is: why should a person accept a rational theory? The first section of the present chapter will contain the answer. The second phase is the reply to the objection that the enterprise undertaken here—the justification of rationality—is doomed, because it is necessarily question-begging. The second section shows that this objection rests on a misconception of rationality. The third phase is the consideration of three objections. These have in common that they denigrate rationality on the basis of nonepistemological grounds—that rationality is psychologically damaging, practically inapplicable, and politically dangerous. These objections will be met by showing how they derive from a misunderstanding of rationality.

## Why should a person accept a rational theory?

The answer to this question was well expressed by Aristotle when he said: "For man . . . the life according to reason is the best and pleasantest, since reason more than anything else *is* man. This life therefore is also the happiest." [1] The justification of this answer is the following.

The reason why rational theories should be accepted and irrational ones rejected is that doing so is in the best interest of the agent. It must, therefore, be asked: why is it rational to do what a person regards as being in his best interest? This can be answered by reflecting on the nature of rationality.

The conception implicit in the theory of rationality is that rationality is a method for achieving what is supposed to be in one's best interest. There are other methods, but rationality is by far the best. The claim is not that only a rational policy is possible, but only that such a policy will be in what a person regards as his best interest. So the justification will recommend itself only to those who do wish to act in what they think of as their best interest, whatever that interest is conceived to be. Of course, there are people who due to ignorance, ineptitude, psychological problems, or conscious decision fail to do what they regard as being in their best interest. Such people are paradigmatically irrational.

It is not part of the claim that the only consideration regarding a policy is its rationality. There may be moral, political, religious, and other considerations as well. These may influence what a person does and exert an influence that may conflict with the dictates of rationality. But insofar as these other considerations are supposed to serve the best interest of the agent, there could not be a conflict. For if they issue in a policy that is in one's interest to follow, then they issue in a rational policy.

A quite general characterization of what is regarded to be in one's best interest can be expressed in terms of problem-solving. Whatever an agent recognizes as presenting a problem is what he recognizes to be in his interest to solve. And the more pressing a problem is considered to be the more the agent regards it to be in his interest to solve it. It is not inevitable that if a person acts rationally, he will in

165

fact act in his best interest, for he may be wrong about what he takes to be his best interest. Nevertheless, rationality is the method which has the best chance of leading to the achievement of what a person supposes to be in his best interest.

The strategy, however, was not merely the uncovering of the connection between rationality and problem-solving. The theory of rationality also advocated problem-solving through theories. What can be said to a person who acknowledges that rationality and problem-solving are in his best interest and goes on to disavow concern for theories? Such a view is attributed to the Azande by Evans-Pritchard.[2] It appears to be a logical consequence of the Azande way of identifying witches that no Azande can avoid being a witch; this contradicts their beliefs. Evans-Pritchard's comment is: "Azande see the sense of this argument but they do not accept its conclusions . . . Azande do not perceive the contradiction as we perceive it because they have no theoretical interest in the subject."

The answer to the denial of theoretical interest is to remind ourselves of the nature and purpose of theories. If our lives are disrupted, if expectations are disappointed, if traditional practice breaks down, then one is forced to ask: how can things be put right? The construction of a theory is the first step in the remedial process, for the theory provides a possible picture of the relevant segment of reality. The requirement of the possibilities is that they must provide a schema such that if things were as depicted, then what was previously problematic would no longer be so.

If someone disclaims interest in having theories, then only two alternatives can account for it. Either he has no problems, or he has no interest in solving problems. Both are practically impossible. It is impossible to be a human being and not to have problems. For human beings have goals and purposes which they want to achieve and problems are simply the obstacles that have to be overcome and the choices that have to be made along the way. Nor could it be that a human being has no interest in solving problems. For, to take an extreme case, one may imagine a mystic who aims at total desirelessness, at the repudiation of goals and purposes, but then one imagines a person whose problem is to negate his humanity. And that problem also requires a solution, which mystical tracts and manuals are only too eager to provide. Being human dooms one to having problems, and theories are the most useful devices for solving them. This is borne out by the Azande. For Evans-Pritchard notes that "those situations in which they [the Azande] express their belief in witchcraft do not force the problem [i.e., that everyone is a witch by their reckoning] upon them." [3]

The justification of the Aristotelian view of rationality is that "life according to reason" is the life where problems are solved, and it is "the best and pleasantest" because unsolved problems are physically and psychologically destructive. And "reason more than anything else is man" because the characteristically human device of solving problems through theories is our unique evolutionary gimmick. "This life . . . . is the happiest" because any other life for man is likely to founder on unsolved problems.

## The justification of rationality

The objection which must now be considered is that the project of this book—the justification of rationality—is impossible. For a theory of rationality can certify the rationality of theories, but how can the rationality of the theory of rationality be certified? The problem is that if the theory of rationality guarantees its own rationality, then it seems to be question-begging; and if it does not guarantee itself, then the rationality of theories appears to be judged in an arbitrary manner. In the first case, rationalism is logically untenable; in the second case, the appeal to rationality must be recognized to be no different from appealing to faith, revelation, authority, taste, instinct, or whatnot.

This dilemma is expressed clearly by Trigg in a recent book:

> There must, however, be something wrong with the notion of a *justification* of rationality, because clearly it is itself a concept from *within* rationality. Anyone who wants such a justification wants to stand outside the framework of rationality while remaining inside, and this is obviously incoherent. [4]

If one accepts the conception of rationality implicit in this passage, the incoherence of the enterprise of justification must be granted. However, it is part of the purpose of the theory of rationality defended here to substitute a different view of rationality, and that view permits justification without incoherence. Trigg, in the excellent company of many philosophers, thinks of rationality as a framework. One can be inside of it or elect to stay outside. Some stay out and they want to know why they should go in; some are in and want to know why they should stay in. And in these terms no good answer can be given. According to the present view, however, rationality is a method, not a framework. It is a method that everybody uses, and, in a sense to be explained, everybody must use. The justification of rationality is the justification of the employment of a method. The method is a device for problem-solving and it should be employed because everybody has problems, because it is in everybody's interest to solve his problems, and because rationality is the most promising way of doing so.

The dilemma that the justification of rationality is either question-begging or arbitrary is resolved by opting for the first lemma while denying its implications. Rationality can be justified rationally without begging the question. Self-certification is question-begging only if the standard employed is arbitrary, and it is a failure only if the theory attempting to guarantee itself does not conform to its own standards. The demonstration that neither is the case constitutes the defense of the theory of rationality against this objection.

Why are standards of rationality not arbitrary? What needs to be shown to avoid the charge of arbitrariness is that the standards of rationality are not optional, that there is a sense in which it is not a matter of choice whether or not one conforms to them. It is clear that rationalism is not logically necessary. The denial of any theory of rationality is not self-contradictory. Sceptics deny it without committing any logical solecism.

The necessity involved in the acceptance of standards of rationality is conditional necessity.[5] What this amounts to is the recognition that whether or not certain necessities obtain depends on contingent states of affairs. Conditional necessities are not true in all possible worlds, but only in a world in which a relevant set of facts holds. But

168

provided that these facts exist, it is necessarily the case that certain things follow. The existence of language, for instance, is a contingent matter in our world. But given that there is a language, it is not a contingent matter that at least some symbols in it must be used consistently. A similar status is claimed for standards of rationality. It is a contingent fact that human beings are what they are; the course of evolution could have been different, the process that led to the formation of our solar system could have followed a different course. But given human nature and the environment, rationality is a matter of necessity. For human nature and the environment jointly make it inevitable that human beings have problems which they must solve, and rationality is the method for solving them. The standards of rationality are simply the formulation of the most promising rules of problem-solving. They are not arbitrary, for provided an agent is a normal human being, he is unavoidably committed to problem-solving. Conformity to standards of rationality is not a matter of choice, for provided that one acts in his own interest, he has to act rationally. In another sense, of course, there is a choice involved in acting rationally, for one may elect not to act in his best interest.

If someone were to exercise that choice and refuse to act rationally but follow instead conflicting dictates of faith, instinct, or taste, then the question that must be decided is whether or not he means to act in his best interest. If he does, but his actions, prompted by nonrational considerations, conflict with the dictates of rationality, then his actions are self-defeating. He aims to do something, but goes about it the wrong way. If he does not mean to act in his best interest, then rationality indeed has nothing to offer him. But given that human beings are what they are, such a policy cannot be pursued for long. It leads either to death or to inconsistency. Inconsistency brings him back to rationality, and death removes the option of choosing between the rational and irrational.

There is still the problem left, however, of the rationality of the theory of rationality. A sceptic may accept the necessity of rationality, but see no reason for thinking that the theory of rationality which expresses what is involved in rationality meets the conditions it prescribes for other theories. The sceptic wants it demonstrated that the theory of rationality itself conforms to standards of rationality.

Clearly, the theory of rationality meets the requirement of problem-solving. The all-important problem which it solves is that of providing the best method for acting in one's interest. But does the theory conform to other standards? It certainly aims to be logically consistent and conceptually coherent, and there does not seem to be any indication that it has failed. The theory also has considerable explanatory power. By beginning with the ordinary distinction between the rational and the irrational it explains not just how the distinction can be drawn, but also why it is of such crucial importance. Moreover, it succeeds in this explanatory enterprise where many other attempts have foundered on the sceptical objections. Nor does the theory fail on account of criticizability. There are several grounds on which it might be criticized. First, it might fail to conform to the requirements of formal logic or lead to conceptual absurdity. Second, there might be ordinary facts about rationality that it fails to explain and that it cannot explain. Third, the theory was developed on the basis of the inadequacy of its rivals. If it were found that the criticisms of these rival theories were faulty, then the claims of the present one might be considerably weakened. Fourth, the theory rests on the correctness of the philosophical analysis of such ideas as criticism, explanation, the primacy of common sense, the external-internal distinction, and many others. If these analyses were mistaken, then the theory would suffer correspondingly. It appears, however, that the theory of rationality so far survives these possible criticisms. And that, of course, is part of the reason why it should be accepted.

## Reason and emotion

Rationalism has often been attacked on the grounds that it rests on a mistaken view of human nature. The supposedly errant view will be called the "classical" account and the rationalism associated with it "classical rationalism."

According to the classical view, the human mind has powers or faculties such as emotion, perception, the will, memory, imagination, and reason. The mental life of human beings consists in the exercise of these faculties. Since Plato and Aristotle there has been a supposed hierarchy of excellence according to which the faculties can be ranked. The faculty of reason was awarded the pride of place, because the exercise of reason, alone, was supposed to enable one to contemplate the most worthwhile objects: the Platonic forms. Or as Aristotle sees it: reason is the essence of man, the respect in which he differs from animals, and human excellence consists in the full exercise of the activity proper to our essence.

The Greek view of reason as the most valuable human capacity has persisted. Classical rationalism, based on this psychological description, offers a philosophical theory about the good life. The theory's influence extends into morality, politics, literature, art, and philosophy. There goes with it the sort of rigidity that accompanies a quest: the ideal is clear, what needs to be done to attain it is also clear, although very difficult, and man's highest purpose is to pursue it undeviatingly. Allowances may have to be made for the frailty of the body and for the regrettable intrusion of the lower faculties. But it ought to be recognized that catering to feeling and imagination, giving in to fancy, dreaming, indulgence in nostalgia are weaknesses. Admittedly, the pursuit of perfection may have to be interrupted from time to time, for the rationalist may recognize an obligation to help others to achieve the same end as he himself is working for. But if he sacrifices his own well-being, it is in order to teach others about the ideal.

Classical rationalism has always had its critics, but the various criticisms, coming from different directions, share a common point: an emphasis upon reason at the expense of other human faculties is damaging to man. Mental life is not like a race with many entries, where the philosopher's task is to back the favorite. Mental life is more like a cooperative venture in which success is possible only by a joint effort of all the faculties. The Aristotelian prescription of moderation should apply to the exercise of reason as well.

One important element in the criticisms of classical rationalism may be called psychological. The psychological element, with its strong affinity to existentialism, is one theme of William Barrett's *Irrational Man*. The criticism is expressed at the conclusion of the book:

> We are the children of an enlightenment, one which we would like to preserve; but we can do so only by making a pact with old goddesses.

> The centuries-long evolution of human reason is one of man's greatest triumphs. . . . But do we need to be persuaded now, after all that has happened in this twentieth century, how precariously situated. . . . reasonable ideals are in relation to the subterranean forces of life, and how small a segment of . . . man they actually represent? We have to establish a working pact between that segment and the whole of us. . . . [T]he rationalism of the Enlightenment will have to recognize that at the very heart of its light there is also darkness. It would be the final error of reason . . . to deny that the Furies exist.[6]

The error of classical rationalism, according to these critics, then, lies in the assumption that the dark underside of human nature, the Furies, or less poetically, our instinctive inheritance from the animal past can be controlled by ignoring it. It is naive to suppose that the pursuit of noble ideals will leave no *Lebensraum* for the *Id;* and the facts of history contradict this optimistic fallacy.

The fallacy, they go on, is far more serious than the mere commission of a philosophical error; and it has dangerous consequences. For these subterranean forces are irrepressible. There is no question about whether they will find expression in our lives; the question is about what kind of expression they will find. And since classical rationalism, with its lofty disregard of the demeaning side of our nature, actually abdicates that all-important choice, it leaves us unprepared for the inevitable outbreaks of brutality. But the surprise and shock of the classical rationalist will not be directed only at the deplorable behavior of others, for he, too, is human and subject to the vicissitudes of his own nature. There is a Hyde to every Jekyll.

The remedy seems obvious: we must acknowledge the potentially destructive forces within us and concentrate on allowing their controlled expression. Naturally, to accept the remedy, they would argue, requires us to abandon the classical rationalist ideal: the cultivation of reason at the expense of other faculties.

Friends and foes of the classical view of rationality, thus, take up their respective sides in response to the question of which should prevail in the conflict between reason and emotion. A notable champion of the classical view writes:

> The irrationalist insists that emotions and passions rather than reason are the mainsprings of human action. To the rationalist's reply that,

though this may be so, we should do what we can to remedy it . . .
the irrationalist would rejoin that this attitude is hopelessly unrealistic.
. . . It is my firm conviction that this irrational emphasis upon emotion and passion leads ultimately to what I can only describe as crime.
One reason for this opinion is that this attitude . . . must lead to an
appeal to violence and brutal force as the ultimate arbiter in any dispute.[7]

Thus, it would seem, that the rationalist requires the suppression of
emotion so as to avoid the dangerous consequences of acting on their
basis. And the antirationalist requires that emotions be expressed so
as to avoid the dangerous consequences of their suppression. Is there a
way out of this problem?

One traditional solution is to dispute the possibility of a conflict
between reason and emotion by subordinating the former to the latter. According to this view, reason by itself is capable only of passing
from proposition to proposition in, at best, a logically impeccable
manner. But reason, left to its own devices, is incapable of initiating
anything, since the springs of action are feelings, desires, wants, and
needs. Moreover, reason is incapable of inventing or discovering the
propositions whose connections its task is to explore, for that is the
role of perception and imagination. Reason's proper activity is to
evaluate logically what the passions prompt, the senses perceive, and
the imagination creates.

The best known representative of this psychological doctrine is
Hume:

> We speak not strictly and philosophically when we talk of the combat
> of passion and reason. Reason is and ought only to be the slave of the
> passions, and can never pretend to any other office than to serve and
> obey them.[8]

The psychological doctrine upon which classical rationalism rests is
thus attacked by Hume on psychological grounds. The point of the
attack is not just to quarrel with an allegedly mistaken psychological
theory, but also to safeguard intrinsically valuable human endeavours
that are stifled by classical rationalism. It is psychologically impossible to suppress feeling and imagination. The attempt to do so is not
only futile but also damaging, for it leads to the denigration of those
activities which alone make the exercise of reason possible.

According to this view, reason is a more or less mechanical activity. It is the dry earth-bound accountant of a firm of dashing, brave, imaginative entrepeneurs whose task is the exploration of what there is. The bookkeeping is necessary, but it is a nuisance. When a new adventure beckons, rules must not be allowed to stand in the way. Rules should be adjusted to aid the quest, for otherwise the quest would be impossible.

Defenders of this view would receive with great sympathy Kuhn's account of science. The activity of reason is comparable to the activity of scientists in the long periods of normal science. The scientists are given a paradigm, and so they have an ideal, a key to nature, a sanctioned method, and an example of how to put it into practice. Theirs is the tedious workmanlike chore of assembling small sections of the mosaic, so that it will fit the creative conception of someone else who transcended a period of normalcy. For acts of creativity cannot be achieved by mechanical means; only feeling and imagination are capable of accomplishing them.

Classical rationalism, these critics hold, with its mistaken deification of reason, makes life sterile, boring, constipated. It curtails joy, creativity, and the freedom that comes from the unconstrained exercise of imagination. If classical rationalism had great achievements to its credit, it might be regarded as forcing a choice between the life it recommends and the one its critics favor. But each and every achievement that a classical rationalist can cite in support of his case is made possible only by the employment of those faculties which he relegates to inferiority. There cannot be a case for classical rationalism that is not also a case for feeling and imagination, and thus the "combat of passion and reason" is a myth.

There are several important features of this criticism of classical rationalism. First of all, while it juxtaposes a psychological analysis to the psychological analysis accepted by classical rationalists, the underlying view of human nature is the same. Both parties hold that there are faculties in the mind and that human behavior is to be understood as the effects of the faculties. The dispute is over the question of which faculties are important. The resulting debate about the value of rationality is thus conducted on psychological grounds. The point that will be argued shortly is that the value of rationality is independent of psychological considerations and thus classical rationalists and their critics are fighting the wrong battle.

The second noteworthy feature is that even if one grants the justice of Humean criticisms of the psychological theory implicit in classical rationalism, it is by no means the case that the classical rationalist's apprehensions are thereby proved groundless. Popper thinks that the emphasis upon emotion at the expense of reason leads to irrationalism and thus to the impossibility of resolving inevitable conflicts by civilized means. And Hume, of course, bears reluctant witness to how realistic Popper's fears are. For Hume admits that "if reason be considered in an abstract view it furnishes invincible arguments against itself," [9] and he did reach the melancholic conclusion that

> 'Tis not solely in poetry and music, we must follow our taste and sentiment, but likewise in philosophy. When I am convinc'd of any principle, 'tis only an idea, which strikes more strongly upon me. When I give preference to one set of arguments above another, I do nothing but decide from my feeling concerning the superiority of their influence.[10]

Thus the dilemma of whether to suppress emotions and be thwarted or to express emotions and risk irrationalism persists even after Hume's attempted resolution of it. The way out is to reject the psychologism that classical rationalists and their critics alike share.

As a preliminary to the defense of rationalism something should be said about how such notoriously vague words as "emotion" and "reason" will be used. To begin with "emotion": the term is used extremely generally. "Feeling" would not serve as a synonym, because not everything that is felt is an emotion: physical sensation, for instance, is not. Emotions are felt, but some feelings are not emotions. Nor is "passion" a synonym, for it connotes a great upsurge of feeling and some emotions are calm.

Instead of offering a synonym, the use of "emotion" will be elucidated by indicating the range of experiences that are intended to fall within its domain. Certainly feelings, exclusive of bodily sensations, are emotions. For instance, fear, pique, anger, jealousy, love, joy, pity, sympathy are feelings and hence emotions. But so are agitations such as being anxious, startled, shocked, excited, irritated, and others. Moods are also emotions; for instance, a person being depressed, happy, discontented, indignant, frivolous, is in an emotional state. Moods are short-term, but motives or inclinations are long-term emotions. Ambition, pride, patriotism, vanity, altruism are usually enduring emotions that guide a person through longer periods of his life.[11] The lack of precision in these remarks may be overlooked because the subsequent argument does not hinge on further reducing the vagueness of "emotion."

The imprecise use of "reason" is of a different order. The trouble with "reason" is that it is used to refer to three different sorts of things and as a result of their shared label the three things are not distinguished with sufficient clarity.

The first sense is in which we say that the reason for the bridge having collapsed is corrosion. "Reason" here means explanation. It is enough to merely note this sense; nothing further will be said about it.

The second sense of "reason" is in which it is either a faculty or power of the mind, or the exercise of that faculty or power. When Descartes offers A *discourse of the Method of rightly conducting the Reason,* he means to tell us how to use this faculty or power well. "Reasoning," in this sense, is closely connected with thinking and problem-solving. "Reason" is what is exercised and "reasoning" is the activity of exercising it. It is something human beings have and do; it is what makes them rational animals.

The third sense of "reason" is in which a belief, theory, institution, action, plan, or goal is said to be "in accord with reason," be "reasonable," or "rational." In the second sense, "reason" is the agent and "reasoning" the activity yielding the products—beliefs, theories, etc.—which may or may not be reasonable or rational in the third sense. In the second sense, "reason" is a psychological agency or process; in the third sense "reason" is an epistemic property. To mark these two senses, "reasoning" is used to refer to the psychological process and "rationality" is used to designate the epistemic property.

In the light of this distinction, the question can be sharpened; we need to ask: is there a conflict between reasoning and emotion, and is there a conflict between rationality and emotion? The two-part thesis that will be defended is that while there may be a conflict between reasoning and emotion, it is in everybody's interest to resolve it in

176

favor of reasoning and that not only is there no conflict between rationality and emotion, but it is logically impossible that a conflict could occur.

The distinction between reasoning and rationality, however, may be attacked on the ground that the sense in which beliefs, actions, theories, or goals can be said to be rational is dependent on the sense in which people can be said to be rational. That this view is still prevalent is attested to by the unapologetic manner in which it is simply assumed. "I shall presuppose," writes a recent author,

> that it is primarily to the individual that we ascribe rationality. To speak of rational action, or rational activity, or a rational morality, or a rational society, is to speak of rationality in a way which must be derived from our conception of a rational individual or person.[12]

The claim that rationality is ascribed *primarily* to individuals and that the sense in which actions, societies, etc., can be said to be rational *must be* derivative can be interpreted either logically or historically. If it is interpreted logically, it is false. For whether or not a belief, theory, or action enjoys a certain epistemic status is logically independent of the psychological process occurring in any individual. A belief or action may be rational even if everyone, including their author, regards them as irrational and they may be irrational even though everyone thinks that they are rational. If, on the other hand, the claim is that in the development of language "reason" and its cognates were first ascribed to individuals and only secondly to the cognitive products of individuals, then it has no philosophical importance. For the distinction between reasoning, the psychological process, and rationality, the epistemic property, is not supposed to be warranted by the history of usages, but by there actually being a difference. When the difference was first noticed is only of anecdotal interest.

Part of the significance of the theory of rationality defended here is that the conflict between rationality and emotion disappears. Classical rationalists and their opponents share a fundamental error. They suppose that the question about the supremacy of reason can be settled by examining human nature. Given a true account of human psychology, according to their mistaken common assumption, we can decide whether reason is or should be the queen of faculties. In fact, however, the make-up of human beings has only the most tenuous connection with rationality or rationalism. Certainly, rationalism is accepted, rejected, or entertained by human agents, and they have to have appropriate psychological capacities to consider such issues. However, this rather trivial claim holds equally of all theories and so the exploration of the connection between rationalism and psychology is not going to be illuminating.

Classical rationalism and its opponents agree about conceiving of rationality as the exercise of the faculty of reason. They disagree only about its excellence. Rationality, as we have seen however, is a method whereby problems can be solved. Classical rationalism is unavoidably committed to a psychological picture of man. Rationalism, however, can and should be quite impersonal. The primary concern of the rationalist is with the rationality of particular theories; they are rational if they conform to the standards of rationality. The existence of people, their psychological constitution, their capacity to reason and its relation to other capacities are completely irrelevant to the rationalist's primary concern. For the rationality of a theory is logically independent of the rationality of the people who accept, reject, or entertain the theory. A theory can be rational even if everybody rejects it, and it can be irrational and be enthusiastically embraced by all.

There is a connection between the rationality of theories and of persons, but it runs in the opposite direction than the one supposed by the classical rationalist. It is a mistake to think that what makes a theory rational is that it has been excogitated by the faculty of reason. That faculty cannot produce guaranteed offspring; its products, like those of other mental activities, must earn the favored epithet. The rationality of a theory has nothing to do with where the theory comes from; it has to do with whether it conforms to standards of rationality. A person, however, has a good claim to being rational if he holds only theories whose rationality he has ascertained. Part of the error of classical rationalism is the supposition that the rationality of a theory depends upon the rationality of its author, whereas, in fact, the dependence is just the opposite.

It is a consequence of the view of rationality defended here that the question of a theory's rationality must be distinguished from the question of the theory's source. It makes no difference whether the theory is the product of reason, imagination, passion, intuition, prejudice, or whatnot. The rationality of a theory depends on what happens after its formulation. And this consideration should remove all the reservations about rationality that critics of classical rationalism hold. For rationalism neither prescribes nor proscribes any method of theory construction, it does not curtail creativity, and it does not impoverish emotional life. There may and should be freedom in feeling and imagination and also in the process of creation. Rationality is neither a recipe for creativity nor a mode of consciousness: it is a method of evaluating, from the point of view of problem-solving, some products of the human mind.

Given these arguments, it follows that there could not be a conflict between rationality, an objective property of theories, and emotion, a kind of mental state and activity, for they are not the kinds of things that could conflict. But is there a conflict between emotion and reasoning? Both of these are mental states or activities, so that categorial differences do not prevent the possibility of there being a conflict.

Let us suppose that a classical rationalist finds himself convinced by these arguments. How far could he reconcile his previous position with rationality being an objective property of theories? He could argue that reasoning is the highest mental activity for man, because it is most likely to lead to rational theories. Having rational theories is in the best interest of everybody, for such theories are solutions to whatever problems people have. So that if reasoning is the best way of arriving at rational theories, then any conflict with reasoning ought to be resolved in its favor, for other alternatives would lead to the perpetuation of those very problems that one meant to solve by the mental activity.

Critics of classical rationalism can contest this claim by denying either that reasoning is the best way of arriving at rational theories, or by arguing that even if reasoning is necessary for arriving at rational theories, it is not sufficient, for its mechanical operations must be based on such other mental processes as imagination, perception, emotion, and will. Classical rationalism, they will say, overemphasizes the importance of reasoning in arriving at rational theories. The result is that the chances of reaching a rational theory are diminished because the stress on reasoning stifles other, equally necessary, mental activities.

The most important feature of this debate is that it is empirical. Philosophers *qua* philosophers, therefore, are not going to have anything illuminating to say about it. The debate originated at a time when philosophical and psychological questions had not been distinguished, and it reached its crescendo in the eighteenth and nineteenth centuries when philosophical and psychological questions were systematically confused. The resolution of the debate depends on answering such empirical questions as whether actions can be prompted purely by reasoning or by emotion; whether the springs of actions are mixed; whether reasoning is capable by itself of producing theories; what is the optimum mixture of mental activities that will produce rational theories; does the production of rational theories differ for people with different personalities; or, indeed, whether the mental activities of a person have any bearing on the chances of his producing a rational theory.

Needless to say, these are unanswered questions. But this fact should not be viewed by philosophers as an invitation to step into the breach. Common sense, though, permits some reflections. Obviously, reasoning has to do with thinking, reflection, weighing alternatives, being judicious. A person proceeding in this manner is more likely to find a good solution to his problems than one who is imbued by emotion or is carried away by imagination. So it is just plain common sense that reasoning about a problem is the best way of solving it. Reasoning is a virtue, in the Aristotelian sense. Equally obviously, however, it has a corresponding vice: it is the mechanical, unfeeling, wooden-minded employment of a technique. The man whose mind works like a computer can solve only those problems that a computer can solve. There are, to put it mildly, others as well. So classical rationalists seem to be right in insisting on the importance of reasoning, and their critics are right in fearing its exaggerated employment. But one must emphasize that this conclusion is warranted only by common sense and so it lacks philosophical or scientific credentials.

The answer to the question of whether there is a conflict between rationality and emotion is that there is no such conflict, because there could not be. The rationality of theories does not depend on the mental processes of their authors, but on the problem-solving capacity of the epistemic fruits of these processes. And the answer to the question of whether there is a conflict between reasoning and emotion is that there may be, but both assertions and denials of its existence are dubious in the absence of solid empirical evidence. Common sense, in the meantime, dictates that if a man has a problem, then he should reason about solving it rather than rely on his emotions or follow his fancy.

The conclusion which has immediate bearing on the issues discussed in this paper is that the fears, criticisms, and reservations about rationalism are misdirected. If rationality is a method of problem-solving, then anyone having problems has it in his best interest to embrace rationalism. And this conclusion follows regardless of what the problems are, for rationality is neutral in this respect. The precondition of its employment is only that there be room for the interposition of a theory between pressures exerted by problems and the demands of solving them. The unique benefit man has gained from evolution is that there is this room and so we can try out in theory first what we must risk in action later. The best interpretation of the sense in which man can be said to be a rational animal, in contradistinction with other animals, is that man is unique in having available to him the device of solving problems through theories. The possession and application of this device, and not the mental state he is in, is what guarantees rationality. Classical rationalists and their critics are alike in mislocating the area where rationality can be found.

There is, however, another consequence of the removal of the conflict between rationality and emotion. It is that the question of the justification of emotions can now be raised without absurdity. If rationality were the slave or competitor of emotion, then using one to judge the other would be an error. But as we have seen, this is not so. Rationality is a method and there is no reason why it could not be used to judge the reasonability, appropriateness, excessiveness, or justifiability of feeling in certain ways in certain situations. This possibility will be explored in Chapter Twelve.

## Rationality and practice

A critic of rationalism may concede everything that has been said in support of the theory of rationality and go on to argue that the sceptical challenge still cannot be met, because the theory presents an ideal that is never applied in practice. What is the use of having a device for evaluating theories when in fact theories are judged on quite different grounds? How many philosophical, moral, historical, or aesthetic theories have been abandoned by their champions, it may be asked, because they came to see the irrationality of their theories? And those who think that scientific theories fare better should take to heart Planck's remarks:

> A new scientific truth does not triumph by convincing its opponents and making them see the light, but rather because its opponents eventually die, and a new generation grows up that is familiar with it.[13]

Darwin at the end of his *Origin of Species* agrees:

> Although I am fully convinced of the truth of the views given in this volume. . . . I by no means expect to convince experienced naturalists whose minds are stocked with a multitude of facts all viewed, during a long course of years, from a point of view directly opposite to mine. . . . [B]ut I look with confidence to the future,—to young and rising naturalists, who will be able to view both sides of the question with impartiality.[14]

And Kuhn, who quotes both of the above passages, writes:

> Copernicanism made few converts for almost a century after Copernicus' death. Newton's work was not generally accepted, particularly on the Continent, for more than half a century after the *Principia* appeared. Priestly never accepted the oxygen theory nor Lord Kelvin the electromagnetic theory.[15]

What can the rationalist say to accommodate the fact that people are irrational and that they frequently ignore the reasons against the theories they hold?

The first thing to notice is that objections to a theory may simply escape notice. There need be no willful ignoring of counterevidence, no hiding of logical inconsistency. A theory may be widely accepted, there may be no particular reason for questioning it, such criticisms as are available the theory may seem to have successfully met, and there may be no serious rival on the horizon. Perhaps it will be discovered only after generations of orthodoxy that the theory is incapable of explaining some of the facts that it was meant to explain. Newtonian physics was in this position.

Second, the question of whether or not a theory is rational may be very controversial. Witness, for instance, the contemporary debate about the criticizability of psychoanalytic theory. Such debates are extremely complex. Psychoanalysts may well accept the standard of criticizability and hold that their theory passes that test. There may be agreement about the standards and disagreement about their application.

Third, irresolution of the rationality of a theory may be due to disagreement about the standards of rationality themselves. It could be that a theory, held to be rational on the basis of a mistaken theory of rationality, would be irrational if the correct theory was applied to it. Disputes of this sort can be settled only if disputes about rationality themselves are resolved.

But none of these possibilities alters the undeniable justice of the observation that frequently theories are adhered to even though their lack of rationality has been abundantly demonstrated. There can be no question but that this shows the irrationality of their stubborn champions. It remains to be seen, however, whether this fact is capable of supporting the sceptic's position.

What is at issue between scepticism and rationalism is the rationality of theories. Sceptics deny and rationalists accept that it is possible to determine whether or not a theory is rational. And the rationalist's contention is that the standards of rationality can be used for that purpose. Now as an objection to this claim the sceptic cites the fact that many people are irrationally attached to their theories. But it is easy to see that this objection is way off the mark. For the rationality of theories is independent of the rationality of the persons who hold theories. The sceptic's point derives from the same confused psychologism that was the mainspring of both classical rationalism and of the traditional criticisms directed against it.

This reply, however, will not satisfy the sceptic. For his point is that rationality cannot accomplish its purpose, namely problem-solving, unless the method is employed. The irrationality of many people is not an objection to determining the rationality of theories, but it is an objection to the possibility of solving problems by the application of rational methods. No matter how excellent a method is, it requires people to put it into practice. If people are irrational, the method will not be used, and so it is as if it did not exist.

At this point, however, scepticism has ceased to be an objection and has become a complaint. Scepticism now comes down to regret for the fact that there is a technique of problem-solving which could serve the best interest of anyone who uses it and that many people perversely fail to do so. One can agree with the sceptic in regretting human irrationality. One may even try to do something about it. But the philosophical task ends when the theory of rationality is successfully defended. Some may think, as Plato did, that the duty of philosophers is not just to design and defend theories that make it possible to understand our experience of the world, but also to advocate them. Philosophers may be obligated to return to the cave. Be that as it may, the obligation is, at best, moral; it can come only when the intellectual task has been completed. And the sceptical challenge was originally directed against the possibility of accomplishing the intellectual task. The very posing of this objection tacitly acknowledges that what the sceptic held to be impossible, namely, a justification of rationality, is not only possible but also desirable.

## Rationality and politics

Michael Oakeshott's "Rationalism in Politics" echoes the classic Burkean warnings: rationalism leads to tyranny, just as the Enlightenment led to the French Revolution. Rationalists accept only the tribunal of reason and so the restraining influence of tradition, custom, and habit are allowed only so long as they pass rational scrutiny. The rationalist aims at problem-solving and his credo is that reason is capable of solving all problems. The inevitable result of this program is loss of liberty.

Oakeshott argues that when rationalism is applied in politics the seeds of repression are planted at the start: social problems supposedly arise because the existing institutions are inadequate to their task. Rationalism, therefore, begins with a prejudice against the past and the *status quo* and its goal is the replacement of traditional institutions with ones arrived at by a rational plan, an ideology. The rationalist encounters political problems, devises an ideological solution, and imposes it upon the problem-situation.

Rationalism is connected to *a priorism*. Perhaps it need not be as extreme as Descartes, Leibniz, and Spinoza supposed; rationalism need not denigrate experience. But it is characterized by a marked willingness to ignore the messiness of particular cases in favor of the large design, the overall theory. As Oakeshott puts it: rationalism shows "an irritable nervousness in the face of anything topical and transitory." [16]

The essence of rationalism, according to Oakeshott, is the combination of the search for perfection and for uniformity. If reason is the best guide, then it must be possible to find the perfect theoretical solution to any problem. And since theories are abstractions from particular cases, all the cases can be treated uniformly by a satisfactory theory. The rationalist's vision for society is the construction of a general theory in accordance with which a society can be firmly organized and put on the road toward perfection:

> From this politics of perfection springs the politics of uniformity; a scheme which does not recognize (particular) circumstance can have no place for variety. . . . If the rational solution for one of the problems of society has been determined, to permit any relevant part of society to escape from the solution is, *ex hypothesi,* to countenance irrationality. . . . Political activity is recognized as the imposition of a uniform condition of perfection upon human conduct.[17]

What underlies this attitude, according to Oakeshott, "is the preoccupation of the Rationalist with certainty." [18] Rationalism and the hankering after certainty both derive from a doctrine about human knowledge. There are, Oakeshott thinks, two sorts of knowledge: technical and practical. Technical knowledge is gained by reflecting upon practice. The result of such reflection may be a set of clearly articulated rules or principles for guiding practice. Practical knowledge is unreflective and is not formulable in rules or principles. It is knowledge of how to do something. The skill involved is entirely that of doing, the skill of the craftsman, which can be learned by imitation, by observation, by doing the task oneself. Technical knowledge is book knowledge, practical knowledge comes only with experience.

Oakeshott's case can be strengthened by noticing that technical knowledge both temporally and logically presupposes practical knowledge. For the former is an abstraction made possible only by the existence of the latter. The principles abstracted from practice are of necessity less than adequate to their source. They are generalizations of the best way of treating usual cases. But what makes some practitioners masters is that they know how to deal with unusual cases. There can be no technical knowledge of that, because principles can be derived only from usual cases. A manual can teach the skill of driving, but it cannot teach the skill of meeting emergencies. There are no rules for emergencies, for they signal the inapplicability of rules.

Oakeshott's claim is that the rationalist's mistaken search for certainty comes from equating knowledge with technical knowledge.

> Technique and certainty are, for him, inseparably joined because certain knowledge is, for him, knowledge which does not require to look beyond itself for its certainty. . . . And this is precisely what technical knowledge appears to be. It seems to be a self-complete sort of knowledge because it seems to range between an identifiable point . . . and an identifiable terminal point, where it is complete.[19]

The rationalist achieves certainty, only at the price of ignoring the source of the only kind of knowledge he recognizes. His blinkers allow him to consider only those cases to which his generalizations apply. The exception escapes his ken; variety is, for him, an irritant, an aberration that needs to be overcome.

These epistemological limitations have dangerous consequences when rationalism is applied to social issues, Oakeshott argues. The intolerance for the particular case and the quest for perfection and uniformity inevitably lead to the diminution of liberty and to the repression of dissent. If all cases are to be treated alike, then the exceptional is merely an obstacle. Moreover, if the scheme, in accordance with which uniformity is to be imposed, is thought of as the best solution of problems, then the exceptional cases are naturally regarded as aberrations and impediments to perfection.

The danger cannot be avoided. For rationalism

> is without power to correct its own short-comings; it has no homeopathic quality; you cannot escape its errors by becoming more sincerely or more profoundly rationalistic . . . the Rationalist has rejected in advance the only external inspiration capable of correcting his error; he does not merely neglect the kind of knowledge which would save him, he begins by destroying it. First he turns out the light and then he complains that he cannot see.[20]

Thus, to sum up, rationalism, prompted by a mistaken theory of knowledge, attempts to impose a uniform and supposedly perfect ideology upon society. The ideology is believed to lead to the solution of problems because it is demonstrably certain. Certainty is the product of technical knowledge which yields a technique for dealing with problems: social engineering. Since these inevitable aspirations of rationalism are destructive of liberty, rationalism should be abandoned.

The kind of rationalism Oakeshott attacks rests on an indefensible theory of rationality. While this theory of rationality recognizes that rationality is a method for solving problems, it identifies rationality with the employment of logic, where "logic" is used in a wide sense so as to include not just mathematical logic, but also the logic of scientific method. The theory then recognizes as rational all and only solutions arrived at by logic. Social problems are merely a species of problems, so it is a perfectly warranted implication of this theory of rationality that social problems are open to rational solution only by bringing to bear upon them the methods sanctioned by logic. The threat of social engineering, the prohibition (always in the interest of the people, the state, the society) of "irrational" behavior naturally arises. Let us call this theory of rationality "positivistic."

Oakeshott, then, can be thought of as offering three criticisms of the positivistic theory of rationality: it makes unsupportable claims to certainty, and it is from this that the quest for perfection and uniformity follows; it lacks any means of self-correction and so tends to the delusion of omniscience and consequent dictatorial pretensions; it

187

rests on a mistaken theory of knowledge and fails to recognize the inevitable uncertainty and fallibility that it brings with it from this flawed starting point. Though the positivistic theory of rationality can counter the first objection, it succumbs to the last two.

There is no reason why a positivistic rationalist would have to make a dogmatic claim to certainty. No doubt, the Utopian aspirations of Robert Owen, the doctrine of human perfectibility advocated by William Godwin, the discernment of the inevitable course of science by Comte, of evolution by Spencer, of history by Marx have in fact pretended to cerainty. But a more modest claim would serve just as well. Positivistic rationalists can simply hold that logic is the only rational method of problem-solving. It may not guarantee success, but it is the best hope for it. The irrationality and moral reprehensibility of deviant behavior follows with even greater force from the more modest claim. For the best policy should be even more jealously guarded if it is vulnerable. So a positivistic rationalist need not be committed to the certain success of the application of logic, and he can still pursue his utopian dream with unabated vigor and self-righteousness.

The other two objections, however, are far more serious. Oakeshott points out, quite rightly, that what sanctions the method of positivistic rationalism is the practice that existed before the method was extracted from it. Problems did not start to be solved only upon the formulation of the principles of logic, for the principles are derived from successful instances of problem-solving. Their adequacy depends on whether or not they continue to be helpful. Positivistic rationalists, however, recognize as problematic only situations in which the methods of logic can be employed. Problems not amenable to logical solution are regarded as pseudoproblems. Genuine problems are solvable either scientifically or by the application of formal techniques. But this approach is made possible only by the distortion of the original prepositivistic problem-situation. For, the truth is, people are concerned with problems other than those that fit into the categories devised by positivism. No doubt some problems can be solved logically, but some others may not be so tractable. By ignoring the latter kind, positivistic rationalism renders itself immune to refutation, for it refuses to take cognizance of problems which might show up the inadequacy of its method. And that is the reason why positivistic rationalism is in principle incapable of self-correction.

The point of this criticism need not be based on the contention that there actually occur genuine problems incapable of logical solution. The existence of such problems can be prudently left open. The telling part of the objection is that positivistic rationalism would be incapable of dealing with such problems if there were any. And the significance of this is that positivistic rationalism becomes dogmatic, for it has protected itself from the very possibility of criticism, and hence of the possibility of improvement. That it tends to become dictatorial, therefore, should cause no surprise.

It should by now be obvious, however, that the theory of rationality defended here does not share the shortcomings of positivistic rationalism. The reason for this is that the theory goes beyond positivism by virtue of its standards of explanatory power and criticizability. The latter guarantees that no rational solution of a problem can be protected against the possibility of criticism. The former, in turn, provides one ground upon which criticisms could be based. For the explanation embodied in a theory must be adequate to the pretheoretical common sense view. Positivistic rationalism has cut itself off from this starting point by recognizing only one kind of problem as genuine, whereas a satisfactory theory of rationality must recognize the problem-situation out of which it grew and the obligation of solving all those problems that initially prompted it.

In conclusion, a rationalist can agree with Oakeshott's criticism of positivistic rationalism and continue to adhere to rationalism, for only an aberration of rationalism leads to the sort of dictatorial attitude against which Oakeshott rightly cautions. A necessary sense of intellectual modesty is built into any theory of rationality that accepts criticizability as a standard of rationality. Furthermore, the recognition of the primacy of common sense prevents rationalism from picking and choosing its own problems. The problem-situation is given, not in any absolute sense, but because human beings are what they are.

One final remark needs to be made. Oakshott regards rationalism as having an antihistorical, antitraditionalist bias. He thinks that rationalism is naturally allied to a radical-reformist frame of mind and finds its natural enemy in the traditionalist-conservative camp. This is a mistake. Rationalism, as has been pointed out before, is axiologically neutral. Radicals and traditionalists agree that problems need to be solved, hence, they both ought to avail themselves of rationalism. Of course, it always needs to be decided whether the best solution of a particular problem is the patching up of an existing institution or the establishment of a new one. But rationalism *per se* has no bias in either direction. It is merely a method for choosing the most acceptable and by no means infallible solution in any given situation. Rationalism is indeed a technique, but it is a criticizable, fallible, self-correcting technique. Liberty is not endangered by it.

## Conclusion

The three phases of the argument for the value of rationality have now been completed. The first phase was a consideration of why a person should accept a rational theory. The answer was that the acceptance of rational theories is in the best interest of each and every person for such theories constitute the best attempts at solving whatever problems anyone may have.

The second phase was a demonstration that the objections to the very attempt of justifying rationality rest on a misunderstanding of the nature of rationality. Rationality is a method for solving problems. It is not, as many take it to be, a framework. If it were a framework, then it might exist side by side with such other frameworks as mysticism, art, commerce, and so on. And then it could be thought of as competing with them. This is an error. Rationality is a method that anybody in any framework should use if he wishes to act in what he takes to be his best interest.

Furthermore, the justification of rationality is not question-begging, for if the standards of rationality are applied to judge the rationality of the theory of rationality defended here, then that theory turns out to be rational. There is no logical difficulty in applying the standards to the theory which advocates those very standards, because the standards have been justified independently of the theory. The justification of the internal standards is that they help to solve problems and the justification of the external standard is that it is in everybody's interest to accept it and the failure to do so leads to the frustration of the goals that the agent pursues.

The third phase examined three nonepistemological arguments against rationality. Each of these arguments was shown to rest on a misconception about the nature of rationality. The first charged that rationality is psychologically damaging because it stifles emotions. Rationality, however, is not a mental state but an epistemological property, and so this alleged conflict could not occur. The second doubted that rationality has any practical value, since people rarely use it. This was seen to be irrelevant to the epistemological merits of rationality. The theory of rationality defends an ideal that sceptics hold to be impossible. The ideal is available, whether people follow it is independent of its value. The third objected to rationality on the grounds that it leads to tyranny, because it rigidifies thinking by the imposition of inflexible procedures and rules and thereby makes dissent impossible. This objection finds its mark in those theories of rationality that equate rationality and logic. The theory defended here, however, has a built-in defense against this danger, because it contains the standard of criticizability and because it does not include a blueprint for the nature of problems that it could attempt to solve.

# The state of
# the argument:
# the theory of
# rationality and
# the refutation
# of scepticism

The aim of Part Three has been to present a theory of rationality and to defend it against objections. The question of what makes a theory rational has been answered by the proposal of a *philosophical* theory of rationality. And that means that the theory does not rest on the discovery of new facts: no new psychological, anthropological, scientific, or historical data have been presented. What has been accomplished is the development of a new way of thinking about facts that are familiar to everybody.

The outstanding facts requiring explanation have to do with the distinction that we make all the time between rational beliefs, theories, products of mind and society, and irrational ones; and with the fact that we hold what is judged to be rational in higher regard than what is judged as irrational; and also with the fact that following a rational policy seems to be more rewarding than following an irrational one. These facts are widely believed and the beliefs in them are almost universally supposed to be legitimate.

The sceptic attacks the supposed legitimacy of these beliefs; he demands a justification for them. He claims that it has not been shown that we, including himself, have a better epistemic right to these beliefs than people have to irrational beliefs. Ultimately, the sceptic claims, all beliefs are unjustified. And the facts surrounding the practices which we label "rational" do not have the kind of explanation that rationalists seek. Our practices, including the sceptic's too, are arbitrary and, in the last analysis, they cannot be justified.

The sceptic's case is further strengthened by his successful criticism of such theories of rationality as the postulational and analytic ones (discussed in Chapter One), or of the coherence theory of rationality (discussed in Chapter Six), or of the classical and positivistic theories of rationality (discussed in Chapter Ten), or of the appeals to pragmatic considerations, common sense, ordinary language, and science (discussed in Chapters Two, Three, Four, and Five).

The reason for the failure of these theories of rationality is twofold. First, each concentrates on some one element of rationality and either excludes or drastically deemphasizes other elements. This makes them wrong, but not totally wrong, for the elements these theories single out as *the* core of rationality is indeed *a* core, but not only one. These theories have something to offer, and what they have offered, we took, but their offering is only part of the solution.

The second reason for the failure of these theories of rationality is that they offer only an internal descriptive account of rationality. Once again, the description of the standards appealed to is a necessary part of a theory of rationality. But a purely descriptive account cannot satisfy the sceptic. For what he disputes is not that this is how we do things, but that our way of doing things is better justified than other—perhaps irrational—ways of doing things.

A successful theory of rationality must provide a descriptive internal account of rationality in which the various standards are all recognized and none is emphasized at the expense of others. And it must also provide an external defense of the standards in terms of which our practices can be justified and conflicting practices criticized. This has been the aim of the theory of rationality presented here.

The refutation of scepticism, however, has not been completed. The sceptic might accept this theory of rationality and hold that when it is applied no theory is found to be rational. So that we have gained the rather empty triumph of being able to say what a rational theory would be like if we had any. But since we do not, our various beliefs and theories are still in the same equally unjustified epistemic position regardless of whether we claim they are rational or irrational. The sceptic can thus claim that it does not follow from having a theory of rationality that anything conforms to it. And the sceptic's claim is not based merely on an abstract possibility. His contention is given substance by the supposed irrefutability of solipsism and by the alleged indefensibility of presuppositions.

The sceptic may make his case by attacking two assumptions to which all theories with factual content are committed. The first is that there exists something outside of the mind of the person who entertains the theory. The second is that it is possible to defend rationally the various presuppositions to which all theories are inevitably committed. The attack upon the first assumption calls into question the rationality of the belief *that* there is an external world; the version of scepticism that argues for it will be called "solipsistic scepticism." The attack upon the second assumption focuses on the supposed impossibility of rationally deciding between various accounts of *what* the external world is like; the form of scepticism that advocates this will be referred to as "metaphysical scepticism." To complete the refutation of scepticism both solipsistic and metaphysical scepticism have to be countered. This will be done in Part Four.

# PART 4
# THE REFUTATION OF
# SCEPTICISM

# 11 A refutation of solipsistic scepticism

*"It still remains a scandal to philosophy and to human reason in general that the existence of things outside us . . . must be accepted merely on faith, and that if anyone thinks good to doubt their existence, we are unable to counter his doubts by any satisfactory proof."*—Immanuel I. Kant, *The Critique of Pure Reason*

## Solipsism and scepticism

The problem of solipsism is one consequence of the Cartesian program of beginning with what is known with certainty and then attempting to deduce the rest of reality from it. If this program is accepted and the mind and its attributes are taken as the philosophical starting point, then it is natural to ask how the existence of anything outside of the mind can be established. Solipsism is the philosophical theory that denies the possibility of rationally demonstrating the existence of the external world.

There are, however, two grounds upon which the denial can rest: one weak, the other much stronger. The weak version of solipsism arises out of the ontological thesis that reality comprises only a solitary mind and its attributes. The world that is commonly thought to be external to the mind is merely an appearance created by the mind in question.

No philosopher of importance has held ontological solipsism; it is not a defensible position. The strongest case that can be made for solipsism in general is that the interpretation it offers of one's experience is as cogent as any other interpretation. Ontological solipsism goes far beyond this by claiming that all other interpretations can be shown to fail. There is no warrant for this claim. Ontological solipsism, therefore, has come to be regarded more as a threat than a serious alternative. The threat is constituted by the inevitable absurdity of any philosophical theory that can be shown to have ontological solipsism as its consequence.

The stronger, more defensible version of solipsism makes the epistemological claim that there is rational warrant for believing only in the existence of a solitary mind and its attributes. There is no rational way of deciding between various interpretations of one's experience of what seems to exist externally. Where ontological solipsism holds that only a mind and its attributes exist, epistemological solipsism argues that there is reason for accepting the existence of only one mind and its attributes.

Epistemological solipsism ("solipsism" from now on) and scepticism are mutually supporting. Scepticism, of course, maintains the impossibility of rationally defending any theory. Solipsism can be thought of as a special application of scepticism to the view that there exists anything external to a solitary mind. But the support solipsism provides for scepticism is far stronger than what is offered by such other limited forms of scepticism as, for instance, moral scepticism or scepticism about the past. For the existence of the external world is presupposed by nearly all theories with factual content. If solipsism were correct, then all theories presupposing the existence of the external world would be rationally unacceptable. Consequently it would be of little use to have a theory of rationality to decide whether or not a theory is rational. No theory could then offer a rational solution of any problem that arises out of an attempt to cope with one's surroundings, because all theories would rest on the undefended presupposition that one's surroundings exist. A sceptic could thus argue that the theory of rationality shows what *would* make a theory rational, but solipsism shows that nearly no theory *is* rational. This version of solipsism will be called "solipsistic scepticism," and the task at hand is to refute it. The aim of the argument, expressed more positively, is to show that it is rational to hold that there is an external world.

## The strategy of the criticism

Solipsistic scepticism is rarely taken seriously. The usual attitude toward it is to declare its absurdity, like that of ontological solipsism, and then waste no more words on it. But this procedure goes a long way toward reinforcing the fundamental sceptical point that reason is a poor way of coping with problems. For sceptics and irrationalists can triumphantly point at Kant's "scandal of philosophy" and conclude that a fundamental presupposition of rationalism is just as arbitrary, rests just as much on faith, as do the fundamental presuppositions of other ways of life.

The feebleness of the usual responses to solipsistic scepticism becomes quite apparent if three routine rejoinders are examined: the therapeutic, the pragmatic, and the psychological. The therapeutic approach is to confront the solipsistic sceptic with his inability to specify the kind of argument that he would accept in favor of the presupposition he questions. It is supposed somehow to follow from the lack of answer that solipsism is illegitimate, absurd, meaningless, and can thus be made to go away. But, of course, solipsism remains because there are at least two interpretations of the situation in which a question may be asked and it does not seem to be possible to specify what sort of answer would be acceptable. The first is that the question is illegitimate, but the second is that it is fundamental, searching, and difficult. To opt for the first without having excluded the second is an unjustifiable step.

There are two *prima facie* considerations for thinking that the solipsist's question is of the second sort. One is that the solipsist is raising doubts about a very fundamental presupposition indeed, and the more fundamental a presupposition is the more difficult it is to know how to go about defending it. For the defense involves appealing to presuppositions and there is a scarcity of presuppositions that do not rest on the one that the solipsist questions. The second consideration is that solipsism is stated in the context of general doubts about the possibility of giving satisfactory rational answers to any questions, so it would be perverse to hold it against the solipsist that he fails to be able to specify the kind of rational answer that would satisfy him.

The pragmatic rejoinder is to point out that the belief in the existence of the external world is useful, and so solipsism is refuted on pragmatic grounds. But this rejoinder fails for two reasons. The first is that since there are not supposed to be any factual differences between solipsism and its rivals, acting on solipsistic assumptions ought to prove to be just as useful as acting on nonsolipsistic assumptions. For both solipsism and its rivals are possible explanations of common human experiences. Success in action is not in doubt between them; the doubt arises over the explanation of the success. The second reason for the failure of the pragmatic rejoinder is that the solipsist questions the rationality of the belief in the existence of the external world. Since an irrational belief may seem to be successful, at least in the short run, merely to point at the usefulness of the belief in question is a *non sequitur*.

The psychological rejoinder accuses the solipsist of an inconsistency between the beliefs he avows and the actions he performs. Since the solipsist acts like nonsolipsists do, it is said, he really holds the same beliefs as nonsolipsists do. Apart from the fact that the solipsist could simply reverse the argument and refute his opponents, the rejoinder misses the point of solipsism. For the question to which solipsism is an answer is: what philosophical account is consistent with the experiences that one has? The actions that one seems to perform are part of what needs to be explained, so there is nothing in solipsism that would oblige a consistent solipsist to behave differently than a nonsolipsist does. Moreover, the kind of solipsism that is examined here does not claim that only its own interpretation is correct. What is claimed is that there is no rational way of choosing between conflicting interpretations of one's experiences.

One successful refutation of solipsism is based on the idea that the theory is incapable of explaining all the facts that it is supposed to explain, consequently it is rationally unacceptable. This conclusion can be reached by an improved version of the paradigm case argument.

The facts that solipsism must explain comprise the common sense view of the world, and at the core of its explanation is the assumption that only a solitary mind and its attributes exist. The objection to solipsism, then, is that the existence of language is one of these facts, but it cannot be explained by solipsism. For the existence of language entails the existence of the external world.

Of course, the existence of language cannot be coherently denied for the denial must take a linguistic form. So any attempt to dispute that there exists a language immediately leads to conceptual absurdity and through it to the violation of one standard of rationality: conceptual coherence.

# The refutation of solipsistic scepticism

Solipsistic scepticism founders on the implications of the fact that there is language. Without undertaking the hopelessly difficult task of defining "language," it is possible to note some minimal conditions that must be fulfilled by anything that is to count as language. It is, of course, possible to imagine borderline cases in which it would be difficult to know what to say about some quasilinguistic activity. Fortunately such cases are irrelevant in the present context because the solipsist must agree that one of the facts of experience is that he uses language and that he means by "language" what is ordinarily meant by it.

First of all, then, the use of English involves the use of spoken or written *symbols,* which happen to be words. It is perhaps possible to do many things that language is used to do without using symbols, but it is not possible to use English without using written or spoken words. Marks on a paper or sounds in the air are not yet words; they become so only if they are used in accordance with *rules.* English has many different kinds of rules, but it is unnecessary to attempt a general account of them. It suffices to note that there must be rules guiding the consistent use of words if one is to be said to be using English. A language user need not be able to articulate these rules; his practice, however, must reflect their tacit acceptance. The use of language does not force the user to employ words consistently, but a person would not be using English unless he was consistent more often than not. He may, of course, be doing something else.

The third condition is that the use of English is normally an activity that is performed for a *purpose;* it is not just something that happens to people on certain appropriate occasions, like adrenalin secretion. Typically, language is used as a means towards an end. It is a conscious, deliberate, learned activity whose performance is warranted by its usefulness. One of the uses of English is descriptive, its purpose being to identify, classify, give information, make assertions with various degrees of confidence about what is taken to be some feature of reality.

The fourth condition is inherent in the previous three: the use of English requires that there be a distinction between *correct and incor-*

*rect uses of words.* The use of English is learned, and learning it involves making mistakes. A mistake would be to use a word in violation of the rules that guide its application. The use of a word in accordance with a rule essentially involves making choices. The choice concerns a decision about what word to use, about what rule should be—tacitly—invoked in different situations. The typical competent user of English has learned to make appropriate decisions. He uses words, by and large, correctly, and he is capable of recognizing incorrect uses.

There will be two arguments offered against solipsism here. The first contends that solipsism is incapable of accounting for the existence of the descriptive use of language. The second convicts solipsism of an incapacity to distinguish between correct and incorrect uses of words. The implication of both arguments is that soilpsism cannot reconcile the existence of language, given the minimum conditions of being a language, with the assumption that reality consists only of a solitary mind and its attributes. Another common point between the arguments is that they face the same difficulty: it seems that they both rest on the extremely questionable verifiability principle. These arguments against solipsism will be telling only if they are shown to be independent of the verifiability principle.

## The first argument: solipsism is incapable of accounting for the descriptive use of language

The existence of the external world is a necessary condition of expressions having a descriptive use. The reason for this is that it is not possible to learn the use of descriptive expressions unless some expression or another is associated with something in the external world. Expressions used for describing the world in any one of the sense modalities presuppose that at least one language user at one point correctly perceived the object to which reference is made. Unless this is supposed, it is not possible to explain how the expression has come to be used to refer consistently to a particular feature of what seems to be the external world. The use of subsequent descriptive expressions can be mastered with reference to those that happen to function as primitive expressions, but such primitive expressions must exist for each of the sense modalities. It follows, therefore, from some expressions having a descriptive use that the external world not only seems to exist, but actually does. To deny this is to make it impossible to explain how language could have a descriptive use, and a consequence of this is the failure of solipsism to account for all facts in the common sense view of the world.

An obvious reply would be to provide alternative accounts of how the descriptive use of language is acquired, and thereby to call into question the alleged necessity of having to associate some expressions with features of reality in order to learn their descriptive use. It is conceivable, for instance, that the skill of using expressions descriptively is not learned but innate or that it is imprinted upon the brain by drugs or surgery.

In reply, it should be remembered that what is involved in the normal descriptive use of expressions is their use in accordance with rules for the achievement of certain purposes. Expressions may be used correctly or incorrectly, depending upon whether the rules are followed or violated.

The crucial question about a person whose skill is supposed to be innate or imprinted is whether he can make a mistake. If he cannot, then he is not really a language user. His performance is more like a reflex act—of the order of an eyeblink or kneejerk—than it is the conscious, deliberate, purposeful act of following a rule. Totally mistake free, innate or imprinted, automatic performances are physiological events that happen to people, not acts that are voluntarily performed to accomplish intended goals. Of course, the use of language could be like this. But if it were, it would be necessary to rethink what we now mean by "the descriptive use of language." Given the present meaning, to which the solipsist must do justice, it is essential that a person should be capable of erring and then of correcting himself in the descriptive use of language.

But what if the innate or imprinted skill has the built-in versimilitude of allowing for the occasional violation of the rules. In that case, however, violations must be both discoverable and be capable of correction. If they were not discoverable, then the achievement of the intended purpose would be frustrated. And if they could not be corrected, then the use of language would be a self-defeating enterprise. The fact is that in the last analysis both the discovery and the correction are possible only by checking the use of the expression against its intended referent. And that is possible only if there existed something external to the mind of the language user.

A solipsist can reply by accepting that the skill involved in the descriptive use of expressions has to be learned and be capable of misuse and by denying that this necessitates the existence of the external world. The descriptive use of expressions, it might be said, is learned with reference to the mental states of the language user, which may be the only existing things.

A forceful statement of this defense of solipsism is made by Stroud.[1] The defense is an attempt to force a wedge between it being a necessary condition of the descriptive use of language that it should be *believed* that true and false descriptions can be distinguished and that the belief should be *true*. The belief in itself, regardless of its truth or falsity, satisfies the condition necessary for descriptive use and is still compatible with solipsism, since the belief may be false. In order to rule out this possibility it is necessary to show that the belief is not just held, but that it is true. That requires showing that the distinction between true and false descriptions can actually be drawn. The solipsist may concede, for instance, that in order to learn the use of color-descriptions some color-expressions must actually be associated with color. This condition, however, can be met by the mere appearance of a color. So the existence of colors is not necessary for learning the use of color-expressions. The world that language describes may be entirely in the mind of the describer.

A successful argument against solipsism requires an additional premise: it is not possible for there to be a descriptive use of language unless it is possible to establish that some descriptions are actually true. This premise, Stroud points out,

> would have to be strong enough to include not only our beliefs about what is the case, but also the possibility of our knowing whether these beliefs are true. . . . But to prove this would be to prove some version of the verification principle.[2]

The objection, then, is that the argument against solipsism presupposes the verifiability principle. If the principle is successful in depicting the relation between language and reality, then solipsism is directly refuted and no additional argument is needed. If the principle fails, then the refutation of solipsism—having the principle as a premise—fails with it.

The reply will be postponed until the consideration of the second argument against solipsism which encounters the same difficulty.

# The second argument: solipsism is incapable of distinguishing between correct and incorrect uses

The argument is that if solipsism were correct, then at least one condition of the existence of language could not be fulfilled and so solipsism could not explain part of what it sets out to explain. The solipsist's world may be described as self-created. All his experiences, mental states, dispositions, everything that exists, is supposedly produced by the one mind. In an extended sense, the solipsist's world is entirely imaginary, for it is the product of the solipsist's mind. In a world like this it is impossible to distinguish between the correct use and what only seems to be such. As a result, incorrect use may seem to be correct, and consequently correct and incorrect uses cannot be distinguished.

Why can there be no distinction for the solipsist between uses that seem correct and uses that are correct? As a first approximation, it might be said that if everything is imaginary, then one reference to these imaginary things is as correct, faithful, or true as any other. In an entirely imaginary world, to be is to seem to be, and there is nothing to which a reference can be true. What seems correct is correct.

But this is a mistake. There is something to which references can be true, namely, the mental states to which, according to solipsism, references are bound to be made. Up to now no reason has been given why a solitary mind could not distinguish between using a word in accordance with a rule to refer to a mental state and only seeming to do so. After all, even a solitary mind can distinguish between different mental states. One mental state may seem like a veridical perceptual experience and another may seem like dreaming. The solipsist can choose to believe one and disbelieve the other. It might be argued therefore, in defense of solipsism, that the distinction between correct and incorrect uses can be drawn on the basis of the different ways in which mental states appear to the solitary mind.

The objection to solipsism can now be sharpened. The reason why there could not be a distinction between correct and seemingly correct use is that there could not be a distinction between a mental state being of a certain sort and it only seeming to be of that sort. Consequently, there could not be a distinction between believing truly and believing falsely that a mental state is of a certain sort. If there existed only a solitary mind, then what seemed to it to be so would be indistinguishable from what in fact was so, for the only basis upon which it could make a judgment is how things seemed to itself to be. And since what seems to be so need not be so, it becomes impossible to distinguish between correct and incorrect uses.

Defenders of solipsism can reply by attacking an assumption implicit in the argument. The argument, it might be said, foists on solipsism the alleged necessity of independent checking. It is assumed that unless independent checking were possible, correct and seemingly correct uses could not be distinguished. Since in a solipsistic world there are no checks independent of mental states, for *ex hypothesi,* only mental states exist, solipsism supposedly fails. There are at least three ways in which solipsists may try to accommodate the problem of independent checking.

The first is to argue that independent checking is possible for a solitary mind because one mental state can be used to check the correctness of the identification of another. For example, if a mental state is identified as of a certain kind, then the possibility of independent checking may rest on memory. The reason for identifying the mental state as of that kind is not just that it seems like that kind, but also that the mind remembers it as such.

This way of saving solipsism fails. Memory can be used as an independent check only if it is possible to distinguish between remembering correctly and only seeming to do so. If the distinction cannot be drawn, then there is no way of telling the difference between remembering and misremembering. For memory to be usable as an independent check, there would have to be an independent check of memory as well. Given the solipsistic assumptions, however, there cannot be a check independent of mental states. The dilemma solipsism faces is this: either there are independent checks of the identification of mental states or not. In the first case, mental states cannot be the only existing things and so solipsism fails. In the second case, correct and incorrect uses cannot be distinguished and so solipsism fails again.

The second attempt to rescue solipsism tries to minimize the force of this dilemma. The solipsist may accept that independent checking of mental states is impossible and go on to argue that the same objection holds of nonsolipsistic theories. The constant demand for independent checking leads to infinite regress. There must be a point, the solipsist would argue, beyond which it becomes unreasonable to ask for additional independent checks. And this point may well be the identification of a mental state as being of a certain kind. It is arbitrary and question-begging to restrict independent checks to checks independent of mental states. Even if they were so restricted the threat of infinite regress would not be avoided. So the dilemma, according to the solipsist, is based on an unreasonable interpretation of independent checking.

But what is it then to have independent checks? The checks in question, it should be remembered, are checks of following a rule. They are supposed to determine whether or not a person's impression that he is following a rule is correct. The check is independent if its application does not rest upon the rule that the person has an impression of following.

The solipsist is quite right in pointing out that if one were to accept only those independent checks that have been independently checked, infinite regress would follow. The solipsist is also correct in arguing that there must come a point beyond which demand for further checking is unreasonable. His mistake is to suppose that this state of affairs is sufficient to establish an analogy between independent checking in a solipsistic world and in a world which is roughly as common sense depicts it. The crucial difference is that in a solipsistic world independent checks are logically impossible, while in a common sense world they are logically possible. If only a solitary mind existed, it would be logically impossible to have an independent check of the identification of any mental state, because only mental states are supposed to exist. If the common sense view was supposed to be correct, then independent checking would be possible, because the identification of mental states could be checked with reference to the physiological and both verbal and nonverbal behavioral correlates of mental states.

The third objection against the refutation of solipsism is directed at the alleged necessity of independent checking. Why, it might be said, could not a solitary mind, or for that matter anybody, proceed on the assumption that what upon careful and painstaking examination seems correct is correct? The assumption that there is something more needed rests on the belief that the respectability of an assertion depends, in part, on the possibility of testing it. This belief, however, is simply the verifiability principle in yet another cloak, so the defense of solipsism against both the first and the second argument rests upon the claim that critics appeal to the verifiability principle. The next step, therefore, is to examine that claim.


## Does the refutation of solipsism depend on the verifiability principle?

The difficulty is that if the refutation depends on the verifiability principle, then it inherits the very great problems that this principle faces. If, on the other hand, the refutation is independent of the principle, then the question arises of upon what other ground can the requirement of independent checking be defended and how can the possibility be excluded that the descriptive use of language is learned with reference to imaginary cases.

The difficulty can be handled in at least two ways. One is to attempt to defend the verifiability principle. This approach, however, will be presumed to have failed. For even though assiduous and highly sophisticated attempts have been made, there exists no satisfactory formulation of the principle. It seems to be impossible to construct a logically tight, neither too inclusive nor too exclusive, criterion for the cognitive meaning of empirical statements. The epitaph for the verifiability principle has been written—fittingly—by Hempel: "I have serious doubts as to the possibility of formulating a satisfactory general criterion for statements with empirical import." [3] The problem is compounded by Popper's demonstration that "arch-metaphysical" assertions about God turn out to be meaningful on Carnap's meaning criterion. [4]

A more promising way is to find something better than the verifiability principle to which appeal can be made. The verifiability principle attempts to explain the relation between the descriptive use of language and reality in terms of meaningfulness. The present approach is to explain that relation in terms of rationality.

The appeal to rationality is based on the assumption that the descriptive use of language is normally a problem-solving activity. The purpose of this use of language is to identify and say something about what is taken to be some part of the external world. The reason why this goal is normally pursued is the belief that in this way the initial problem can be solved. Problems can be solved through the use of language only if language is a suitable instrument. The suitability of language for describing what is taken to be the external world depends upon the possibility of describing some feature of the external world successfully. The test of successful description is that the problem that prompted the use of language becomes more tractable as a result of its use. If there were no evidence for the success of the activity, then there would be no way of telling whether the problem has been solved. Since the purpose of using language was to solve the problem, its use, then, would prove to be quite futile. So the use of language is rational only if some descriptions are at least sometimes successful.

The descriptive use of language is a means towards problem-solving, and its being a means requires that true and false descriptions be distinguishable. The reason for accepting the distinction is not the questionable verifiability principle, as Stroud has it, but the following consideration. The possibility of the distinction between true and false descriptions explains what otherwise could not be explained, namely, how it is possible to do what we seem to be doing all the time: solving problems by the use of language.

The direct consequence of the possibility of the distinction is that descriptions must be criticizable. For the purpose of the distinction is to help solve a problem. This is accomplished if the description succeeds in being true. A true description, however, is incompatible with some states of affairs, namely, with the truth of other conflicting descriptions, and those other descriptions are potential criticisms of the one in question.

The reason for the failure of solipsism is that descriptions made in circumstances required by solipsism are uncriticizable. In the world of the solipsist what seems to be the case is indistinguishable from what is the case. Since what seems to be the case may not be, true and false descriptions cannot be distinguished. Solipsism starts off with the assumption that there is no rational way of choosing between the belief that the descriptive use of language refers to the external world and the belief that it refers to the mental states of the language user. The fatal objection to solipsism is that one of the facts that it must explain, namely, that language has a descriptive use, can not be explained unless solipsism is mistaken. For only if true and false descriptions can be distinguished can there be a descriptive use, and the distinction can be drawn only if there is a way of criticizing some descriptions. But the only way of criticizing some descriptions is with reference to the external world, where the distinction between what is the case and what seems to be the case can be drawn. And that is possible only if solipsism is mistaken.

## An analogy

An analogy will help to bring out in another way what is wrong with solipsism. The use of language is in some ways very much like playing chess. As there are words and rules in language, so there are pieces and rules in chess. As language is normally used for a purpose, so playing chess is normally for a purpose. As words in a language can be used correctly and incorrectly, so pieces in chess can be moved correctly and incorrectly. But it is not ordinary chess that supplies the analogy. There are some experts who can play chess blindfolded. What this comes to is that an expert can play chess in his head without having to look at the pieces. Now such an expert can play chess with ordinary players who need a chessboard, he can also play with another expert, and they can both play blindfolded. The situation needed, however, is when an expert plays chess by himself without a board and pieces. He plays both sides himself and does it in his head without recourse to the vulgarity of a tangible chessboard.

There is, of course, no reason why an expert could not do this. He could have trained himself to speculate about possible moves so far ahead that he does not need to go through the routine handling of the pieces. However, he has trained himself by extrapolating from actual situations involving an actual chessboard. He comes to be able to discard the board and the pieces, because he no longer needs them, even though he needed them when he was a novice. But now imagine an expert who was not trained by the use of a chess set—perhaps he is congenitally blind, paralyzed, and very good at abstract thinking. He is taught the rules, the names of the pieces, and he practices blindfolded with actual opponents who may also play blindfolded.

What is needed, however, to have an analogy with the solipsist's view of the use of language is to suppose that the congenitally blind chess expert was never taught chess and has never practiced with anybody else. He himself made up for himself the game with its rules, pieces, and purpose. The solipsist's view of language is like this man's view of chess. But just as this man could not play chess, so the solipsist could not use language.

The chess expert knows that some moves are correct, in accordance with the rules, and some others are not, just as the solipsist knows that some uses to which words are put are correct, in accordance with the rules, and some others are not. The chess expert, of course, will make only those moves that seem correct to him, just as the solipsistic language user will use words only in ways that seem correct to him. However, especially at the time when the chess player is just a novice at the game, a move that seems correct to him may not be correct. Similarly, the solipsist may seem to himself to be using a word in accordance with the rules, but his use of words may in fact be incorrect, especially when he is just acquiring the language. Now unless on these occasions there is a way of correcting the incorrect move, or the incorrect use of a word, the novice chess player or a language user will not and cannot become a chess player or a language user. For playing chess or using language is performing in accordance with rules. But neither the chess player nor the solipsist can ever correct the mistakes they inevitably make when they are endeavoring to acquire their respective skills, because they cannot know when they have made a mistake. They cannot know whether or not they are following the rules that they made up for themselves. Since the reason for following the rules is to achieve certain purposes, they also cannot achieve the purpose for which the game was invented and the language was designed.

Playing chess or using language has a point only if behaving in these ways is instrumental in realizing the purpose for which the behavior was intended. Whatever purpose a language user has in mind, it can be achieved by the use of language only if he is using it in accordance with rules. But the solipsistic language user could not know whether or not his use was in accordance with the rules, and so he could not have a reasonable expectation that he would achieve the intended purpose. The purpose can be achieved only if violations of the rules can be discovered, only if there is an independent check of the use that seems correct. Given the assumptions of solipsism, there could not be an independent check, and so the solipsist's use of language could not help him to realize his goals. A solipsist would not use language if he wanted to achieve something, because if his assumptions were correct, there would be no reason for using it.

# 12 Metaphysics, rationality, and vision

*"One of the broadest and surest generalizations that anthropologists can make about human beings is that no society is healthy or creative or strong unless that society has a set of common values that give meaning and purpose to group life, that can be symbolically expressed, that fit with the situation of the time as well as being linked to the historical past, and that do not outrage men's reason and at the same time appeal to their emotions."* —Clyde Kluckhohn, *"Culture and Behaviour"*

## Metaphysics and scepticism

The refutation of solipsistic scepticism does not put the sceptic completely out of commission. He can retreat to the position that while there are rational grounds for the belief *that* there is an external world, there is no way of rationally deciding between various accounts of *what* the external world is. Such world views as provided by science, mysticism, Christianity, materialism, idealism, Marxism, phenomenalism are competing interpretations of what there is. They can be thought of as solving a problem, namely, the provision of an intelligible pattern for understanding the nature of reality, and they can be made to be logically consistent and conceptually coherent. But, it may be argued, they fail to be rational because the explanations offered by these metaphysical theories are equally vacuous or equally all-inclusive and one logically tight metaphysical theory is no better than any other. Moreover, metaphysical theories are uncriticizable, for what evidence could there be for or against a view that is supposed to be an interpretation based on all evidence?

The aim of metaphysics is to provide a coherent and comprehensive way of thinking about what there is. A successful metaphysical theory will provide a rational answer to the perennial question of what reality is like and of what our place is in it. The possession of this answer will make it possible to understand the significance, is any, of one's life, while the lack of an answer may render it chaotic, unfocused, arbitrary. Of course, it is possible to supply nonrational or even irrational accounts of what there is, and such accounts may give direction to one's life. But only a rational account makes it possible not to live at odds with the world, for only a rational account can succeed in ascertaining what there is. The point of metaphysical scepticism is the denial that a rational metaphysical theory is possible. The implication of this denial is that any attempt to understand the scheme of things is doomed to failure because reason cannot go beyond the trivial guarantee that something, whatever it is, exists outside of one's mind. Man may and does delude himself by dreaming up countless ingenious theories of the beyond. But whatever guise they come in, be it metaphysics, art, religion, mysticism, or science, they are one and all arbitrary. For they rest upon unsupported visions whose only warrant is their intensity and they make *a priori* assumptions certified neither by logic nor by experience.

The refutation of metaphysical scepticism requires a rational defense of both the visionary and the *a priori* components of metaphysics. The visionary aspect can be brought under rational control if it is possible to show that the merits of various visions can be argued. This task will be undertaken in the present chapter. The rationality of the *a priori* element will be discussed in the next one. These two chapters aim to demonstrate how metaphysical theories can conform to the standards of explanatory power and criticizability and, therefore, how they can be rational.

Ours is not a metaphysical age and this makes it necessary to emphasize what has appeared obvious in the past: metaphysics is one of the formative influences upon mankind. Metaphysics exerts its influence not directly, but through its effects upon religion, science, politics, morality, and art. Christianity, for better or worse, has been a major force in history and the thought of Plato, Aristotle, Augustine, and Aquinas left an indelible mark upon Christianity. Communism derives its theoretical backing from that errant Hegelian: Marx. Locke and Mill exercised a profound influence upon the development of liberal democracy. Aristotle, Bacon, and Descartes mapped out the course science followed for generations after them. Hume, the Encyclopedists, and positivists dealt a blow to religion and as a result it affects our lives less and less. Kierkegaard, Nietzsche, and Schopenhauer revived the antiacademic, antirationalistic intellectual tradition that through existentialism and other channels has had an important influence on the contemporary intellectual climate. Dewey's ideas changed the education and consequently the mores of several generations of Americans. History without the history of ideas would be impossible. But the history of ideas is, to a very large extent, the history of the way in which various metaphysical views have shaped the beliefs and actions of people.

It is one thing to acknowledge the importance of metaphysics and quite another to applaud it. In fact, many philosophers, and not just sceptics, abhor it. Metaphysics is frequently regarded as harmful, because it is suspected of being rationally indefensible. Metaphysical theories, on this view, are cosmic superstitions, "haunted universe doctrines," speculations that by their very nature lead to a cloud-cuckoo land where evidence can no longer be had. Can metaphysics be defended against these charges?

## Metaphysical vision

A definition of metaphysics at this point may be too broad, including within its scope all that has been called metaphysics, or too narrow, excluding enterprises that some have held to be metaphysical, but since this is a matter of reasoned disagreement, the question is not properly answered by legislation.

Some measure of agreement could be obtained by citing historical instances. Few would disagree that Plato's theory of universals, Spinoza's pantheism, Descartes' dualism, Hegel's biography of the absolute, and Russell's neutral monism are metaphysical theories. But this will not go very far, for although nobody can now pretend not to know what kinds of things are metaphysical theories, it is still not known what makes them that kind. There is the beginning of a list, but there is no rule prescribing how to add to it over and above a few obvious cases. Does Freud's psychoanalytic theory belong? What about Kierkegaard on man and God? Should logical positivism be added? What should be done with theology, the theory of evolution, the indeterminacy principle; are proposals for utopias metaphysical?

The best way is to find general characteristics that metaphysical theories have and to protect oneself against exceptions by a *ceteris paribus* clause. The general description will, of course, have to be made more and more specific to escape triviality; this will be accomplished by showing the respects in which metaphysical theories differ from other things.

Metaphysical theories are attempts to understand reality. Plato, Leibniz, Spinoza, and Hegel offer systems in terms of which sense can be made out of previously uninterpreted or differently interpreted phenomena. A metaphysical theory provides a possible way of explaining the scheme of things—it tells us how things really are.

Lofty as this aim is, it is not very informative to remark upon it, since there hardly is a theory of which it is not true that it is an attempt to understand reality. The difference between metaphysical and other theories starts to emerge if it is noticed that metaphysical theories are extremely general as a rule, while other theories interpret only some more or less limited segment of reality.

But this will not do. There are some all-embracing non-metaphysical theories. It is not easy to find something more general than recent cosmological theories about the allegedly expanding universe, for instance, or to duplicate the comprehensiveness of mystical apperceptions of the essential oneness and goodness of everything. But the all-inclusiveness of some aesthetic, scientific, mystical, or moral views does not necessarily make them metaphysical. So while it is true that metaphysical theories usually aim at the presentation of a general and comprehensive view of reality, it is also true that this feature does not distinguish metaphysical and nonmetaphysical theories.

Metaphysical theories occupy, then, a middle position between very general scientific theories and mystical, moral, or aesthetic visions. Metaphysics shares with art, mysticism, and poetry the feature of being visionary. A good initial characterization of this aspect is offered by Waismann in a slightly different context:

> When I say "vision" I mean it: I do not want to romanticize . . . it is the piercing of that dead crust of tradition and convention, the breaking of those fetters which bind us to inherited preconceptions, so as to

attain a new and broader way of looking at things. . . . from Plato to Moore and Wittgenstein every great philosopher was led by a sense of vision: without it no one could have given a new direction to human thought. . . . What is decisive is a new way of seeing and, what goes with it, the will to transform the whole intellectual scene.[1]

Metaphysics, then, is visionary, but it is also more. As mystical or aesthetic visions are permeated by passion and a sense of awe or beauty, so metaphysical theories are permeated by argument. The mystical and artistic products of vision are, as it were, their own warrant. Metaphysical theories stand in need of and are always meant to have rational support. Metaphysical visions shake our shackles, but they are never revolts against rational restraint in general, only against specific categorial confinements.

Metaphysical visions are revolutionary. They are implicit rejections of the traditional ways of thinking about the world. The rejection stems from difficulties with the tradition and from the availability of a new, better, or at any rate different, alternative. Revolutions are followed by periods of consolidation during which the new vision acquires currency, its details are worked out, it is systematized. Eventually, the erstwhile revolution becomes the orthodoxy; what began as individual vision ends up as the commonly accepted world view of an intellectual epoch.[2]

Imagination has a major role in metaphysical vision. There are at least three different but related areas of human experience that are labelled imaginative. The first is in which imagination is intimately connected with memory. The conjuring up of images is the attempt to see with the mind's eye what is no longer in front of the actual eyes. The task of imagination, in this respect, is to reproduce what happened in the past. In its second role, imagination is closely related to error. If a person is described as imagining that something is so, it is frequently implied that he is deceived; he takes as real what is not. The third role of imagination has to do with invention, creativity, ingenuity. One who is imaginative in this sense goes beyond the reproductive aspect and produces something new. These three aspects or roles are, of course, connected. For the present purposes, however, it is the third role of imagination that is important.

Metaphysical vision results when creative imagination is applied to the task of making sense out of reality. The product of this use of creative imagination is the new way of thinking that Waismann regards as at least one essential function of metaphysics. A metaphysical theory is a particular vision surrounded by arguments whose aim it is to show that reality can be understood in terms of the theory. Vision without argument is mysticism, poetry, or art. A metaphysical theory without vision is a logical skeleton: bare, cold, awaiting to be enlivened and rendered vulnerable to critical appraisal. But it is necessary to be more concrete; how does having a vision show? What difference does its possession make?

Consider the lives of a Christian and an atheist. Observation of their behavior may not make it possible to identify them, because behavior is not always hallmarked as Christian or atheistic. Indeed, apart from a direct avowal of their convictions, it may not be possible to find any behavioral grounds upon which to judge their religious leanings. The difference between them does not come from what they do, but from how they think and feel about what they do: their inner lives differ. The Christian regards his life as a preamble to eternity which he hopes to spend in the proximity of God. His moral convictions receive their ultimate sanction from a transcendental authority. He fears, trusts, loves God and recognizes His universal jurisdiction. The feelings of the atheist are not invested in any transcendental authority; he believes that his present life is the only one he has. His moral convictions may be determined by his judgment about what is likely to be beneficial for mankind. The Christian regards humanity, good and evil, the past, present, and the future of man as but the observable, sometimes mysterious, sometimes understandable, unfolding of a divine plan. For the atheist there is no plan; there is only choice and chance, and there is no design behind the obstacle race that mankind runs.

Part of the difference between these two men lies in their feelings about their lot, their relation to the universe, the kind of place they take the universe to be. These are metaphysical sentiments. Such sentiments constitute a species of feeling one of whose chief characteristics is prolonged endurance through time; they are the emotive component of such attitudes as pessimism or optimism, stoicism or hedonism, anxiety or trust, awe or irony. Another main feature of metaphysical sentiments is that the object toward which they are directed is the universe. The feelings are, thus, quite general in their direction. When they are expressed with reference to a particular object, the selection of the object depends on it being perceived as an instance of something far more general. Anxiety, pessimism, or awe are metaphysical sentiments only if it is the scheme of things, and not particular objects, that makes one anxious, pessimistic, or awestruck. Metaphysical sentiments frequently prompt and almost invariably color one's attitudes toward reality and the perception of one's relation to it. It is partly in terms of such sentiments that one answers what Kant presented as one of the three main questions of philosophy: for what may I hope?

The metaphysical theories of the Stoics and Locke, of Spinoza and John Stuart Mill, of Aquinas and Hobbes, to offer some obvious contrasts, differ not only because they assign different importance and truth-value to the same propositions, but also because to accept one rather than another metaphysical theory is to feel one rather than another way about reality and man's place in it. This is the reason why understanding a metaphysical theory is an intellectual matter, while accepting it is to such a great extent also an emotional issue. This explains why we can appreciate, say, the austerity and nobility of Spinoza's metaphysics, while recognizing that it does not survive objections. It explains also why a Christian may refuse to abandon his beliefs even though he accepts the inadequacy of the arguments supporting his position. And it is why a person might say that the arguments for materialism are strong, but he would not like materialism to be true. The simple fact is that we hope for the success and correctness of some metaphysical theories and fear and recoil from the implications of others.

Philosophers, however, are disposed not to take official cognizance of this commonplace. Like the rope in the hanged man's house, metaphysical sentiments are rarely mentioned in philosophical arguments. Possibly what underlies this widespread aversion is the suspicion that these feelings are no more than large-scale prejudices. Intellectual integrity requires that one be on guard against what he wishes to be true and to pursue arguments even if they lead to deplorable conclusions. However, in striving to avoid wishful thinking, all too many philosophers have come to ignore an important aspect of metaphysics. It will be said in reply that metaphysical sentiments ought to be ignored. Metaphysics, after all, purports to be a rational enterprise, it aims to tell the truth, and metaphysical sentiments are neither true nor false.

Feelings, metaphysical or other, have indeed no truth-value, but they may still be appropriate or inappropriate. Furthermore, a person may be concerned with rationally appraising the appropriateness of his feelings, and he may be prepared to curtail or inhibit them if they are judged to be inappropriate.

Consider, for instance, an atheist who happens also to be a materialist. Suppose that over a period of time he meets one misfortune after another through no fault of his own. People he loves die, he is seriously injured in an accident that he was not responsible for causing, lightning destroys his house, he is falsely and unjustly accused of a crime, and so on. He may well develop a feeling of resentment against the scheme of things. His previous feeling of nature's neutrality turns into anger mixed with fear; he resents the unfairness of it all. These feelings, of course, are inappropriate—given that he is a materialist. Nature cannot be both impersonal and unfair, nonsentient and a proper object of anger and resentment. One can understand how he came to feel in these ways, but one must recognize that it is unreasonable both to have these feelings and to accept materialism. Given materialism, his feelings convict him of the Monte Carlo fallacy writ large. Recognition that his feelings are inappropriate will not make the feelings cease, but it may be the first step toward controlling them.

It is one thing to say that metaphysical sentiments may or may not be appropriate and quite another to give an account of how their appropriateness is to be rationally appraised. Here is a suggestion: the rational appraisal of metaphysical sentiments depends upon the correctness of the metaphysical theory to which the owner of the sentiments is committed and in terms of which the sentiments are expressible. So the judgment of appropriateness is shifted from feelings to theories. Theories, presumably, can be evaluated upon rational grounds, and so perhaps can be those feelings that are constitutive of the theory. If it is a reasonable belief that reality is impersonal, morally neutral, devoid of design, then resenting what happens is inappropriate. If it is reasonable to believe in the God of the Bible, then it is proper to stand in awe of Him.

The rational appraisal of metaphysical sentiments may proceed in terms of two crucial questions: first, what would the world have to be like for this metaphysical sentiment to be appropriate? and second, is there good reason for thinking that the world is like that?

The consideration of the first question leads back to vision and creative imagination. For in the light of the preceding remarks about metaphysical sentiments it becomes possible to understand one of the mainsprings of the exercise of vision. The impetus behind the individual discovery and the subsequent general acceptance of a vision embodied in a metaphysical theory is the attempt to reconcile one's feelings with the traditional interpretation of reality that one has accepted. For these not infrequently conflict, and the conflict is a disturbing, emotionally bothersome, occurrence. The materialist whose life is beset by ill-luck, the Christian who encounters genuine evil, the moral agent who becomes impressed by the inexorability of the laws of nature are ripe for metaphysics. In each case the probably unreflective, traditionally received metaphysical belief—in materialism, in the existence of God, in human freedom—exerts a force in one direction, while feelings—resentment, abhorrence, helplessness in the face of scientific dicta—exert a counterforce. It is not easy to ignore such conflicts, once they are perceived, for one's most fundamental convictions are being challenged. Part of the function of metaphysical vision is to reconcile these conflicts. A vision expresses a picture in which the world is so interpreted that one's metaphysical sentiments are appropriate to it. A vision is usually prompted by a conflict between feelings, generated by one's perception of the world, and the hitherto unquestioned tradition, and it aims at a conflict-free coherent picture of reality.

It is worthwhile to reflect upon the connection between having such a picture of reality and happiness. Intelligence, maturity, self-interest require that in day-to-day life the world should not be treated in terms of how one fears or wishes it to be, but in terms of how one believes it to be. We need to be objective and we must not allow ourselves to react on the basis of anxiety, desire, fantasy, hope, and the like. But after having acted reasonably, the feelings remain. Not to have the feelings is to be an automaton; to have the feelings, but never to express them is to be doomed to frustration. Both alternatives deprive men of happiness. Unless a way is found to express these feelings one cannot be happy. The acceptance of a metaphysical vision, reconciling some of these feelings with beliefs about the nature of the world, affords a way of expression. Poetry and art provide other channels. But metaphysical theories do not just provide objects upon which accumulated feelings can be vented, they also provide rational sanction for some feelings and a ground for criticizing others; they are the touchstones of the appropriateness of metaphysical sentiments. And in being this, they also provide ideals that man can live by. The possession of an attainable ideal together with the means and the possibility of approximating it, an ideal that has, in addition, rational warrant, is surely not far removed from the proximity of happiness.[3]

## The rationality of metaphysical vision

But now we must pass from description to defense and face the second question posed above—a question that many would regard as a devastating objection against much of what has been said up to this point. It might be granted that the appropriateness of metaphysical sentiments can be judged in terms of a coherent vision of the nature of reality, but how is the rationality of that vision to be judged? What is the difference between vision and fantasy? One can admit that it is emotionally satisfying to accept a metaphysical theory and that this might even make a contribution to the happiness of its adherents, but do we, can we, have *reasons* for believing that reality corresponds to a particular metaphysical theory?

These questions can be sharpened by considering them in terms of the distinction between discovery and rational defense. The point of the distinction is to keep apart the nonrational factors that influence a man in his discovery of a theory and the rational considerations by which the theory is judged. It should be acknowledged that psychological and sociological causes influence the way a man thinks and that prejudice, luck, coincidence play roles in the process of discovery. But while these factors and others may operate in the discovery of a theory, none of them is relevant to its rationality. The rationality of a theory depends upon its conformity to standards of rationality, and that is totally independent of what anybody thinks or feels. Of course a man, may be led to err because his judgment is colored by nonrational considerations; he might mistakenly regard a theory as rational or irrational when it is not. This possibility, however, still has no bearing on the rationality of the theory—it merely reflects adversely upon the person who is led astray by such irrelevancies.

In the light of this distinction, the discussion up to now can be characterized as belonging to the context of discovery. Metaphysical sentiments, vision, imagination may indeed play a role in the discovery and formulation of metaphysical theories, but they are irrelevant to the process of rationally appraising such theories.

Should it be concluded then that metaphysical theories cannot be rationally judged? This might be an attractive suggestion, for one could agree that metaphysical sentiments, vision, the exercise of creative imagination are necessary for human happiness, but then go on to deny that these activities should be accompanied by rational pretensions. Metaphysics, then, could be thought of as one of those luxurious artifices that accrue from having escaped the struggle for survival. Metaphysics could take its place beside art and poetry, and that is not such bad company. However, part of the present purpose is to resist this conclusion by arguing for the rationality of at least some metaphysical theories.

There are two ways in which this argument might proceed. One way might be a concern with the rationality of the *acceptance* of a metaphysical theory. The other might be concerned with the rationality of the *proposal* of a metaphysical theory. The idea underlying the first procedure is that while metaphysical theories are *a priori* and consequently untestable, they give rise to testable empirical theories. Thus it is possible to give reasons for the acceptance of a metaphysical theory by comparing the success and failure of empirical theories suggested by it with the success and failure of those suggested by its rivals. This approach will be explored in the next chapter.

The possibility that will be argued for here is that there are rational considerations guiding the *proposal* of metaphysical theories as well. If this can be shown to be true, it will have considerable importance. If it is possible to eliminate some metaphysical theories prior to the slow and indecisive process of awaiting the outcome of empirical theories suggested by them, then many philosophical problems can be solved. Examining this possibility, of course, is just another way of tackling the question posed previously: how do we decide between conflicting metaphysical visions?

The difficulty that has to be overcome is that the field of reasons for proposing metaphysical theories seems to be preempted. On the one hand, there are plenty of nonrational considerations that enter into the proposal of a theory—considerations that have been relegated to the context of discovery. On the other hand, even those who are willing to admit that there may be reasons for metaphysical theories tend to regard them as reasons for accepting and not for proposing a metaphysical theory. Thus regardless of whether or not the distinction between discovery and rational defense is acceptable, it seems that there are nonrational factors guiding the proposal and rational factors guiding the acceptance of metaphysical theory. Is it not the case that what makes the proposal of a theory reasonable is that the theory might prove to be acceptable?

There are two considerations that dispose one to search out reasons for proposing as opposed to reasons for accepting theories. The first is that not infrequently a theory is proposed, it is judged to be reasonable, and upon examination turns out to be unacceptable. Since reasonable proposals may turn out to be unacceptable, there must be reasons for proposing that are not reasons for accepting a theory.

The second consideration is that if there are no acceptable explanations leading to the resolution of a metaphysical conflict, then practically any theory proposed to resolve the conflict could be judged to be as good or as bad as any other. Suppose, for instance, that there is hard evidence for the occurrence of telepathy. This requires some sort of explanation. The possibility of nonphysical communication or the existence of as yet undiscovered powers of the brain are possible explanations. But of course there are others. Telepathy may be attributed to playful angels relaying information; or it may be accounted for by supposing that human beings draw information from a cosmic information-bank and telepathy is due to an error whereby the same information is given to two customers at the same time. The last two theories are unreasonable, the first two are not. But how could such judgments be made if there were no reasons for proposing theories that are not also reasons for accepting them? *Ex hypothesi* there are no reasons now for the acceptance of any one of the four theories, yet some of these proposals are more reasonable than others.

If it is accepted that there may be reasons for proposing a theory that are not also reasons for accepting it, there still remains the crucial question of what these reasons are. The proposal of a metaphysical theory is the proposal of an explanation. The explanation is prompted by a conflict and it is composed of metaphysical sentiments, vision, and arguments. The purpose of the explanation is to provide a way of understanding reality that avoids, dissolves, or minimizes the conflict and is, at the same time, logically consistent, conceptually coherent, and criticizable. It follows from the nature of the case that the kind of explanation that metaphysical theories initially offer always breaks new ground. For what the conflict has shown is that the traditional way of looking at things is inadequate—this, to a large extent, is the reason why metaphysical conflicts are so troubling. How is the rationality of breaking new ground to be judged, if not by testing the adequacy of the new explanation?

If we consider again the four options for explaining the postulated occurrence of telepathy, we judge the first two explanations as being serious contenders and the last two as not. What, if anything, is behind this intuitive judgment?

One suggestion is that Occam's razor renders the first two options preferable. It is simpler to suppose that human beings have a mind capable of nonphysical communication or that the brain has hitherto undiscovered powers than to postulate the existence of playful angels or of a cosmic information-bank. Simplicity requires that one's theory should have as great an observational content as possible. Unobserved entities and processes need, of course, to be postulated, but it is better to have less than more of the observationally uncertifiable. Undiscovered mental activities or brain processes are unobservable, but they are linked to observation, which information-relaying angels and cosmic information-banks are not.

As it stands, this answer will not do. Parsimony is no doubt an extremely important heuristic device in science, but metaphysics is not science. If Occam's razor were an acceptable metaphysical argument, then one could resolve the disputes between monism and pluralism, materialism and dualism, monotheism and polytheism without having to look at arguments. The general difficulty is that Occam's razor is acceptable in metaphysics only if it is supplemented with the claim that reality is simple. And this claim would have to postulate that reality is such that always the metaphysical theory will be most reasonable whose vision is accompanied by the greatest observational content. But this claim is itself a metaphysical theory and it has to be supported without begging the question. It does not sufficiently justify the intuitive rejection of angels and the information-bank to say that their existence would complicate matters.

What underlies the appeal to simplicity as well as the intuitive preference for some proposals over others can be brought out by reflecting on the context in which metaphysical conflicts occur. The conflict arises, because the existing metaphysical outlook is no longer capable of reconciling the conclusions presented by the empirical theories the metaphysical outlook prompted with the vision of reality that the outlook embodies. The proposal, whose rationality needs to be appraised, offers a possible way of removing the conflict by extending one of the available metaphysical options so that it can accommodate empirical evidence with as little alteration as possible. The thrust behind the proposed explanation is the need to remove the conflict; the limitation upon it is that it can count as an explanation only if it does not depart from the traditional vision too radically, for something counts as an explanation if it tells us how an apparent anomaly can be reconciled with the existing outlook.

Consider, for instance, mechanistic determinism. It is committed to the existence of laws to account for the occurrence of every event, and it is committed also to the view that science is the best method for discovering these laws. For a long time it was part of mechanistic determinism that the sought-for laws were causal. Quantum mechanics cast serious doubt on the possibility of finding causal laws to account for the behavior of all particulars in its domain. Mechanistic determinism was thus correspondingly extended so as to include statistical as well as causal laws. The vision has been retained. Laws are still believed to exist behind every event, but since the laws are statistical, they have less effect on individuals. In this manner mechanistic determinism is extended, by an extension of the category of law, to account for empirical evidence.

But not all extensions of metaphysical theories are reasonable. Determinism can accommodate statistical laws, but its extension to include a class of chance events would amount to the abandonment of the original vision.

It may not be possible to find a clear-cut rule to determine how far a theory can be stretched before it loses its original form, but that does not mean that the situation is hopeless. The rule that does emerge is that a proposal to extend a metaphysical theory is reasonable if the extension is compatible with the vision the theory expresses. The greater the extension, the more it departs from the vision and the less reasonable the proposed extension is. This rule is insufficiently precise to be a logical principle. It is comparable to a principle in common law that rests on precedent. It is like the principle that unless there is reason to the contrary a man is taken to intend the immediate consequences of his actions. The rule cannot be applied mechanically, but it may be applied reflectively. Its successful application requires judgment shaped by a thorough understanding of the metaphysical theory.

Telepathy, to return to the hypothetical case, presents a challenge both to dualism and to materialism. Both metaphysical theories could be extended so as to take account of telepathic communication. Dualism would have to postulate the possibility of minds communicating without the mediation of bodies and materialism would have to assume the existence of undiscovered physical powers of the brain. There is, of course, no factual warrant for these extensions. The point, however, is that if telepathy occurs, these metaphysical theories can accommodate it without doing violence to their original vision. The dualistic vision of man as partly spiritual and partly material would not suffer if it turned out that minds did not need bodies to communicate. But the existence of angels, let alone playful ones, has no role in dualism. Not that dualism rejects their possible existence, rather there is no reason for supposing that they exist. The occurrence of telepathy does not present such a reason, since it could be accounted for by an extension of dualism that is in conformity with the original vision. The same is true of materialism. Materialism envisions man as being totally part of nature. This vision is not undermined if man turns out to have undiscovered physical powers. But cosmic information-banks are not warranted by anything in materialism. The leap from the original vision to the existence of information-banks is unnecessary; there is no connecting link between the vision and the new extension.

A metaphysical theory, it has been argued, is an answer to the question: what would reality have to be like for a particular metaphysical sentiment to be appropriate? Once the answer is given, its rationality needs to be judged. In the end, a judgment about the acceptibility of the theory must be rendered on the basis of whether the theory survives criticism. But this end, in the case of metaphysical theories, is not easily reached. The evidence presented by empirical theories is seldom decisive. Metaphysical theories most frequently die because their usual empirical nourishment is appropriated by a rival.

In the meantime, before trustworthy evidence becomes available, the rationality of the proposal of a new metaphysical theory still needs to be and can be judged. What makes the proposal of a new metaphysical theory rational is that it solves the problem that prompted it and it is logically consistent, conceptually coherent, criticizable, and capable of providing an explanation of the nature of reality. The explanation starts with an existing metaphysical outlook and extends it in order to remove those conflicts that beset the original outlook. The extension, however, has limitations imposed upon it by the vision embodied in the original theory.

Metaphysical theories are bridges between tradition and new knowledge. Their goal is to reconcile past beliefs with new evidence, so that a rational view of reality emerges. Their method is creative imagination tempered by arguments.

But could not the tradition be mistaken? Could it not be that the vision permeating the existing outlook is a chimera? Of course. But the fact that a tradition exists in a given intellectual epoch determines the point of departure. The outlook one starts with may be mistaken, but what is problematic and what is novel or irrelevant or surprising must be judged against a background and that is tradition. One cannot think without a tradition. But we can guard against mistakes by holding the tradition open to criticism, by not letting it become dogma. One way of doing that is by doing metaphysics.

# 13 Metaphysics, rationality, and presuppositions

*"In every state, not wholly barbarous, a philosophy, good or bad, there must be. However slightingly it may be the fashion to talk of speculation and theory, as opposed (sillily and nonsensically opposed) to practice, it would not be difficult to prove, that such as is the existing spirit of speculation, during any given period, such will be the spirit and tone of the religion, legislation, and morals may even of the fine arts, the manners, and the fashions. Nor is this the less true, because the great majority of men live like bats, but in twilight, and know and feel that philosophy of their age only by its reflections and refractions."*—Samuel Taylor Coleridge, *Essays on His Own Times*

## Introduction

Metaphysical theories are often suspect because it is supposed that their visionary and *a priori* elements are irrational. As we have seen, however, it is possible to judge at least some visions on rational grounds. The task of this chapter is to argue for the rationality of the *a priori* components of metaphysical theories.

Metaphysical theories share an important feature not just with aesthetic and mystical visions but also with such large-scale scientific theories as cosmological speculations about the expanding universe, the theory of evolution, the conservation of parity, and the theory of relativity. This shared feature is the goal of offering a comprehensive explanation of what there is. But, of course, metaphysics is not science. Perhaps the most significant difference between them is that unlike scientific theories, metaphysical theories are largely *a priori*. Scientific theories attempt to provide an explanation by trying to make sense out of observed phenomena. Metaphysical theories explain by providing schemes in terms of which phenomena, whatever they

230

may turn out to be, could be explained. Scientific theories are based on facts in that they are verified or falsified by facts. Metaphysical theories are not based on facts in this sense, although, as it will be argued, facts are not irrelevant to their rational appraisal.

The explanatory schemes offered by metaphysical theories are *a priori* presuppositions. They are *a priori* without being analytic or empirical. If they were analytic, their denial would be self-contradictory, and if they were empirical, they would have to be verifiable or falsifiable by observation. It is a notorious feature of metaphysical theories that they are observationally uncertifiable. Consider, for instance, materialism, dualism, or determinism. The view that everything is ultimately composed of matter, or that there are two fundamentally irreducible substances or qualities in reality, or that there is a law behind the occurrence of every event, are not meant to be true by definition. There are alternatives to each of these and it is an altogether unsatisfactory defense to claim that the alternatives are self-contradictory merely because they are at odds with a favored metaphysical theory. On the other hand, metaphysical theories are not supposed to be empirical either. There is no fact that would show that materialism, for instance, is mistaken. If a fact was found that was apparently unanalyzable in material terms, the materialist, who in this respect is typical of all metaphysicians, would ascribe it to human ignorance or to insufficient understanding. It is, of course, just this apparent immunity to refutation that prompts the attempted assimilation of metaphysics to art, mysticism, or poetry.

The rationality of metaphysics and the refutation of metaphysical scepticism thus depend upon the possibility of showing that the *a priori* components of metaphysical theories—presuppositions—are rational.

## Collingwood's account of metaphysics

Collingwood's brilliant, careless, and suggestive theory is developed in *An Essay of Metaphysics*.[1] Every statement, according to Collingwood, is an answer to a question. A person in making a statement need not be aware of the question, but what gives point to a statement is the question to which it provides an answer. Questions arise against the background of presuppositions. Presuppositions prompt questions, for only if it is supposed that something is so, or not so, may that something become questionable. Presuppositions are either relative, in which case they themselves are answers to more fundamental questions, or they are absolute, that is, they prompt questions, but they are themselves not answers to any question. Absolute presuppositions are unquestioned, not unquestionable. Any systematic inquiry rests on absolute presuppositions, but a presupposition that is absolute in one inquiry may come to function as a relative presupposition in another inquiry. To question the absolute presuppositions of an inquiry is to undertake another inquiry.

Suppose the behavior of my car forces me to assert, perhaps in my heart only, that there is dirt in the fuel tank. The unspoken question in the background is about the jerky progress of the car. A relative presupposition involved is that the malfunctioning of the car, in the absence of external interference, is caused by some internal mechanical defect. If the inquiry were pursued in a philosophical spirit, after a series of more and more fundamental relative presuppositions, one might arrive at the absolute presupposition that every event has a cause. Presuppositions, relative and absolute, not only underlie questions, they also suggest the kind of answer that would prove satisfactory; presuppositions shape the nature of an inquiry.

A declarative sentence, according to Collingwood, is a statement if, *inter alia,* it is an answer to a question that arises. A question can arise only if a presupposition prompts it. Since no question arises, within an inquiry, about the absolute presuppositions of that inquiry, absolute presuppositions are not statements, they have no truth-value in that inquiry. Thus relative presuppositions are either true or false, while absolute presuppositions are neither. They are merely supposed and accepted unquestioningly.

Collingwood is short on examples, but the orderliness of nature for eighteenth-century science, explanations partly in terms of final cause for Aristotelian metaphysics, the existence of a spiritual element in reality for orthodox Christianity would qualify as absolute presuppositions. Collingwood's own example is that "every event has a cause" is an absolute presupposition of Kant's system.

Absolute presuppositions occur in clusters; the combination of them determines the nature, purpose, and the scope of a particular way of looking at the world. To understand a world view is to understand the absolute presuppositions that underlie it. Collingwood conceives of the task of metaphysics as the achievement of this understanding. The method of metaphysical inquiry is to render explicit the implicit presuppositions of a particular world view.

Absolute presuppositions are unquestioned fundamental assumptions; to articulate them is to make them possible objects of scrutiny. As soon as that possibility is realized, the presuppositions cease to be absolute. Metaphysical inquiry thus tends to be historical; it is usually not one's own, but the presuppositions of other ages that are examined.

Since absolute presuppositions are neither true nor false, metaphysics is essentially a descriptive enterprise. Its purpose is not to discover whether any absolute presupposition is true or false, since it is neither; rather it is to describe what Collingwood calls the constellation of absolute presuppositions of a world view. A metaphysician has to learn to think within the world view he studies, to ask and to answer questions as proponents of that world view would; that and only that is the task of metaphysics.

There is a very great deal in Collingwood's account of metaphysics that is acceptable. It is beyond argument, for instance, that the thinkers of any intellectual epoch take for granted certain fundamental assumptions. Nor does it require much persuasion to recognize the intellectual interest in studying these fundemental assumptions. One is tempted to say, however, that such study already exists; it is intellectual history or the history of ideas. Yet Collingwood desires to call the study metaphysics. If Collingwood is right, then much that has gone under the name of metaphysics must be dismissed as nonsense, or as Collingwood calls it, "pseudo-metaphysics."

A major ambition of many metaphysicians, of Descartes, Spinoza, the early Wittgenstein among others, was to construct a metaphysical theory of the nature of reality on the basis of a few true principles.

They were at pains to formulate and to argue for absolute presuppositions. Now these metaphysicians may have been wrong in thinking that what they took to be absolute presuppositions were really that, but they unquestionably insisted on the necessity of proving the truth of absolute presuppositions. According to Collingwood, in doing this, they are doing pseudo-metaphysics.

Perhaps so. Collingwood here yields to none in criticizing metaphysics. But if the criticism is accepted, if absolute presuppositions are neither true nor false, if they are merely supposed and accepted unquestioningly, then they are indistinguishable from articles of faith. Indeed, they are worse, since articles of faith are at least made explicit, while absolute presuppositions tend to be implicit. And if Collingwood is correct in thinking that absolute presuppositions underlie all systematic thought, then the conclusion is inescapable that all human thought rests on irrational commitment.

Thus the two major weaknesses of Collingwood's theory are its failure to do justice to the traditional conception of metaphysics and its commitment to the ultimate failure of rationality. These features, of course, are weaknesses only if metaphysics, as it has been conceived of traditionally, is possible, and if the rationality of fundamental commitments can be defended.

There is, however, another consequence of Collingwood's argument that statements can be understood only in the context of the question to which they are answers, and that the questions themselves arise only against the background of presuppositions. Different metaphysical theories have different absolute presuppositions. So questions that are formulated by the use of roughly the same expressions in different metaphysical theories have, in fact, radically different import. Thus, for instance, when Plato, Duns Scotus, and Wittgenstein address themselves to the problem of universals, they are not giving different answers to the same question. Their presuppositions are different, hence they cannot ask the same questions, nor have the same problems.

Thus Collingwood attacks yet another cornerstone of metaphysics, namely, that there are stock metaphysical problems to which metaphysicians have offered various answers throughout the ages. Problems concerning God, freedom, and immortality, and those about universals, appearance and reality, the nature of value, and many others are not enduring metaphysical questions; they are different problems couched in the same guise. So if Collingwood is right, not only are metaphysical beliefs ultimately irrational, but these irrational beliefs are not even continuous from age to age. Argument about different metaphysical theories is impossible because absolute presuppositions are neither true nor false, and because two people in different metaphysical frameworks could not ask the same question.

# The nature of presuppositions [2]

Metaphysics is the study of presuppositions: Collingwood is right in this. But metaphysics is not merely a descriptive-historical study, nor are presuppositions necessarily irrational. What, then, are presuppositions, and what makes them rational?

It sounds less dogmatic if instead of "absolute" presuppositions we discuss "fundamental" presuppositions. Fundamental presuppositions are basic theoretical commitments in systematic inquiry. An inquiry is systematic if it has a purpose, if the purpose is the solution of some problem or problems, and if the relevance of questions and answers that occur in the inquiry can be judged with reference to their tendency to contribute to the solution of the original problem. Thus in the course of a stroll, idly noticing the landscape, wondering about the names of some trees, or musing about the fauna does not constitute systematic inquiry. Conducting a murder investigation, looking for treasure, trying to understand a poem, and checking a theory by experimentation normally are systematic inquiries.

What makes some presuppositions fundamental is that they are unquestioned in a particular systematic inquiry. But saying this is not yet a sufficient characterization of them. Consider, for instance, an historian examining fifteenth-century incunabula in the hope of shedding light on the life of an historical figure. There is a staggering number of presuppositions involved, but let us take only two. The historian assumes that printing has been invented before the fifteenth-century and also that it is possible to have knowledge of the past.

Both of these presuppositions are unquestioned in the inquiry, yet there is a sense in which the latter is fundamental while the former is not.

If the historian's assumption about printing is questioned, the doubt can be removed by further historical inquiry. But no amount of historical investigation is capable of resolving doubt about the possibility of historical knowledge. Generally, a presupposition is fundamental to an inquiry if without assuming it to be true, the inquiry could not reasonably be conducted, and if its truth is questioned, the question is about the very possibility of the inquiry, and thus it is unanswerable within that inquiry. This is the sense in which the resemblance of the future to the past is fundamental to scientific inquiry, the responsibility of normal human agents is fundamental to the present legal system and the perfectibility of man is fundamental to contemporary educational theories.

Fundamental presuppositions are theoretical, as opposed to psychological, commitments. Thus the supposed object of metaphysical inquiry is not the psychological process of presupposing, but those basic propositions whose truth is taken for granted in particular systematic inquiries. It is possible, indeed it is likely if Collingwood is right, that the thinkers of an age are unaware of many of their fundamental presuppositions. The discovery that a person is committed to fundamental presuppositions and that he has never questioned them need not therefore be a sign of dogmatism.

In retrospect, we can note for instance that Hume was committed to the apparently unquestioned possibility of there being a Newtonian science of the mind. If our interest is in the history of ideas, or more particularly the history of Hume's ideas, it is easy to understand and indeed sympathize with Hume's commitment by viewing it against the background of the amazing new Newtonian cosmology. A reasonable and lettered man would have thought as Hume did in those times. But if our interest is in metaphysics, then our question is about the correctness of the assumption that there can be a Newtonian science of the mind. That question is not answered by analyzing Hume's states of mind, nor by imaginatively entering the *Zeitgeist* of the Enlightenment.

Collingwood holds that it is futile to try to answer the question in

236

any other way. No doubt part of the reason for this pessimism is that Collingwood did not see how it could be done. But there is a way. The argument, in short, is that metaphysical theories are rational and *a priori* because of fundamental presuppositions. Fundamental presuppositions are the *a priori* components of metaphysical theories, and they are formulable as rational propositions which are neither analytically true nor empirically testable. There are at least three types of fundamental presuppositions: regulative, categorical, and ontological.

## Regulative presuppositions

A number of philosophers have argued recently that metaphysics can be reinterpreted to exclude its untestable, irrational elements. The suggestion is that metaphysics should be understood as heuristics: rational metaphysical theories should be conceived of as scientific research programs. The role of a metaphysical theory, they hold, is the provision of methodological rules to direct scientific inquiry. The principle of causality, for instance, should be thought of as an injunction always to inquire into the cause of every event; determinism should be interpreted as the prescription always to research into the laws guiding the behavior of particulars; nominalism as the advice to transpose the material into the formal mode. Thus metaphysics is rational if it can be reformulated in heuristic terms, and if it cannot be, then it fails to be rational. Metaphysics tells us not what the world is like, but what procedures science should follow in order to discover what the world is like. Not the least advantage of this suggestion is that if it is accepted, metaphysics becomes open to rational appraisal on the basis of the success or failure of the scientific investigation that it prompted.

This interpretation of metaphysics seems to have been adopted by Popper:

> Not a few doctrines which are metaphysical could be interpreted as typical hypostatizations of methodological rules. An example of this . . . is called the "principle of causality." . . . Another example . . . is the problem of objectivity. . . . It might indeed be said that the majority

237

of the problems of theoretical philosophy, and the most interesting ones, can be reinterpreted in this way as problems of method.[3]

Popper's suggestion is amplified and worked out in greater detail by Watkins, Agassi, and Lakatos.[4]

Carnap's principle of tolerance is an expression of the same attitude. Carnap writes:

> It seemed important to me to show that many philosophical controversies actually concern the question whether a particular language form should be used. . . . For example, in the controversy about the foundations of mathematics, the conception of intuitionism may be construed as a proposal to restrict the means of expression and the means of deduction . . . while the classical conception leaves the language unrestricted. . . . I wish to show that everyone is free to choose the rules of his language and thereby his logic in any way he wishes. This I called "the principle of tolerance" . . . . In this way, assertions that a particular language is the correct language . . . are eliminated, and traditional ontological problems . . . are entirely abolished.[5]

At another place Carnap writes:

> The acceptance of a linguistic framework must not be regarded as implying a metaphysical doctrine. . . . An alleged statement of the reality of the system of entities is a pseudostatement without cognitive content. To be sure, we have to face at this point an important question; but it is a practical, not a theoretical question; it is the question of whether or not to accept the new linguistic forms. The acceptance can only be judged as being more or less expedient, fruitful, conducive to the aim for which language is intended.[6]

Metaphysical problems are thus either eliminated or reinterpreted as problems of method. The *a priori* schemes produced by metaphysical theories are regulative or methodological presuppositions.

Consider materialism: it provides a framwork, an interpretive scheme in terms of which we can speculate about the nature of reality. In practice, this comes to the application of materialism to special areas of inquiry. For example, Hempel's covering law model of historical explanation, the identity theory of the mental and the physical, a Hobbesian political theory are all special applications of the general theory of materialism. These special theories function as intermediate links between a metaphysical theory and testable, empirical—first-order—theories.

The identity theory, for instance, is accepted, at least for methodological purposes, by such empirical theories as those concerning the treatment of mental illness through chemical and behavioral therapy or those attempting to construct a cybernetic model of human behavior.

A regulative presupposition of materialism is that all phenomena should be explained in scientific terms. The presupposition determines the problem, the direction of the inquiry, and the nature of the sought-for explanation. It will seem natural to regard as problematic those observed phenomena that lack or do not seem amenable to scientific explanation. The inquiry will have been thought successfully completed if such an explanation is found.

Regulative presuppositions are *a priori;* they are formulable as conditional statements whose antecedent is the goal of the inquiry, namely, having a rational interpretive scheme of the nature of reality, and whose consequent is a research program. The statement of the regulative presupposition of materialism is clearly not analytic, since it can be denied without self-contradiction; dualists, for instance, do so. Nor is the statement empirical, since no conceivable set of observations could verify or falsify it. That many phenomena have been explained in scientific terms does not constitute evidence for the assumption that all phenomena are so explainable. And that many phenomena have not been explained in scientific terms does nothing to show that all phenomena are not so explainable. Given that the number of phenomena is indeterminable, it is in principle impossible to verify or falsify, by empirical testing, the regulative presupposition of materialism, or indeed of any metaphysical theory.

Regulative presuppositions are based on the nonanalytic and nonempirical assumption that the method which proved successful in one area of inquiry will prove successful in many others. Contemporary materialists are impressed by the great success of scientific explanation, so they strive to apply it to history, politics, psychology. But materialists are not unique in this. Aristotle found teleological explanation useful in biology, so he attempted to give it at least a partial explanation of all phenomena in terms of final cause. Marx found explanation of political behavior in economic terms useful, so he applied it to all behavior. Pythagorians and their rationalistic successors found some remarkable mathematical regularities in nature, so they supposed that all reality is mathematically ordered. What makes regulative presuppositions *a priori* is the rationally controlled imaginative leap involved in extrapolating from a few cases of one kind to cases of all possible kinds.

The problem concerns the rationality of this leap. The objection might be that the precise feature which renders regulative presuppositions *a priori*—the untestable extrapolation of method—is the feature that renders them nonrational. There is nothing, it might be objected, that is allowed to count against the research program. Phenomena that resist explanation in terms of the methodological prescription will not be treated as counterinstances but as outstanding problems to be resolved when greater knowledge, sophistication, and ingenuity are achieved. Regulative presuppositions are uncriticizable; the conditions under which they would be abandoned, so it might be argued, are unspecifiable.

But this is a mistake. It is true that regulative presuppositions cannot be verified or falsified, but they can be criticized. It should be remembered that regulative presuppositions occur in the context of theories. Theories are constructed for the purpose of solving a problem. The presupposition recommends a method. The rationality of regulative presuppositions depends on the success of the theory in solving the problem by relying on the research program implicit in the presupposition. Thus a condition in which a regulative presupposition would be abandoned is if the theory accepting it was persistently unsuccessful in solving its problem, while another theory, constructed on the basis of another presupposition, had remarkable success in solving the same problem.

Given one regulative presupposition of materialism, for instance, it ought to be possible to construct a purely mechanistic model in terms of which human behavior could be explained. The most sophisticated model now available is provided by cybernetics. Suppose that after decades of intensive attempts no satisfactory cybernetic model had been constructed and that interactionistic explanations prompted by dualism had been signally successful. The reasonable procedure would then be to abandon the search for mechanistic explanation. This, of course, would not mean that the identity theory, and through it materialism, had been refuted. Metaphysical theories are not refuted if their regulative presuppositions become untenable, for it is always possible to retreat to the position that another, not-yet-discovered model would make a mechanistic explanation possible.

Though it begins to look as if metaphysical theories may be irrational after all, since they can be held in the face of persistent failure, this is not the case. Even though metaphysical theories cannot be refuted, they can still be undermined. They can be made to die a death by a thousand qualifications. This is the kind of demise that vitalism had, that theism and dualism are having, and that behaviorism will, with any luck, have. Metaphysical theories disintegrate slowly: they wither away.

The key to the rationality of metaphysical theories is the recognition that they are not gratuitous speculations of idle minds, but passionate attempts to make sense out of reality. If they fail in this, they may linger on, but their *raison d'etre* is removed. Dogmatists and wishful thinkers may hang on to them, but this merely demonstrates the irrationality of some men and not the irrationality of metaphysical theories.

It would be tempting to stop here, identify the salvagable part of metaphysics with heuristics and conclude that since regulative presuppositions can be rationally appraised, metaphysics is an intellectually respectable enterprise. The temptation, however, has to be resisted, for while metaphysics is heuristics, it is also more than that. The suggestion of Popper and Carnap is not mistaken, but incomplete. Several considerations ought to incline one toward this conclusion.

First, it is historically inaccurate to suppose that materialism, for instance, is merely a methodological prescription. Leucippus and the atomists, Hobbes, and contemporary materialists do not just recommend a method. Their recommendation stems, at least in part, from the supposed truth of the ontological assumption that the nature of reality is material. It would be incredible to suppose that every single metaphysician—painstakingly analytical and self-conscious thinkers—was wrong, and wrong exactly in the same way, about what he was doing. Metaphysicians certainly meant to do more than prescribe a method. It remains, of course, an open question of whether it is possible to do more while staying within the bounds of reason.

The second reason why it is a mistake to identify metaphysical theories with methodological prescriptions is, as Watkins [7] points out, that it is perfectly consistent to reject the ontological assumption of a metaphysical theory and simultaneously applaud the methodological principle with which it is supposedly identical. One can deny, for instance, that materialism is correct and still think that the search for the scientific explanation of every phenomenon should continue.

The minimal purpose of a metaphysical theory is to provide a rational explanation. The next two arguments are based on the recognition that if metaphysics were identified with heuristics, then it could not achieve its purpose. The proposed identification would doom rather than rescue metaphysics.

If a metaphysical theory were identified with a regulative presupposition, then it would be irrational to accept it. Suppose it is granted that the form of a metaphysical theory is a conditional statement whose antecedent expresses a goal and whose consequent expresses a method for achieving the goal. A rational agent should be able to provide reasons for preferring the goal he pursues to alternative goals. The difficulty produced by the identification of a metaphysical theory with a regulative presupposition is that the possibility of arguing for the goal expressed by the antecedent is removed.

The identification is on secure grounds if a potential critic challenges the consequent of the conditional. If the statement, "If reality is to be understood, follow the scientific method," is objected to on the grounds that prayer and meditation would be better methods, then its champions can defend its rationality by tolerantly calling for testing.

A sophisticated critic, however, would attack the antecedent instead. He would suggest that reality should not be understood, because the required effort diverts attention from the essentially important and only worthwhile activity, namely, understanding God. And prayer and meditation are much better ways of doing that than the pursuit of the scientific method is. As a sign of tolerance, the critic, too, can then call for testing.

If metaphysics were merely heuristics, how could such fundamental, indeed "metaphysical" disagreements be settled? Clearly, empirical testing is irrelevant, for the question is about the appropriateness of such testing. If we suppose that both of the competing goals can be expressed in logically unobjectionable language, then, given this conception of metaphysics, there is no way of rationally settling fundamental conflicts about such general types of activity as scientific investigation, prayer and meditation, the pursuit of pleasure, power, sainthood, or racial superiority.

The result is that in the last analysis no argument can be given for preferring one goal to another. Since the pursuit of a goal is rational only if arguments can be given for preferring it to other goals, the pursuit of no fundamental goal is rational. Thus the identification of metaphysics with heuristics leads to the inescapable conclusion that no activity is rational.

Another difficulty with the identification of metaphysics and heuristics is that it becomes impossible for a metaphysical theory to explain anything. Suppose that the conditional, "If reality is to be understood, follow the scientific method," is accepted, and it works. It does indeed prompt fruitful inquiries and, as a result, life becomes better.

The difficulty is that it has now become impossible to explain the success of the inquiry. The methods work, but why do they? The natural answer is no longer available. It cannot be said that adherence to the scientific method is useful because it reveals the nature of reality. For, as Carnap tells us,

> An alleged statement of the reality of a system of entities is a pseudo-statement without cognitive content. . . . To be sure, we have to face at this point an important question; but it is a practical, not a theoretical question. . . . The acceptance cannot be judged as being either true or false because it is not assertion. It can only be judged as being more or less expedient, fruitful, conducive to [our] aim. . . .[8]

What has happened is very fundamental and very mistaken. We are invited to sever the connection between the rational grounds upon

243

which a metaphysical theory is to be accepted or rejected and the verisimilitude of the theory.

The last two objections against the identification of metaphysics and heuristics become one. If the goal of an activity is not rationally supportable, then the only way of judging behavior is with reference to its propensity to achieve the goal for which it was performed. All attempts at rational evaluation become internal: one is presented with a coherence theory of rationality. And just as the coherence theory of truth licenses any logically consistent system, so the coherence theory of rationality permits all activities that bring about their goal. So long as they are internally coherent and efficacious, the lives of the mystic, the sadist, the saint, the poet, the tyrant, the sage, and the fool are each as rationally respectable as another.

The situation has an interesting parallel with the difficulties of the early logical positivists. The spirit of positivism lives on, for as the meaning of propositions was identified with their method of verification, so the rationality of a metaphysical theory is identified with its method of verification. The thinking that leads to the identification of metaphysics and heuristics reveals the same habit of thought as the one that produced the verifiability principle. It is not surprising that Carnap had a major share in both.

The result is too restrictive and because of it metaphysics becomes incapable of achieving its task: the provision of a rational explanation of the nature of reality. The analysis, criticism, and rational defense of regulative presuppositions is a part of metaphysics, but it should not be supposed that it is the only part; there are other presuppositions as well.

## Categorical presuppositions

The second kind of presupposition consists of the categories that are taken for granted in a metaphysical theory. Questions that arise in the course of inquiry must be stated in terms of the categories, but the categories themselves are not questioned in that inquiry. The problem, once again, is to show that categorial presuppositions are formulable as rational and *a priori* assertions. The first task, however, is to indicate what categories are.

Passmore's discussion of the difficulties involved in clarifying the notion of category concludes with a sound recommendation from Fowler's *Modern English Usage:*

> For the sake of precision it would be better if category was used by no one who was not prepared to state (1) that he does not mean *class,* and (2) that he knows the difference between the two.[9]

To discover the classes to which a person is committed one has to look at the way in which he classifies particulars. Whether or not a particular belongs to a class is, on the simplest level, an empirical question, like, for instance, are dodoes birds? The question is settled by ascertaining whether the particular possesses or fails to possess the characteristics requisite for class membership. The problem involved in classification, however, may be more complex. Suppose that the question is whether Alsace-Lorraine is French or German. The point is not to indicate uncertainty about a fact of geography, but rather to inquire what should count as determining national affinity. The argument then is about the characteristics that should determine membership in a certain class. Some hope of settling such arguments may come from a discussion of the history of the principles guiding inclusion in the class and also from a discussion of the purpose of the classification. There is, however, an even more difficult problem. Suppose that the argument is about the kind of classes that could be used for classification. The problem then may be to determine the point of view from which particulars should be classified. Such points of view may be historical-genetic, scientific, aesthetic, religious, and the like. The system of classes that are chosen will, of course, reflect the point of view that is accepted. A measure of agreement can again be reached if it is recognized that classification from one point of view does not exclude classification from other points of view. Alternative points of view may coexist, because classification in their terms may be dictated by different nonconflicting purposes.

The problem that is of immediate concern, however, is if a disagreement arises about alternative and conflicting systems of classes where classification has the same purpose. Disputes of this kind are typically metaphysical. The different points of view that prompt the adoption of conflicting systems of classes are metaphysical theories whose purpose is the achievement of a rational understanding of reality. It is such very general and fundamental disputes about classification that will be understood by categorial disputes. By "category" will be meant such a class that if a person were to give up classifying particulars in its terms, then he could no longer hold the metaphysical theory with which he began.

It may be that there are categories which all metaphysical theories share, and perhaps must share, in common. Perhaps the categories of quality, quantity, and relation are of this sort. Be that as it may, the relevant consideration is that conflicting metaphysical theories differ at least about some categories. Consider, for instance, the conflict between dualism and materialism. The latter is committed to classifying particulars in physical terms, whereas the former is committed to classifying the same particulars in physical and mental terms. The dispute between materialism and dualism is, *inter alia,* over the question of whether or not the classification of particulars into mental and physical is an irreducible requirement of understanding reality. If a materialist were to accept the irreducibility of the mental to the physical, or if a dualist were to admit that the mental could be completely understood in physical terms, each would have abandoned his original metaphysical position.

The categories to which a person is committed can be discovered by determining what it is that he regards as a category mistake. Consider the following case.[10] Suppose you and I put a book on the table, leave the room, return in a few minutes, and look for the book which is not where we left it; we cannot find it. I wonder who took it, and you say nobody. I wonder whether perhaps it has slipped down from the table, but you say it has not. I suspect my memory, but you assure me that we did leave the book there. So I exclaim in frustration: but it could not have disappeared without a trace! And you say: Why not, that in fact is exactly what happened. If you mean what you say, we have a serious disagreement. Most people would regard the statement things may disappear without a trace as inadmissible. But this may be either because they think that experience teaches us that the statement is false, or because our category commitments exclude the possibility of something happening without an explanation. To say that the statement is false is to admit the possibility that it might be true, that is, reality could be such that things disappear without a trace. On the other hand, to maintain that the statement involves a category mistake is to deny that this sort of thing could ever happen. The denial is not empirically based, it is an *a priori* assumption about the nature of reality.

All metaphysical theories are committed to regarding some statements as category mistakes, simply because all metaphysical theories involve category commitments that can be violated. When there is intelligent disagreement about the question of whether a statement is false or embodies a category mistake, the disagreement is metaphysical.

It might be argued, however, that such disagreements always show the lack of rationality of the category commitment, for what possible nonempirical justification could there be for thinking that something logically possible could not happen? Categorial presuppositions may be *a priori,* it might be objected, but precisely because they are *a priori,* they are also nonrational. Can the rationality of categorial presuppositions be reconciled with their being also *a priori?* The clue to their rationality is found in the continuity that persists through changing categorial commitments.

There is a sense in which early Greek materialism is quite different from contemporary materialism. In another sense, however, they are not all that different. What makes Leucippus, Hobbes, and J. J. C. Smart all materialists is their commitment to the categorizability of all particulars in terms of the concept of matter. What sets them apart is their conception of matter. They accept the fundamentality of the concept, but they differ about the criteria that guide its application. All materialists agree that particulars should be analyzed in terms of the ultimate constituents of matter, but they conceive of these constituents differently. The Greeks thought of "atoms" as unobservable, but inferable, having such spatial dimensions as shape and size. Contemporary materialists think of the ultimate constituents also as unobservable and inferable, but deny that they need have spatial dimensions. There is change in the concept of matter, but there is also continuity.[11]

The study of the changing criteria for the application of the concept of matter (or force, cause, velocity, etc.) is a study in the history of ideas. But changes in criteria are not historical accidents, they are prompted, indeed forced, by the success and failure of those first-order theories that make use of the criteria. We have to think differently about the concept of matter, because the facts presented first by nineteenth-century chemistry and then by twentieth-century physics can make sense only if we revise our categories. The rationality of categorial presuppositions is based upon their criticizability in the light of evidence presented by first-order theories. Categorial commitments have to be altered, because as knowledge of particulars grows, the facts no longer fit our *a priori* schemes. After a while a set of categories no longer prompts the right questions, but constrains inquiry. When that point is reached, the categories have to be revised.

Consider vitalism as a case in point; it has been fatally weakened, although it has not by any means been proven false. Recent research in the biological sciences indicates that the property of being alive can be materialistically analyzed. The distinction between living and nonliving particulars thus no longer needs to mark two fundamentally different categories. Vitalism is committed to the fundamentality of this category distinction, materialism is committed to its denial. First-order theories favor materialism.

Vitalism is undermined, but not refuted. It is possible after all to continue to insist upon the fundamental difference between the animate and inanimate. But such insistence is no longer in the service of the original purpose of vitalism. That purpose was to provide a rational theory to account for the difference between two kinds of particulars. The problem motivating the theory has been solved in terms of another theory. Vitalism may linger on, but it no longer serves a philosophical purpose.

Thus metaphysical theories are rational, partly because they are criticizable through their categorial presuppositions. The criticism takes the form of showing that the problem that the metaphysical theory was supposed to make more tractable is solvable by first-order theories that presuppose the categories of a competing metaphysical theory.

It might now be suggested that metaphysical theories should be regarded as fundamental classificatory schemes combined with methodological prescriptions about the direction in which first-order inquiries should proceed. With the acceptance of this suggestion metaphysical theories would acquire that harmless heuristic aura that positivists and pragmatists wanted them to have all along. But it would be a mistake to regard metaphysicians as merely extending an invitation to all those interested to look at reality through their kaleidoscope. There is more to metaphysics than the recommendation of one set of categories, or of one method of inquiry over another.

Two considerations force the rejection of the heuristic interpretation of metaphysics. First, its rejection is tacit in practically all metaphysical works. Plato, Aquinas, Descartes, Spinoza, Leibniz, Kant, Hegel and many others are very clear in that they are making ontological claims. They mean to tell us what there is.

It has been suggested that these ontological commitments are not rationally supportable, but even if that were conceded, it cannot reasonably be denied that they are made. There have been attempts, as we have seen, to rescue metaphysicians from the folly of their assumptions by reformulating them in innocuous, ontologically astringent language. Thus Descartes may be taken to recommend that we think of reality in terms of the spiritual and the physical, Plato can be interpreted as offering a logical analysis of universals, and materialists may be taken to do nothing but recommend the methods of science. Let us overlook the historical inaccuracy as well as the semantic infidelity of such an undertaking and suppose for a moment that such reformulations are possible. There is still a problem which constitutes another reason for having to take ontological commitments literally and for rejecting the heuristic interpretation of metaphysics.

If metaphysical theories did not involve ontological assumptions, it would be impossible to see why one consistent system of categories and regulative presuppositions should be preferred to any other. The reason for accepting a system of categories is that particulars are as some categories depict them. And the reason why following a regulative presupposition leads to understanding and success in coping with the world is that particulars are as they are supposed to be by the regulative presuppositions. Vitalism fails because there is no reason for thinking that *elan vital* exists, and dualism and theism would fail

249

too if there existed no spiritual element in reality, and materialism would not be adequate if there existed nonmaterial particulars.

## Ontological presuppositions

Metaphysical theories are committed to ontological presuppositions as well as to regulative principles and categories. This commitment cannot be dismissed. The types of ontological commitment that metaphysicians have undertaken are, as it were, metaphysical themes of which their exemplifications in particular metaphysical theories are but variations. The way in which a metaphysical theory handles the distinction between appearance and reality determines, in part, the nature of its ontological commitments. Is the world as we perceive it through the senses and scientific instruments the only proper object of metaphysical speculation, or is there a suprasensible world transcending experience that is penetrable, if at all, only by pure reason? In the first case ontological commitments will have to be related, no matter how tenuously, to the possibility of experience; the metaphysics embodying the commitment is immanent. In the second case the ontological commitments need bear no relation to the possibility of experience, even though they may have been prompted by the confusion that prevails in the world of experience. Their object is, at best, contemplatable, but never, even indirectly, experienceable. This type of metaphysics is transcendent.

The distinction between transcendent and immanent metaphysics is blurred. It is best to think of ontological commitments as ranging along a continuum extending from something like direct realism to mysticism or speculation about the ineffable. At one extreme, everything is as it seems to be, the senses are accepted as a sure guide; at the other extreme, nothing is what it appears to be, and the senses merely obscure vision.

It is the extreme form of transcendent metaphysics that has given the subject a bad name. Wittgenstein's advice should be heeded: "Whereof one cannot speak, thereof one must be silent." The present defense of metaphysics is not all-inclusive; it is meant to argue only

250

for the rationality of those metaphysical theories whose relation with experience has not been severed: theories must be subject to criticism by experience.

Particular ontological presuppositions are formulable as existential propositions that range over everything that exists. Such propositions, of course, are not supposed to be true by definition—their denial is not self-contradictory; nor are they empirical, since it is logically impossible that any set of observations would prove or disprove, verify or falsify them. The propositions used for expressing ontological presuppositions can be instantiated; it is possible to find particulars that fall within their range. The existence of such particulars, however, constitutes no evidence whatsoever for the claim that all particulars, past, present, and future, are like the examined ones. The problem, then, is to show how ontological presuppositions can be rational. What are the circumstances in which particular ontological presuppositions would have to be abandoned?

The three types of presuppositions are not all on the same level. Categorical and regulative presuppositions themselves presuppose certain ontological presuppositions. The commitment, say, to the categorizability of all particulars in material terms and to the universal applicability of the methods of science, is understandable only in the light of the even more fundamental commitment to the existence of nothing but matter. Of course, it is precisely this ontological commitment that critics find unacceptable. Categorical and regulative presuppositions may be deformed to look like heuristic devices justified by the success of the inquiry that rests upon them, but ontological presuppositions cannot similarly be justified. Nonverifiable and nonfalsifiable existential propositions go against the grain.

But now the question must be asked: what is the reason for this aversion? The old answer, that it is the verifiability principle that prohibits rational commitment to ontological presuppositions, suffers from the great weakness that even after decades, no satisfactory formulation of it exists. It is simply vain effort to try to so specify the notion of empirical testing that it covers all and only those instances that positivists are disposed to admit into the fold.

All the same, it might be said, positivism contains an essential insight: rationality demands that speculation be tempered by the possibility of relating it to experience. That insight is correct. But, as it happens, it is possible to reconcile the acceptance of the insight with the rationality of metaphysics. Wherein, then, consists the rationality of ontological presuppositions?

In the first place, by accepting the truth of an ontological presupposition it is possible to explain the success of an inquiry that is based on categorial and regulative presuppositions. Ontological presuppositions are not made in a vacuum, their acceptance is warranted, partly, because they offer an explanation of a state of affairs that is otherwise inexplicable. The truth of ontological presuppositions can account for the success of some inquiries, and their falsity can account for the failure of others.

Of course, there is no logical compulsion to try to explain the success of an inquiry. Doing metaphysics can be eschewed, but only at a great cost. For while it is of great importance to solve practical problems, it is, as we have seen in the course of criticizing pragmatism, no less important to understand why some practical solutions succeed where others fail.

In the second place, ontological presuppositions are criticizable: not that they can be proven true or false, but they can be seriously weakened. As first-order inquiries rest partly upon regulative presuppositions and categorial distinctions, so regulative presuppositions and categories rest partly upon ontological presuppositions. Since inquiries are conducted in order to solve problems, the persistent failure of a type of inquiry reflects adversely upon the presuppositions of that type of inquiry. The situation in which a particular ontological presupposition should be abandoned is when the inquiry committed to the presupposition fails to solve the problem that prompted it, while another inquiry committed to a different ontological presupposition is successful in solving the problem.

Vitalism is an obvious example of a metaphysical theory whose ontological presupposition is mistaken. The attempt to draw a fundamental categorial distinction between animate and inanimate fails, because no qualitative difference has been found, and because all the differences that have been found can be accounted for in materialistic terms. The regulative presupposition that prompts the search for the quality or substance that is life has to be abandoned, because persistent search has failed to turn up anything. And so the ontological presupposition, namely, that there exists an *élan vital,* is seriously undermined. It is not refuted though; only a very strong presumption is created against it. There is now a *prima facie* case against vitalism.

The unmaking of ontological commitments does not depend on the unfavorable outcome of a crucial experiment. It depends upon the slow change of the climate of opinion, upon the accumulation of increasingly embarrassing facts, upon the availability of alternative metaphysical views. The process is slow and messy, but it occurs. It is a mistake to conclude from the irrational attachment of some men to unpatchable metaphysical theories that the theories themselves are irrational. Many metaphysical theories are rational, and they do cease to count—only slowly.

# The state of the argument: the rationality of metaphysics and the refutation of scepticism

We began by taking seriously the sceptical challenge to rationality. The challenge and the need to meet it acquired even greater urgency when the usual ways of countering scepticism were seen to have failed. It was possible, however, to rescue some extremely important elements out of the wreckage of traditional arguments, and these were incorporated into the theory of rationality. The theory answered the question of what makes a theory rational, but it did not answer the question of whether any theory, apart from itself, is rational.

Solipsistic scepticism attempted to defend the original sceptical challenge by arguing against many, if not all, theories on the ground that they are committed to the rationally indefensible presupposition that there is an external world. Solipsistic scepticism was refuted, however, by showing that neither ontological nor epistemological solipsism is a viable option. Solipsism requires that all the commonly accepted facts of experience be capable of fitting into the theory that there is no reason for believing in the existence of anything except of a solitary mind and its attributes. One of these facts is the existence of language. But solipsistic scepticism cannot account for this fact because the existence of language entails the existence of the external world.

Metaphysical scepticism was the next line of defense. Its claim was

254

that even if there is reason to believe that something external exists, there is no rational way of deciding which of innumerable interpretations of what it is is the correct one. The refutation of metaphysical scepticism, then, required a way of showing that metaphysical theories can be rational. This was done by demonstrating that metaphysical theories are capable of meeting the five standards of rationality.

The problem metaphysical theories aim to solve is that of having a rational view of reality and of man's place in it. The possession of such a view, as we have seen, is an essential component of happiness and it makes rational action possible.

Insofar as logical consistency and conceptual coherence are concerned, metaphysical theories must, of course, conform to them. But the way in which they do so is no different from the way any other theory with rational pretensions must meet these requirements.

The difference between metaphysical and other theories is due to the way in which the former explain and are criticizable. Metaphysical vision and fundamental presuppositions jointly constitute the explanation provided by metaphysical theories. Their criticizability depends upon the possibility of testing those empirical theories that have been constructed on the basis of the vision and presuppositions embodied in the metaphysical theory.

We have thus an answer to the question of what makes a metaphysical theory rational. And this refutes metaphysical scepticism.

# Conclusion

*"In a world without metaphysics conditions will be more favourable to the development of irrationalism."*—Robin George Collingwood, *An Essay on Metaphysics*

The time has come to state the outcome of the issue between scepticism and rationality. The following points have been established:

1) There is a form of scepticism that denies the possibility of rationality. The denial rests on the contention that the rationality of any theory, system of beliefs, or way of life depends upon its conformity to some standards of rationality, but the standards themselves are arbitrary, for they lack rational justification. Hence the appeal to reason is exactly in the same position as are the appeals to faith, revelation, instinct, taste, and the like.

This form of scepticism is free from the shortcomings that beset previous versions. It is not rigid about the number of possible forms of reasoning, for all forms are attacked. It does not claim that justification falls short of certainty, for the very possibility of justification is doubted. It does not attack the reliability of the products of reasoning, for it is the process by which they are arrived at that is suspect. It is not a psychological attitude which, if genuinely held, ought to result in inconsistent behavior, for scepticism is an epistemological doctrine about the arbitrariness of standards of rationality. The sceptic may behave just like everybody else, he merely denies that rational warrant can be found for doing or believing anything.

Scepticism is not just an epistemological bogey, but a widespread and spreading attitude which ought to countered. It results in the impossibility of settling conflicts in a civilized manner. It encourages the appeal to prejudice and the use of force, propaganda, and dogmatism. It is an attack on what is finest in the Western tradition.

2) The usual philosophical arguments do not refute scepticism. The justification of rationality on the grounds of its usefulness fails, for

256

usefulness is judged on the basis of the facility with which some goal is approximated. But since the pursuit may be for an irrational goal, usefulness it not a sufficient basis for judging the rationality of an enterprise. The refutation of scepticism on the grounds that common sense contradicts it is question-begging, for the sceptic calls into question the rationality of common sense as well. The attempt to render the sceptical challenge illegitimate by appealing to the logic of ordinary language founders, for ordinary language is compatible not just with common sense but with solipsism as well. The use of science as the rational enterprise *par excellence* does not survive the recognition that science rests upon presuppositions that also need to be defended and cannot, except by question-begging, be scientifically defended. The argument that rationality is a notion internal to each way of life and so the sceptical question about the rationality of a whole way of life is misplaced actually strengthens scepticism, for the sceptic's point is that rational choice between ways of life is impossible.

3) The problem presented by scepticism was partly solved by the construction of a theory of rationality. The theory defends an external standard of rationality which anchors rationality to an objective feature of the world that remains constant throughout changing times, cultures, and commitments. The theory also defends four internal standards of rationality by showing how they are grounded upon the external standard. The five standards jointly guarantee the rationality of a theory that conforms to them.

The external standard of rationality is problem-solving. A class of problems—problems of life—and the need to solve them are objective in the sense that all human beings are bound to have them. Such problems as the satisfaction of physiological needs, the reconciliation of conflicts between self-satisfaction and the demands of one's society, finding a way of being happy are shared by all human beings. Another class of problems—problems of reflection—arise when the luxury of choosing between various solutions to problems of life has been won. Problems of life occur because human nature and the environment are what they are; such problems are unreflective, extratheoretical, and independent of history, culture, and context. Of course, the

257

solutions of these problems are very much bound up with habit, custom, and tradition.

Some problems of life and reflection are removable, others are enduring. The solution of removable problems results in the disappearance of the problems. Enduring problems, however, persist and solving them requires the development of a policy about how to cope with such problems. Because enduring problems exist, problem-solving can never be a purely technological operation.

Rationality is not optional, for solving their problems is in the best interest of all human agents. Being rational and acting in what one regards as his best interest are two ways of describing the same policy.

Conformity to the external standard is necessary but not sufficient for rationality. The theory of rationality is not pragmatism in a new guise. If problem-solving were identical with rationality, then any solution to a problem would have to be regarded as rational. The internal standards go beyond expediency and help to decide between various solutions by supplying further conditions of rationality.

Internal standards are related to problem-solving in two ways. First, they act as restrictions upon it. Internal standards require the fulfillment of additional conditions by a solution, if the solution is to count as rational. The additional requirements are that the solution be logically consistent, conceptually coherent, have sufficient explanatory power, and be criticizable. The second way in which internal standards are related to the external one is that the latter is the ground upon which the former are justified. The justification of internal standards is that adherence to them aids problem-solving, or, that observing them is in the best interest of the agent.

4) Rationality is a method for solving problems. It is not a state of mind brought about by the exercise of the faculty of reason. Nor is it a doctrine about the good life or a recipe for political action. Of course, whether the method is put to use and the use to which it is put do have psychological, moral, and political consequences. But these consequences are not intrinsic to the method, they follow from the context in which the method is employed.

258

Standard objections to rationality on account of the supposed encouragement it gives to political rigidity, its purported tendency to favor part of our psychological repertoire at the expense of emotion and imagination, its alleged impracticality, are all misplaced. These objections may be telling against mistaken theories of rationality, but the conception defended here is free from these objections. Rationality is axiologically neutral. Moreover, no personality is likely to have a special affinity with or aversion to its employment, since the only prerequisite for rationality is that the agent should have problems he desires to solve, a condition fulfilled by all human beings.

It is this conception of rationality that is capable of countering the sceptical challenge.

5) The sceptic may renew his attack by joining forces with solipsism to argue that rationality is inapplicable in practice because its application presupposes the rationally unjustifiable belief in the existence of an external world. Solipsism, however, is refuted on the grounds that it violates a standard of rationality and so it is irrational. Solipsism is obliged to explain all facts in the common sense view of the world in accordance with the assumption that only a solitary mind and its states exist. But it is incapable of discharging this obligation because the existence of language entails the existence of the external world.

6) If it is acknowledged that belief in the existence of the external world is rational, it may still be doubted that rational justification of various metaphysical theories concerning the nature of the external world is possible. Metaphysical theories are combinations of imaginative vision and *a priori* presuppositions, and, it may be objected, neither can be rationally supported. Consequently all ways of looking at the world are equally respectable.

Against this, it has been shown that both the visionary and the *a priori* components of metaphysical theories can be rational. The rationality of metaphysical vision depends upon the rationality of the proposal of the metaphysical theory of which the vision is part. The rationality of the proposal depends upon the success in reconciling the tradition and the challenge to it that forms the problem to which the metaphysical theory is a solution. The rationality of *a priori* presuppositions depends upon the success or failure of first-order theories based on the presuppositions.

7) The refutation of scepticism depends upon the combination of the theory of rationality and metaphysics. The theory of rationality defends the standards which guarantee the rationality of a theory that conforms to them. Metaphysics provides the theory. The reason why scepticism can be refuted only by a rational metaphysical theory is that the *a priori* presuppositions underlying all theories must be defended and this can be done only by metaphysics.

The reply to the sceptical challenge depends on the availability of a rationally controlled vision of the world. The vision informs feeling, imagination, and thought. It is rational if it reconciles the tradition and the challenges to it that prevail in an epoch; if it conforms to logic; if it presents a framework in terms of which the scientific, historical, moral, and political, in a world, the cultural facts of the epoch can be explained; and if it is held open to criticism and challenge.

Rationality, metaphysics, and the refutation of scepticism thus stand or fall together.

# Notes

Introduction

1. Lionel Trilling, "Mind in the Modern World," *The Times Literary Supplement,* No. 3689 ( 17 November 1972), p. 1382.

2. Bertrand Russell, *Human Knowledge, Its Scope and Limits* (New York: Simon and Schuster, 1967), p. xi.

3. Kai Nielsen, *Scepticism* (London: Macmillan, 1973), p. 2.

Chapter 1

1. There is an excellent discussion of Hume's scepticism in Richard H. Popkin's "David Hume: His Pyrrhonism and His Critique of Pyrrhonism," *Philosophical Quarterly* 1 (1950): 385–407.

2. David Hume, *A Treatise of Human Nature,* ed. L. A. Selby-Bigge (Oxford: Clarendon, 1958), p. 183.

3. *Ibid.,* p. 218.

4. *Ibid.,* p. 183.

5. *Ibid.,* p. 183.

6. *Ibid.,* p. 268.

7. David Hume, *Enquiries Concerning Human Understanding and Concerning the Principles of Morals,* ed. L. A. Selby-Bigge (Oxford: Clarendon, 1961), p. 165.

8. For a detailed discussion of this point, see James Opie Urmson's "Some Questions Concerning Validity," in *Essays in Conceptual Analysis,* ed. Antony Flew (London: Macmillan, 1956).

9. There is an admirable discussion of this in John W. N. Watkins's "Confirmable and Influential Metaphysics," *Mind* 67 (1958): 344–365.

10. Ludwig Wittgenstein, *The Blue and Brown Books* (Oxford: Blackwell, 1958), p. 17.

11. Ludwig Wittgenstein, *Philosophical Investigations* 66, tr. Gertrude Elizabeth Margaret Anscombe (Oxford: Blackwell, 1958).

12. This discussion is indebted to William Warren Bartley, *The Retreat to Commitment* (New York: Knopf, 1962), especially chapters 4 and 5, and "Rationality versus the Theory of Rationality," in *The Critical Approach,* ed. Mario Bunge (New York: Free Press, 1964).

13. Alfred Jules Ayer, *The Problem of Knowledge* (Harmondsworth, Middlesex: Penguin, 1956), pp. 74–75.

Chapter 2

1. Herbert Feigl, "De Principiis Non Disputandum . . . ?" in *Philosophical Analysis,* ed. Max Black (Englewood Cliffs, N.J.: Prentice-Hall, 1963), pp. 113–147.

2. Rudolf Carnap, "Empiricism, Semantics, and Ontology," *Revue Internationale de Philosophie* 4 (1950): 20–40; reprinted with some revisions in *Meaning and Necessity,* 2nd ed. (Chicago: University of Chicago Press, 1956). Page references are to the latter version.

3. *Ibid.,* p. 206.

4. *Ibid.,* pp. 213–4.

5. *Ibid.,* p. 206.

6. *Ibid.,* p. 214.

7. *Ibid.,* p. 206.

8. *Ibid.*, p. 212.
9. *Ibid.*, p. 206.
10. *Ibid.*, p. 206.
11. *Ibid.*, p. 214.

Chapter 3

1. George Edward Moore, "A Defence of Common Sense," in *Contemporary British Philosophy,* 2nd series, ed. J. H. Muirhead (London: Allen & Unwin, 1925), pp. 193–223. It is reprinted in G. E. Moore's *Philosophical Papers* (London: Allen & Unwin, 1959), pp. 32–59. Page references are to the latter edition.
2. George Edward Moore, *Philosophical Papers,* pp. 32–5.
3. *Ibid.*, pp. 32–3.
4. *Ibid.*, pp. 35–6.
5. *Ibid.*, pp. 36–7.
6. *Ibid.*, p. 37.
7. George Edward Moore, "Some Judgments of Perception," *Philosophical Studies* (London: Routledge, 1922), p. 228.
8. George Edward Moore, "Hume's Philosophy," *Philosophical Studies* (London: Routledge, 1922), pp. 147–167.
9. *Ibid.*, p. 164.
10. George Edward Moore, "Proof of an External World," *Philosophical Papers,* pp. 127–150.
11. *Ibid.*, pp. 145–6.
12. *Ibid.*, p. 146.
13. *Ibid.*, pp. 148–9.
14. *Ibid.*, p. 150.

Chapter 4

1. The derivation is attempted by Norman Malcolm in "Moore and Ordinary Language," in *The Philosophy of G. E. Moore,* ed. Paul A. Schilpp (New York:

262

Tudor, 1942), pp. 345–368. Future references will be to this article. The best available attempt to sort out the differences between appealing to common sense and to ordinary language is Vere C. Chappell's in "Malcolm on Moore," *Mind* 70 (1961): 417–425.
2. Norman Malcolm, "Moore and Ordinary Language," pp. 352–3.
3. See Alfred Jules Ayer, *The Foundations of Empirical Knowledge* (London: Macmillan, 1940), pp. 44–5, quoted by Malcolm, "Moore and Ordinary Language," on pp. 353–4.
4. Norman Malcolm, "Philosophy for Philosophers," *The Philosophical Review* 60 (1951): 329–340; see especially pp. 338–9.
5. See Malcolm's "Philosophy for Philosophers," and "The Verification Argument," in *Philosophical Analysis,* ed. Max Black (Englewood Cliffs, N.J.: Prentice-Hall, 1950), pp. 229–279. As for critics of the PCA, see John W. N. Watkins, "Confirmable and Influential Metaphysics," *Mind* 67 (1958): 344–365; Alfred Cyril Ewing, "Pseudo-problems," *Proceedings of the Aristotelian Society* 57 (1956–7): 31–52; Charles Arthur Campbell, "Common-Sense Propositions and Philosophical Paradoxes," in *Clarity Is Not Enough,* ed. Hywel David Lewis (London: Allen & Unwin, 1963), pp. 217–238.
6. See Chappell, "Malcolm on Moore," especially pp. 423–4.
7. For an account of how this interpretation limits the PCA, see James Opie Urmson's "Some Questions Concerning Validity," in *Essays in Conceptual Analysis,* ed. Antony Flew (London: Macmillan, 1956), pp. 120–133.
8. Malcolm seems to accept this in "Philosophy for Philosophers."

9. Malcolm, "Moore and Ordinary Language," pp. 356–7.

10. See Max Black's "Making Something Happen" in *Models and Metaphors* (Ithaca: Cornell University Press, 1962), pp. 153–169, especially Part I.

11. See John L. Cobitz, "The Appeal to Ordinary Language," *Analysis* 11 (1950): 9–11.

12. Roderick Chisholm, "Philosophers and Ordinary Language," *The Philosophical Review* 60 (1951): 317–328.

13. Malcolm, "Moore and Ordinary Language," p. 361.

14. John W. N. Watkins, "Farewell to the Paradigm Case Argument," and "A Reply to Professor Flew's Comment," both in *Analysis* 18 (1957): 25–33 and 41–2.

15. Antony Flew, "Philosophy and Language," in *Essays in Conceptual Analysis,* ed. Antony Flew (London: Macmillan, 1956), pp. 1–20; "Farewell to the Paradigm Case Argument: A Comment," *Analysis* 18 ( 1957): 34–40; and "Again the Paradigm," in *Mind, Matter, and Method,* eds. Paul K. Feyerabend and Grover Maxwell (Minneapolis: University of Minnesota Press, 1966), pp. 261–272.

16. Watkins, "Farewell to the Paradigm Case Argument," p. 29.

17. *Ibid.,* pp. 27–28.

18. See Robert J. Richman, "On the Argument of the Paradigm Case," *Australasian Journal of Philosophy* 39 (1961): 75–81 and "Still More on the Argument of the Paradigm Case," *Australasian Journal of Philosophy* 40 (1962): 204–7.

Chapter 5

1. Popper's view of rationality is to be found in "Oracular Philosophy and the Revolt Against Reason," Chapter 24, *The Open Society and Its Enemies,* 4th rev. ed. (London: Routledge, 1963), pp. 225–258; "On the Sources of Knowledge and Ignorance," pp. 3–30, (abbreviated as SKI); "Three Views Concerning Human Knowledge," pp. 97–119, (abbreviated as TVCHK); "Truth, Rationality and the Growth of Knowledge," pp. 215–250, (abbreviated as TRGK); all these in *Conjectures and Refutations* (New York: Harper Torchbooks, 1968), (abbreviated as CR).

2. *The Logic of Scientific Discovery* (London: Hutchinson, 1959), p. 19, (abbreviated as LSD), and "A Realist View of Logic, Physics, and History," in *Physics, Logic, and History* (New York: Plenum Press, 1970), eds. W. Yourgrau and A. D. Brook, p. 5.

3. Popper, Section VI of TRGK in CR.

4. Popper, Section 6 of TVCHK, also Section VII of "Science: Conjectures and Refutations," both in CR.

5. For a detailed account of falsifiability, see Popper, Chapter IV of LSD.

6. For an account of Popper's rejection of the verifiability criterion, see "The Demarcation Between Science and Metaphysics," in CR.

7. From Popper's rejection of verificationism there follows the rejection of probability as a criterion for the appraisal of scientific theories. For Popper's views on induction and probability, see LSD, especially Chapter X.

8. For a detailed statement of Popper's views on refutation, growth of knowledge, and truth, see TRGK.

9. For a discussion of verisimilitude, see Popper, Sections XI–XIV of TRGK.

10. Popper, LSD, p. 31.

11. Popper, Section I of TRGK.

12. Thomas S. Kuhn, *The Structure of Scientific Revolutions* (Chicago: University of Chicago Press, 1962) and "Logic of Discovery or Psychology of Research," in *Criticism and the Growth of Knowledge,* eds. Imre Lakatos and Allan Musgrave (Cambridge: Cambridge University Press, 1970), pp. 1–23, (abbreviated as CGK).

13. This elucidation of the notion of paradigm is Margaret Masterman's in "The Nature of a Paradigm," pp. 59–89 in CGK.

14. Thomas S. Kuhn, "Reflections on my Critics," (abbreviated as RC), p. 264 in CGK.

15. Kuhn, RC, pp. 265–6.

16. Imre Lakatos, "Falsification and the Methodology of Scientific Research Programmes," p. 155 in CGK.

17. See Renford Bambrough, "Universals and Family Resemblances," in *Wittgenstein,* ed. George Pitcher (Garden City, N.Y.: Doubleday, 1966), pp. 186–204, especially pp. 197–8.

18. Frank P. Ramsey, *The Foundations of Mathematics,* ed. R. B. Braithwaite (London: Allen & Unwin, 1931), pp. 115–6.


Chapter 6

1. Peter Winch, *The Idea of a Social Science* (London: Routledge, 1958); abbreviated as ISS. "Understanding a Primitive Society," *American Philosophical Quarterly* 1 (1964): 307–324, reprinted in *Rationality,* ed. Bryan Wilson (Oxford: Blackwell, 1970), page references will be to the latter volume; abbreviated as UPS.

2. Ludwig Wittgenstein, *Philosophical Investigations,* tr. Gertrude Elizabeth Margaret Anscombe (Oxford: Blackwell, 1953); abbreviated as PI. L. Wittgenstein, *On Certainty,* eds. Gertrude Elizabeth Margaret Anscombe and George H. von Wright, trs. Denis Paul and Gertrude Elizabeth Margaret Anscombe (Oxford: Blackwell, 1969).

3. The expression occurs five times in *The Philosophical Investigations:* 19, 23, 241, p. 174, and p. 226. Two recent attempts to explicate Wittgenstein's use of it are: John F. M. Hunter, " 'Forms of life' in Wittgenstein's *Philosophical Investigations,*" *American Philosophical Quarterly* 5 (1968): 233–243, and Patrick Sherry, "Is Religion a 'Form of Life'?", *American Philosophical Quarterly* 9 (1972): 159–167.

4. The examples of forms of life are: science, art, history, religion (Winch, ISS, p. 41 and p. 100); the life of a monk and the life of an anarchist (Winch, ISS, pp. 52–3); and magic in a primitive society, although probably not in ours (Winch UPS, p. 102).

5. The synonyms of "form of life" are: "mode of life" (Winch, ISS, p. 52 and UPS, p. 106); "way of life" (Winch, ISS, p. 53, p. 103 and UPS, p. 94); "mode of social activity" (Winch ISS, p. 88); "form of social behaviour" (Winch ISS, p. 88); "form of activity" (Winch, ISS, p. 89); "category of behaviour" (Winch, ISS, p. 99); "mode of social life" (Winch, ISS, p. 100); "mode of discourse" (Winch, ISS, p. 100); and "universe of discourse" (Winch, UPS, p. 83).

6. Wittgenstein, PI, p. 225.

7. The source for the remarks concerning forms of life is Winch, ISS, pp. 40–2 and p. 100; and for those concern-

ing rules is ISS, pp. 26–33 and pp. 43–4.

8. Wittgenstein, PI, p. 226.

9. Winch, ISS, p. 41.

10. *Ibid.*, p. 15.

11. *Ibid.*, pp. 100–101.

12. Winch, UPS, p. 80.

13. *Ibid.*, p. 82.

14. *Ibid.*, pp. 81–2.

15. *Ibid.*, pp. 99–100.

16. *Ibid.*, p. 99.

17. Wittgenstein, PI, p. 225.

18. Winch, ISS, p. 107 and 109; UPS, p. 93.

19. Winch, ISS, p. 66.

20. *Ibid.*, p. 75.

21. For instance, Dewi Zephaniah Phillips, "Religious Beliefs and Language Games," *Ratio* 12 (1970): 26–46.

22. Kai Nielsen, "Wittgensteinian Fideism," *Philosophy* 42 (1967): 191–209.

23. Winch, ISS, pp. 33–39.

24. The distinction comes from Ian C. Jarvie and Joseph Agassi, "The Problem of the Rationality of Magic," *British Journal of Sociology* 18 (1967): 55–74; reprinted in Bryan Wilson, ed., *Rationality*.

25. Winch, ISS, p. 101.

## Chapter 7

1. See, for instance, Jonathan Bennett's *Rationality* (London: Routledge, 1964), and Roy Edgley's, *Reason in Theory and Practice* (London: Hutchinson, 1969).

## Chapter 8

1. The distinction between external and internal accounts is part of what remained acceptable from Carnap's thesis after the critical discussion of it in Chapter Two.

2. The distinction is Popper's; see "Truth, Rationality, and the Growth of Scientific Knowledge," in *Conjectures and Refutations* (New York: Harper, 1968), especially Sections II and III.

3. "Theory" is used loosely throughout this discussion; it means an explanatory system of beliefs. The looseness is justified, for it prevents the prejudgment of the issue of what types of theory might prove rational. "Theory" thus includes but is not synonymous with "scientific theory."

4. Two examples of this type of argument are Popper's "The Nature of Philosophical Problems and Their Roots in Science," in *Conjectures and Refutations,* and the rejoinder by Agassi, "The Nature of Scientific Problems and Their Roots in Metaphysics," in *The Critical Approach,* ed. Mario Bunge (New York: Free Press, 1964), pp. 189–211.

5. These three problem-areas are similar to Habermas's distinction between three "knowledge-constitutive interests"; see Jürgen Habermas, *Knowledge and Human Interest,* tr. Jeremy Shapiro (Boston: Beacon Press, 1972).

6. The relation between problems of life, theories, and problems of reflection is in some ways very much like Popper's frequently used schema of beginning with a problem, proceeding to a tentative solution, eliminating error, and encountering a new problem that has emerged from the procedure. The main disagreement between the account offered here and Popper's is that according to the former, problems of life are not theory-generated, whereas, according to Popper, there are no such problems. See Karl Raimund Popper, "Epistemology

Without a Knowing Subject," in *Objective Knowledge* (Oxford: Clarendon, 1972), p. 119.

7. The critical discussion of Moore's defense of common sense in Chapter Three yielded the conclusion that common sense is primary. Its primacy was argued there to derive from the universality of the human physiological apparatus and of the problems which must be faced by all human beings. The notion of problem of life derives from and is a systematic development of this Moorean idea.

8. On this point, see Mary Douglas, *Purity and Danger* (London: Routledge, 1966), and Robin Horton, "African Traditional Thought and Western Science," in *Rationality,* ed. Bryan Wilson (Oxford: Blackwell, 1970).

9. John Dewey, Logic: *The Theory of Inquiry* (New York: H. Holt, 1938), p. 104.

10. Moritz Schlick, "The Future of Philosophy," in *The Linguistic Turn,* ed. Richard Rorty (Chicago: University of Chicago Press, 1967), p. 51.

11. Karl Raimund Popper, "The Nature of Philosophical Problems and Their Roots in Science," p. 72.

12. Karl Raimund Popper, "A Realist View of Logic, Physics, and History," in *Objective Knowledge* (Oxford: Clarendon Press, 1972), p. 290.

13. Thomas S. Kuhn, "Reflections on My Critics," in *Criticism and the Growth of Knowledge,* eds. Imre Lakatos and Allan Musgrave (Cambridge: Cambridge University Press, 1970), p. 264.

Chapter 9

1. Peter Winch, *The Idea of a Social Science* (London: Routledge, 1958), p. 100.

2. Edward E. Evans-Pritchard, *Nuer Religion* (Oxford: Clarendon, 1956), see especially Chapter Five, "The Problem of Symbols."

3. Lucien Levy-Bruhl, *Primitive Mentality* (London: Allen & Unwin, 1923), orig. publ.: 1921.

4. It is unclear whether according to Nuer religion there is only one Spirit or there are many Spirits. This unclarity is reflected in the discussion. Evans-Pritchard writes on this point: A theistic religion need not be either monotheistic or polytheistic. It may be both. It is a question of the level, or situation, of thought rather than exclusive types of thought. On one level Nuer religion may be regarded as monotheistic, at another level as polytheistic. . . . These conceptions of spiritual activity are not incompatible. They are rather different ways of thinking of the numinous at different levels of experience." *Nuer Religion,* p. 316. It is difficult to see why the belief that there exists only one Spirit and the belief that there are many Spirits are not incompatible.

5. See *Nuer Religion,* Chapter Thirteen, "Some Reflections on Nuer Religion."

6. *Ibid.,* Chapter Three, "Spirits of the Below."

7. The notion of pragmatic paradox derives from Daniel John O'Connor, "Pragmatic Paradoxes," *Mind* 57 (1948): 358–9; Max Black, "Saying and Disbelieving," *Analysis* 13 (1952): 24–33; and Colin King Grant, "Pragmatic Implication," *Philosophy* 33 (1958): 303–324.

8. See Karl Raimund Popper, "Two Faces of Common Sense," in *Objective Knowledge,* pp. 32–105.

9. This discussion owes much to Alasdair MacIntyre's "Rationality and the Explanation of Action," in *Against*

*the Self-Images of the Age* (London: Duckworth, 1971), p. 244–259; and to Robin Horton's "African Traditional Thought and Western Science," in *Rationality,* ed. Bryan R. Wilson (Oxford: Blackwell, 1970), p. 131–171. Both authors acknowledge indebtedness, as does the present one, to Mary Douglas's *Purity and Danger* (London: Routledge, 1966).

10. Horton, "African Traditional Thought and Western Science," p. 165.

11. *Ibid.,* pp. 153–4.


Chapter 10

1. Aristotle, *Ethica Nicomachea,* Book X., Chapter 7, tr. William D. Ross (New York: Random House, 1941).

2. Edward E. Evans-Pritchard, *Witchcraft, Oracles, and Magic Among the Azande* (Oxford: Clarendon, 1937), pp. 24–5.

3. *Ibid.,* p. 25.

4. Roger Trigg, *Reason and Commitment* (Cambridge: University Press, 1973), p. 149.

5. The term is David Pears's, see his "Critical Study: Individuals," *The Philosophical Quarterly* 11 (1961): 172–85 and 262–77.

6. William Barrett, *Irrational Man* (New York: Doubleday, 1958), pp. 247–8.

7. Karl Raimund Popper, *The Open Society and Its Enemies,* 4th rev. ed. (London: Routledge, 1962), p. 234.

8. *Treatise,* p. 415.

9. *Dialogues,* p. 135.

10. *Treatise,* p. 103.

11. This account of emotion derives from Gilbert Ryle's "Emotion," Chapter IV, in *The Concept of Mind* (New York: Barnes and Noble, 1949).

12. David Gauthier, "Reason and Maximization," *Canadian Journal of Philosophy* 4 (1975): 412.

13. Max Planck, *Scientific Autobiography and Other Papers,* tr. F. Gaynor, (New York: Philosophical Books, 1949), pp. 33–34.

14. Charles Darwin, *On the Origin of Species* (authorized ed. from the 6th English ed.; New York: Appleton, 1889), II, pp. 295–96.

15. Thomas S. Kuhn, *The Structure of Scientific Revolutions,* (Chicago: The University of Chicago Press, 1962), pp. 149–50.

16. Michael Oakeshott, "Rationalism in Politics," *Rationalism in Politics and Other Essays* (London: Methuen, 1967), pp. 1–36, see p. 3.

17. *Ibid.,* pp. 5–6.

18. *Ibid.,* p. 11.

19. *Ibid.,* p. 11.

20. *Ibid.,* pp. 31–32.


Chapter 11

1. Barry Stroud, "Transcendental Arguments," *The Journal of Philosophy* 65 (1968): 241–56.

2. *Ibid.,* p. 255.

3. Carl Hempel, "Empirical Statements and Falsifiability," *Philosophy* 33 (1958): 348.

4. Karl Raimund Popper, "The Demarcation between Science and Metaphysics," in *The Philosophy of Rudolf Carnap,* ed. Paul A. Schilpp (La Salle, Ill.: Open Court, 1965).


Chapter 12

1. Freidrich Waismann, "How I See Philosophy," *Contemporary British Philosophy,* Third Series, ed. Hywel David

Lewis (London: Allen & Unwin, 1966), p. 32.

2. The process from revolution through consolidation to orthodoxy has been outstandingly described, for one aspect of intellectual life, by Thomas S. Kuhn in *The Structure of Scientific Revolutions* (Chicago: University of Chicago Press, 1962). Ernest H. Gombrich's *Art and Illusion* (Princeton: Princeton University Press, 1960) performs a very similar task in the history of visual arts. John Passmore in *The Perfectibility of Man* (London: Duckworth, 1970) traces, *inter alia*, the history of the idea that man is perfectible from its heretic Pelagian origins through seventeenth- and eighteenth-century consolidation to its present-day status as a cornerstone of both liberal democracy and communism.

3. On the subject of this paragraph, see Stuart Hampshire, "Commitment and Imagination," in *The Morality of Scholarship*, ed. Max Black (Ithaca: Cornell University Press, 1957).

Chapter 13

1. Robin George Collingwood, *An Essay on Metaphysics,* Part I (Oxford: Clarendon Press, 1940).

2. This account of presuppositions is indebted to David Rynin's "Donagan on Collingwood: Absolute Presuppositions, Truth and Metaphysics," *The Review of Metaphysics* 18 (1964–65): 301–333.

3. Karl Raimund Popper, *The Logic of Scientific Discovery* (London: Hutchinson, 1959), pp. 55–6.

4. John W. N. Watkins, "Confirmable and Influential Metaphysics," *Mind* 67 (1958): 344–365; Joseph Agassi, "The Nature of Scientific Problems and Their Roots in Metaphysics," in *The Critical Approach,* ed. Mario Bunge (New York: Free Press, 1964); Imre Lakatos, "Falsification and the Methodology of Scientific Research Programmes," in *Criticism and the Growth of Knowledge* (Cambridge: Cambridge University Press, 1970), eds. Imre Lakatos and Allan Musgrave.

5. Rudolf Carnap, "Intellectual Autobiography," in *The Philosophy of Rudolf Carnap* (La Salle, Ill.: Open Court, 1963), ed. Paul A. Schilpp, pp. 54–5.

6. Rudolf Carnap, "Empiricism, Semantics, and Ontology," in *Meaning and Necessity,* 2nd ed. (Chicago: University of Chicago Press, 1956), p. 214.

7. Watkins, "Confirmable and Influential Metaphysics," pp. 356–7.

8. Carnap, "Empiricism, Semantics, and Ontology," p. 214.

9. John Passmore, "Allocation to Categories," *Philosophical Reasoning* (London: Duckworth, 1961), p. 147.

10. The discussion of this kind of presupposition owes much to William Henry Walsh's *Metaphysics* (New York: Harcourt, Brace & World, 1963), especially Chapter 10. The example is Walsh's.

11. For a superb account of the changing conceptions of matter, see Stephen Toulmin and June Goodfield, *The Architecture of Matter* (Hammondsworth, Middlesex: Penguin, 1963).

# Index of names

# Index of subjects

Presuppositions
  absolute, 83, 233-235
  categorical, 244-250
  Collingwood's account of, 231-237
  fundamental, 235-253
  metaphysical, 80-91
  ontological, 250-253
  and rationality, 115, 235-253
  regulative, 237-244
  of science, 80-91
Problem-areas, 122-126
Problems
  and common sense, 46-48
  of life and reflection, 122-126, 133-
    134, 155-156
  metaphysical, 234, 238
  and rationality, 120-132
  removable and enduring, 126-130
  and science, 77-79
  what are, 120-130
Problem-solving
  external standard of rationality, 118,
    120-132
  and logic, 135-149
  and rationality, 91, 118, 125
Psychoanalysis, 11, 215

Questions
  and answers, 232-235
  external, 25-39, 107
  internal, 26-39, 107
  practical, 27, 28, 34
  theoretical, 27

Rationalism
  analytic, 18-19, 93
  classical, 170-181
  critical, 76-91, 107-108
  and empiricism, 7
  and irrationalism, 7
  postulational, 17
Rationality
  and acceptance of theories, 119, 135,
    158, 165-167

and beliefs, 7
and certainty, 12-14, 185-188
coherence theory of, 94-106
and common sense, 48-59
and conceptual coherence, 149-153
and criticism, 76-91, 114-115, 118,
  157-163
criticisms of, 1, 2
and enduring problems, 126-130
and explanation, 113-114, 118, 153-
  156
external account, 111-113, 118-131
and fallibilism, 76-91
formal account of, 116-117
and forms of life, 94-106
ideal of, xiii
internal account, 111-113, 133-163
and justification, 7, 16-19
justification of, 1
and logic, 114, 118, 125, 135-149,
  153
of metaphysical vision, 215-229
and metaphysics, 89, 213-253
and method, 167-170
and ordinary language, 60-75
philosophical account of, 116-117
and politics, 184-190
positivistic, 184-190
possibility of, 8
and practice, 181-184
pragmatic justification, 25-39, 107
and presuppositions, 115, 230-253
and the *a priori,* 230-255
and problems of life, 122-126
and problems of reflection, 122-126
and problem-solving, 91, 118-132
psychological account of, 116-117,
  173-181
and removable problems, 126-130
requirements of theory of, 111-117
and science, 76-91, 130
and self-interest, 165-167
standards of, 7, 8, 17, 117
and success, 39, 114